THE COMPLEAT MUSTARD

THE COMPLEAT MUSTARD

Rosamond Man
&
Robin Weir

CONSTABLE
LONDON

First published in Great Britain 1988
by Constable and Company Limited
10 Orange Street London WC2H 7EG
Copyright © 1988 by Rosamond Man and Robin Weir
Set in Linotron Sabon 11pt by
Rowland Phototypesetting Limited
Bury St Edmunds, Suffolk
Printed in Great Britain by
St Edmundsbury Press Limited
Bury St Edmunds, Suffolk

British Library CIP data
Man, Rosamond
The compleat mustard
1. Mustard
I. Title   II. Weir, Robin
641.3'384

ISBN 0 09 466990 2

For Keith, with love – R.M.

To Elizabeth, Charlotte and Matthew – R.W.

CONTENTS

ILLUSTRATIONS

ACKNOWLEDGEMENTS

So many are the people who have helped with this book, that to list every one individually would overflow our permitted space. But to all of them we give grateful thanks.

Particularly to Henry Poupon, Jean-Pierre Halm, Mme Fouquet and M. Bourget of Moutarde Maille, Dijon; Hélène Boutet, Moutarde Bornibus, Paris; Françoise Turpaud, Européenne de Condiments, Dijon; Bea Slizeweski, The R.T. French Company, Rochester, New York; Dr S. A. R. Cross, Mrs Norma Walker, Don Hoffman and especially John Hemingway of Colman's, Norwich; Enrico Cinquetti Dondi, Dondi Lorenzo spa, Cremona; Giles Tullberg, Wiltshire Tracklements, Shenstone; Charles Gordon, Charles Gordon Associates, Guildford; Shreeram Vidyarthi, Books from India U.K.; Madeleine Blondel, Musée de la vie Bourguignonne, Dijon; K. Becker, FAO, United Nations, Rome; Amanda Courtney, British Trout Association; Lucia Godwin and Lou Powers, Thomas Jefferson Foundation, Charlottesville, Virginia; Terence Charman, Imperial War Museum; Edna Linnell, Tewkesbury Museum; Biddy Cole, Rye Pottery, Rye; W. A. L. Seaman, Archivist, Tyne & Wear County Council; D. W. Liddle, County Librarian, Gateshead; D. J. Butter, County Archivist, Durham; J. Main, Durham County Library; Paula Chesterman, Punch Publications Ltd; C. Anne Wilson, Brotherton Library, Leeds; Miriam Stead, British Museum; Nigel Hepper, Royal Botanic Gardens, Kew; J. C. Pert, Homeopathic Development Foundation; D. J. Wright, British Medical Association; and Adrian Binstead, Food Trade Press, Orpington.

Thanks, too, for permissions to reproduce, or refer to, recipes must go to Henry Poupon, SEGMA Maille, Dijon; Elizabeth Lambert Ortiz (*Japanese Cookery*, Collins, 1986); Gail and Mick Duff (*Food from the Country*, Macmillan, 1981); Victor Gordon (*The English Cookbook*, Jonathan Cape, 1985); Jane Simpson and Gill MacLennan (*The Apple Book*, The Bodley Head, 1984). Thanks for permission to reproduce the illustrations on pages 27, 29, 32, 34, 41, and 61 to Madeleine Blondel, Musée de la Vie Bourguignonne; for those on pages 25, 46, 50, 52, 56, and 183 to Colman's of Norwich; that on page 82 to Punch Publications; and that on page 157 to Alfred Dunhill.

For specialist help of all sorts, we thank Sid Wayne of Stone County Specialities Inc, Ontario; Mike McKirdy, Cooks Books, Rottingdean; Tom Jackson of Ilkley; Jean Rosen of Dijon; Françoise Decloquement; San Firlej; Imogen Olsen; Gerry Coran and Lawrence Cooper; Pepita Aris; Maggie Black; Anna del Coute; Mrs Harold Loasby; Jill Tilsley-Benham; Dr John H. Harvey of Frome, Somerset; Marie-Pierre Moine; Caroline Schuck; Elizabeth Lambert Ortiz; Alan Davidson; and John Lyle of Sidmouth, Devon.

Very special thanks are due to Angus and Gilly Urquhart for Italian research and translations; to Heidi Lascelles and Caroline Liddell – without whose encouragement this book would never have been published; to Robin Baird-Smith for his enthusiasm, foresight and extreme patience; to Caroline Schuck, Jacqueline Korn and Scott Ewing for never-flagging encouragement; to the late James H. Weir, MD, for medical research; to Elizabeth, Charlotte and Matthew Weir for counting, mixing, tasting and helping; to the late Morgan Man for many translations from French, German and Arabic; and to Moira, Kate and Peg Man for tasting, talking and much practical help. Without them, and most especially without the constant support of Keith Perrott – who endlessly ate mustard with everything – the book would never have been written.

Mustard jars from *Essai sur l'Histoire de la Moutarde de Dijon*
E. Jobard (undated)

FOREWORD

Moustarde aprez disner – After meat
comes mustard.

Old French and English proverbs

Venice, for centuries, was queen of the ancient spice trade. How
fitting, then, that she should give birth to the idea of a book on
mustard. After pepper, mustard is the world's second most important
spice. Yet, unlike other spices, mustard has caused no wars: it grows so
obligingly easily that it has always been there, ready to be gathered
when wanted. Man has used it, since time immemorial, in countless
ways. As with any ingredient which becomes familiar in many countries, it took on many personalities, and its appearance was sometimes
highly unexpected. Venice was the scene of one very original marriage.

Dining at the pretty La Colomba restaurant, Robin Weir was
presented with a pudding – and a challenge. Could he guess the secret
ingredient? If so, the dessert was on the house. Creamy in colour and
texture, its appearance gave no clue. The first mouthful revealed a
sweetness, a hint of pears and a slight, but definite, bite. Three helpings
later the secret was still unrevealed. But the old proverb was apt, for
the vital spice was indeed mustard – in the form of the wonderful
Mostarda di Venezia, quinces preserved in a sugar syrup spiced
with white mustard seed. Similar to the better known Mostarda de
Cremona (traditionally served with cold meats) though in purée
form rather than with whole fruits, the Mostarda, in Venice, is served
with a dollop of the rich creamy cheese, *mascarpone*, to produce that
elusive-tasting dessert.

The idea was born, and soon it was mustard in everything: mustard
soups, mustard sauces, mustard ice cream, mustard biscuits. Sacks of
mustard seed sat in all corners of our kitchens, jars of mustard lined
our shelves. And the more we experimented, the more endless seemed
the possibilities.

The research began. The problem was not, as so many had asked, whether there was enough to write a book on mustard, but to know how, and when, to stop.

History turned up fascinating, and often tantalizing, details. Prehistoric man had supposedly chewed mustard seeds. A bag of seed, ready for sowing, had been found at the Mycenaean site of Marmariani in Greece, and mustard had been discovered in a Bronze Age lake dwelling of Morigin at Lake Bienne.

From India, where the plant's early flowering signifies the first sign of spring, came many folk tales, none so charming as that of the grower going to sleep at night, a mustard seed and a drop of water in the palm of his hand. By morning, a large plant had grown.

France had other, less complimentary tales. Their picturesque phrase to describe a vain and stupid man, '*Il est le premier moutardier du Pape*', dates back to medieval times. When Cardinal Jacques Duèse was installed as Pope John XXII at Avignon in 1316, his relatives wasted no time in asking for jobs. One distant cousin from Dijon knew only about mustard, and since the Pope was reputedly mad about the stuff, he was rewarded with his title (another cousin jumping on the bandwagon as 'second mustarder'), and a pretty uniform: pale apple green, a mustard pot slung over his shoulder and the motto 'I tickle the palate and excite the nose.'

Monasteries were large consumers of mustard. The accounts of the Cathedral Saint Etienne, near Dijon, for 1447 show that 'Firstly, the 5th day of September for the day of Clement 7 pints of mustard were made.' The mustard maker returned on 16 October, 2 December and 30 January to replenish the well-used pot.

France inveigled her culture, and her mustard, into Thomas Jefferson's life. On his return home, he adopted many French habits, planted mustard seed in his garden and ordered the condiment (some 5 lbs each, of two types, in 1790) from a Paris grocer. Some seventy years later, wild mustard greens were to provide precious nourishment for many during the Civil War.

We were surprised to learn how high in nutrients mustard is: 25 per cent protein, 29 per cent fat, salts of calcium, phosphorus, magnesium and sulphur, plus Vitamin B – though you would need to eat more than the stomach could cope with, to benefit. Its uses in medicine were ancient and legion, though we doubt its efficacy as an aphrodisiac, especially one eighteenth-century recommendation to apply poultices to the affected area.

Also somewhat surprising was Argentina's love of mustard. Perhaps in view of the magnificent local beef, and the large Anglo community, it is logical. Interestingly both English and Latin tastes are catered for, as not only is the mild condiment Savora (first marketed by Colman's in 1899) very popular but also the fiery English brand. Indeed Colman's largest factory in South America is located in the Argentine. The rest of that vast continent largely ignores mustard, except high in the mountains of Colombia, where it appears in various local dishes.

Mountainous regions would seem to be good for mustard: the tiny country of Nepal grows a staggering 79,000 tonnes a year, making her the world's third largest producer, most of it going to India.

Over half the world's made mustard still comes from the French town of Dijon, although no longer does any one firm list, as in 1780, over eighty different varieties. While we may not have quite that range today, we are again becoming more conscious of mustard's many guises. No longer are we limited to just English or French on the supermarket shelf. There are whole grain mustards, smooth mustards, herby mustards, sweet mustards, mild and hot mustards (though none so hot as the Japanese), mustards made with champagne, mustards made with ale – an age-old combination this, for ale used to be spiced with mustard seed to prevent undue fermentation.

We have tried to paint as complete a portrait of this fiery little plant as space allowed. The journey has been long, sometimes frustrating, occasionally fraught. But it has always been interesting, often exciting and, gastronomically, very rewarding. Mustard is primarily a stimulant. We hope that this book will stimulate you to become, like us, 'enthusiasts'.

Rosamond Man
Robin Weir
Manuden and London, 1988

INTRODUCTION

Botany and horticulture

For high purpose did the gods ordain
the mustard plant to grow beneath
the feet of mortals.

Attributed to Montaigne (1533–92)

Mustard is a very easy plant to grow. It epitomizes the old country saying, 'One year's seed: seven years' weed' – one species in particular can lie dormant for a hundred years in the soil, only to flourish again given the right conditions.

This habit of self-seeding has often made mustard an unconscious recorder of history. In California, for instance, it is easy to trace the steps of one of the early missionaries, Father Junipero Serra. Accompanying the Spanish military on their colonization of Upper California, he set out, in 1768, with Captain Gaspar de Portolá: 'The route of his walk is today the route of the main north–south highway, and it is vividly marked in the spring by the blossoming mustard whose seeds the friar scattered as he went.' (Alastair Cooke, *America*.) Thus was the first network of 'bible-trails' marked out, an ingenious and foolproof method of map-drawing.

By nature, the plant is a biennial, sown one year to produce its flower and seed the next, but as man started to cultivate it in earnest, new annual strains were evolved. It is extraordinarily obliging in its reproduction – indeed for the Hindus it is the symbol of fertility – and a pound of white seed (approximately 70,000 seeds) can produce 55 million seeds by the second generation. A mere twelve ounces of the much smaller black seed produces some 500 million offspring within two seasons – roughly 3,400 'grandchildren' for every seed.

Mustard comes from a very large family – the Cruciferae – and among its relations are the cresses, radishes, turnips, and horseradish.

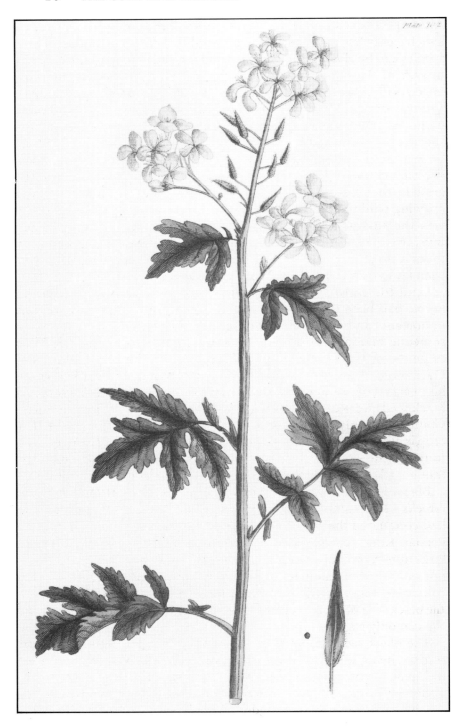

Mustard plant, from *Medical Botany*, 1821

Although a fiery strain runs through much of the family, it is neverthe-less friendly to man, no known member being poisonous. Three species can be classified as mustard and they all belong to the cabbage branch of the family, the *Brassicas*. The white, or yellow, mustard once so familiar to the English countryside is *Brassica alba* (Boiss), *Brassica hirta* or – in its Greek guise – *Sinapis alba* (giving the medical name for the mustard plaster, sinapism). It is the smallest of the species.

Sinapis alba was probably introduced to England by the Romans: it is certainly native to the Mediterranean region, while black mustard grew further east, round what we now call Iran. The mustard found growing wild today in Gloucestershire is the white, and Tewkesbury was the earliest known centre of English mustard making. Black mustard was another import, again probably with the Romans, though maybe at a later date, but by the nineteenth century it had been known as a 'wild' plant for at least one hundred years.

Until the early Tudors, the growing of mustard, as indeed of all herbs, had been the province of the monasteries. That mustard was important can be seen from the fact that they had a 'mustardarius' – someone in charge of growing and distributing the mustard. Then came the rise of Tewkesbury mustard, followed by Mrs Clements of Durham in 1720, and finally Jeremiah Colman. Although few know his exact recipe we do know that Colman's made use of both white and black seeds, very carefully selected, as were the growers. Indeed today, Colman's supply their growers with the seed for growing; the new crop is all delivered to Colman's who again select the seed and return it to the farmers for the next season's sowing. For the last thirty years, though, black mustard has played no part in the famous table mustard.

Black, or true, mustard, *Brassica nigra* (Koch), was known to the Greeks – Hippocrates refers to it – decades before Alexander the Great had conquered the plant's native land. Legend has it that Darius, the Persian King, sent Alexander a bag of sesame seed, to illustrate the large numbers of his army. Alexander returned a bag of mustard seed – not only greater numbers in *his* army, but a greater fieriness. What colour were those seeds? White mustard seed is nearly twice as large as the black; the black is smaller than sesame, and indigenous to the area. We can only suppose . . .

The black seed probably came to Europe via the early Arab spice traders, being shipped from Alexandria. Certainly mustard flourished in Egypt: great quantities were found in the XIIth Dynasty (1991–1786 BC) tomb of Dira Abu'n-Nega, near Thebes, and there are specimens from the New Kingdom Age (1567–1085 BC) at the Dokki

Agricultural Museum in Cairo. The largest of the species, it grows 8–12 ft tall, though its seeds are half the size of its white relative and – confusingly – not black, but a reddish-brown. Nowadays the growers of black mustard are few and far between: England has cultivated none since the Second World War. Only in areas where labour is plentiful and cheap (Sicily, Southern Italy, Ethiopia) is the seed deliberately sown, for *B. nigra* must be gathered by hand. It is all too apt, when shaken, to scatter those minuscule seeds.

Brassica juncea (Coss), brown or Indian mustard, grows 4–6 ft high and presents no problems in harvesting: the monstrous machines that are the pickers of today can easily scoop millions of the seeds in one greedy mouthful. It hails from the Himalayas, spreading westward to the Crimea and eastward to China, and has always been significant in that vast sub-continent – as a seasoning spice, of course, and, before the discovery of chillies in the New World, presumably even more desirable for its pungency than for the nuttiness it gives to so many dishes today. Almost more important was the oil obtained from the seed, particularly favoured for culinary use in Bengal. The leaves are popular as a vegetable in Northern India and also in China (where they are called *Bak-Choi*, much loved fresh and pickled).

Samples found at Channu-Daro Sind in Lower India dating from 3000 BC are almost certainly from the brown species, although there is conflict. One writer says these are *B. nigra*, but all the authorities agree that this is not native to India. Mustard greens are without doubt *B. juncea*, and as the plant's native terrain lies within western China, it is probably the brown seed that is listed in the ancient herbal of Shen Nung, emperor some 5,000 years ago. Pottery vessels containing mustard were also found at Ban Po Village, North Xyan in Shenxi Province, dating back to 5000–4000 BC, so the Chinese were certainly among the earliest cultivators of the plant, if not the first.

Today, the USSR are the world's largest producers; they have extensive areas under cultivation at Sarepta in Southern Russia, where the plant is indigenous. Little appears in the West about Russians and their mustard. They make a great deal of oil from it, which they appreciate highly, using it much as we use the best olive oil. And that they enjoy mustard is obvious from the shortage which developed in the Ukraine in early 1986. Letters to the editor of *Literaturnaya Gazeta* (*The Literary Gazette*), complaining that mustard could only be bought in 3-litre jars, were at first thought to be a hoax. But eventually it was discovered that 'the factory had decided to make the change to cut its workload, by reducing from 10,000 to 333 the number of jars produced from each ton of pungent Soviet mustard'

(94,000 tonnes in 1982, the most recent figure we have). 'The magazine concluded, with a note of despair, that as a result mustard in the giant jars would soon go off, forcing every family to throw it away. Then, once again, the Soviet Union will have another mustard deficit' (*The Times*, 3 February 1986).

Close behind is Canada, with 80,300 tonnes in 1982, and they are the world's biggest exporters of mustard seed. Like Colman's suppliers, the farmers are given the seed, told how many acres to sow, and are paid cash for the crop. It is a thriving business, and some 250,000 acres annually go under mustard cultivation in South Alberta and Saskatchewan, half growing *B. juncea* and half *Sinapis alba*. Most of the white goes across the border into the United States, the world's biggest importer of mustard. Some of the brown goes westward to Japan, where they enjoy a very hot mustard as a table condiment, often mixed with *wasabi* (horseradish) to enliven it further, but the largest importer of Canada's brown seed is France, which grows only about half its mustard seed requirements.

Mustard, together with vines, was introduced into the Dijon area of Gaul by the Romans, whose use of the condiment is well documented by Marcus Gabius Apicius. Living during the heyday of the Roman Empire (80–40 BC), he was fascinated by food. He was also very rich, and spent most of his fortune on his obsession. He left a fascinating record of Roman eating and cooking habits in which mustard is often mentioned – as a preservative, in sauces, with meat, with fish, with vegetables, as a vegetable (still enjoyed as such in a few remote areas of the south). The Romans obviously liked their mustard, though Plautus, 150 years earlier, had so disliked it that he mentions it in two of his plays particularly disparagingly.

Interestingly, almost the entire Arab world has ignored the condiment, although charlock, mustard's wild cousin, is sometimes eaten in Turkey as a young salad leaf, and there is one delightful tale from an English traveller in sixteenth-century Byzantium of the procession through Constantinople of all the traders, including 300 Bulgarian mustard makers. Other than that, the seed hardly appears on the Arab table.

On a more sinister note, mustard has lent its name to another product which employs the same irritant qualities as those produced by mustard oil. Athenas said of mustard that it hurt the eyes because of irritation caused by the pungency of the smell. Mustard gas is much more dramatic. It causes acute conjunctivitis (often followed by temporary blindness), choking, and burning of the skin (Hitler suffered from English mustard gas shells in Belgium four days before

Armistice was declared – 'a few hours later my eyes had turned into burning coals, it had grown dark around me'). However, the Chinese in the fourth century BC, according to Joseph Needham (*Science and Civilization in China*, Vol. IV, Part 2), were actually using mustard precisely for that purpose. 'It is clear that . . . it was customary to use toxic smokes made by burning balls of dried mustard . . . in stoves, the smoke being directed against troops attacking cities, or blown into the openings of enemy sap tunnels.' Once again, the Chinese seem to have been pioneers in the field, but today the gas – dichlorethyl sulphide – is made by adding chlorine to ethyl sulphate, and its effects, unlike those of mustard, are only destructive. Thankfully, mustard seed ends its days more usually in the mustard pot.

Mustard and medicine

I got home at half-past ten,
and mustard-poulticed and barley-
watered myself tremendously.

Charles Dickens, letter to Miss Hogarth,
18 August 1858

Both these remedies, barley water to soothe and revive, a mustard poultice to stimulate the blood vessels and guard against chill, were highly popular with the Victorians – indeed barley water is still seen today on many a hospital bedside table. But it was the heyday especially of the mustard poultice and plaster. The poultice was the milder though both were similarly made by mixing mustard with wheat flour (or linseed meal) to a thick paste with water, the proportions depending on the strength required. Spread on to brown paper, or linen, covered with gauze, the poultice was then applied to the appropriate area – though not left for too long, or blisters could ensue. Ten minutes was the recommended time for people 'with delicate skins . . . ¾ hour for those with very tough, insensitive skins', at the end of which the area would be bright red due to the irritant factor of the mustard on the skin. This caused the blood vessels to open, promoting an increased circulation – hence the redness.

The human body's efficiency in producing a counter-irritant response to mustard being slapped on the skin – a speeding up of the blood circulation – was no doubt largely responsible for the reduction of inflammation. With congestion removed, the nervous pressure is

Original mustard plasters, *c.* 1880

relieved, and thus the pain. Hence, for many years, mustard had also been recommended for rheumatism, which is often distressingly painful, as old Jeremiah Colman well knew. In his will he ordered that mustard oil should be given free to those who asked for it, but when 10,000 people applied following an article in *Truth* magazine Colman's started to sell it through chemists and grocers.

The essential oil of mustard had been noted some two centuries before, by Nicolas Le Febvre, though it was not until 1819 that another chemist, Thibierge, noticed that one of its constituents was the beneficial sulphur. Nonetheless, even without this sophisticated chemical knowledge, the ancients had long preached the virtues of mustard.

For the Greeks, the word came from the Gods. Aesculapius, the Greek god-physician himself, proclaimed the benefits of preparations made from the green plants, and Pythagoras prescribed mustard as an aid to improved memory, and as an antidote to scorpion and serpent bites. Hippocrates (*c*.460–377 BC), the 'Father of Medicine', wrote extensively about mustard and was one of the first to be specific. White mustard was a great cleanser of the alimentary system – both as an emetic, and as a laxative. Crushed, the seed could be drunk in a hot sweet-sharp solution (presumably a sweetened vinegar), or with hyssop as mustard and cress, in warm honey and water.

Dioscorides, writing his *De Materia Medica* in the first century, added that mustard was 'virtuous in ridding one of the superfluous moods of the brain' and also that it was efficacious in removing deafness and a buzzing of the ears. Athenas, in contemporary Rome, echoed these views, adding that Cyprus mustard was the best. The Romans also used mustard to combat stiffness, mixing it with olive oil and rubbing it into the affected parts.

In India, mustard oil has for centuries been used to anoint and massage the body, to soothe and invigorate. Susruta the Elder, the fourth-century physician, also advised that the bed linen and room of the sick should be fumigated with mustard to drive away malignant spirits.

As a native of Asia, brown mustard seed appears also in Chinese medicine, being highly recommended in a sixth-century herbal. One hundred years later, it was specified for treating carbuncles and swellings, in the form of a mustard plaster. Recently, the Chinese have been experimenting again with mustard, this time the white seed. In the case of chronic bronchitis, they have treated approximately 300 patients with a 10–20 per cent solution injected into various acupuncture points, achieving an 80 per cent success rate.

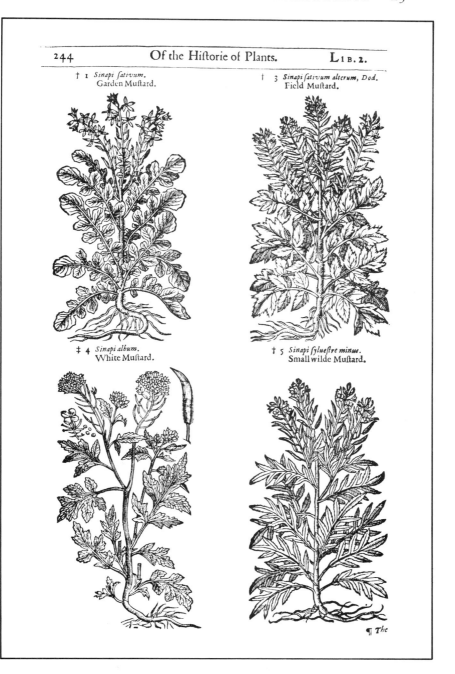

244   Of the Hiſtorie of Plants.   L ɪ ʙ. 2.

† 1 *Sinapi ſativum.*
Gardcn Muſtard.

† 3 *Sinapi ſativum alterum, Dod.*
Ficld Muſtard.

‡ 4 *Sinapi album.*
White Muſtard.

† 5 *Sinapi ſylueſtre minus.*
Small wilde Muſtard.

¶ *The*

Mustard plants in *Gerard's Herbal*, 1597

Western medicine owed much in its early days to the Arab physicians and the Moorish conquest of Spain. And mustard, though hardly cared for as a condiment by the Arabs, had an ancient medicinal history. It is mentioned in several of the great Arabic treatises, particularly that of Al-Biruni (c.AD 1050) who gives its name in various languages and states that 'It is used as a curative in dyspepsia and flatulence.'

Here we would seem to have one of the first specific references to mustard as an aid to digestion. True, Pliny had said that it was wholesome for the body and Hippocrates mentions it as a great internal cleanser. In fact, the same quality of mustard – its irritant ability – is at work in both cases, though to different degrees. For the English herbalists and physicians from Tudor times onward, this gastronomic benefit was to assume as great an importance as its medicinal virtues.

John Gerard praised mustard on both accounts in his herbal of 1597. Not only was it good for the digestion, provoking appetite and warming the stomach, but 'It helpeth the Sciatica, or ache in the hip or huckle bone . . . It also appeaseth the toothache being chewed in the mouth. It helpeth those that have their hair pulled off, it taketh away the blue and black marks that comes out of bruisings.' Interestingly, centuries later, when we went to the Mustard Shop in Norwich, Don Hoffman (the manager) told us he could remember his grandmother using mustard to alleviate bruising.

Dr Thomas Cogan attributed even greater powers to mustard in *The Haven of Health* (1605): 'The force of the seed is perceived by eating mustard, for if it is good in making to weep we are straightway taken by the nose and provoked to sneeze, which plainly declareth that it soon pierceth the brain. Wherefore as it is a good sauce and procureth appetite, so it is profitable for the pulse, and for such students as be heavy-headed and drowsy, as if they would fall asleep with meat in their mouths. And if any be given to music, and would fain have clear voices, let them take mustard-seed in powder, work the same with honey into little balls, of which they must swallow one or two down every morning fasting, and in a short time they shall have very clear voices.' A Dublin receipt of 1778 suggests standing 'garlick and ½ oz of mustard in a quart of white wine for a week, then drink as much as you wish' as a remedy against asthma, and in the nineteenth and early twentieth centuries mustard was being much advised in the treatment of bronchitis, pleurisy and pneumonia. It had long been used for coughs (hiccoughs, too, a pinch of mustard in cold water) – Culpeper mentions mustard mixed with honey as 'good for old coughs', while

Mustard bath advertisement from the *Tatler*, 1927

another ancient remedy has the seed boiled with dried figs in strong ale.

Despite mustard's great helpfulness to the stomach's digestive powers, taken in too large a quantity, it is one of nature's most efficient laxatives (particularly the white seed). It is also a powerful emetic. Indeed it is one of the few emetics which also act as a stimulant, and is therefore extremely useful in cases of poisoning where there is also breathing or heart failure (but we must stress that while a solution of mustard in warm water will, in an emergency, act quickly as an emetic, it is *not* a substitute for a doctor).

On a less dramatic level, mustard baths are still a useful, and relaxing, remedy for stiffness after extreme physical exertion, although for a long soak we would suggest half of one of Colman's packets of specially prepared Bath Mustard, unless you wish to emerge looking like a lobster! For unbroken chilblains, a foot bath is similarly efficacious; mustard ointment was the great eighteenth-century treatment for this unpleasant complaint, both in England and in France. Mustard baths were also advised for those seeking a fine complexion, and since mustard does open the pores, thus allowing the skin to be thoroughly cleansed, it is a reasonable theory.

Today, mustard is not much used in medicine except by the homeopaths, who use mainly the black seed, for ear, nose and throat complaints, though also for colic and urinary problems. The white seed is used for problems with the oesophagus and the middle ear.

Commercial mustard makers: Dijon

Il n'est ville se nom Dijon
Il n'est moustarde que a Dijon.

Fourteenth-century French proverb

The first reference to mustard in the Dijon archives occurs in 1336, when a whole cask was consumed at a banquet. Mustard mills, mortars for making mustard, and pots of mustard are frequently mentioned in wills and inventories, and in 1347, we find in the town records a sum of '12 francs' for sending mustard to the Queen. Dijon mustard was obviously considered the finest: in 1354, the Receiver-General of Burgundy bought mustard seed and vinegar to make 200 lb of mustard, sent in four barrels to King Jean.

Philippe le Hardi, Duke of Burgundy 1364–1408.
It was in 1390 that the first ordinance was drawn up
relating to mustard and vinegar makers in Dijon

The first Ordinance relating to the vinegar-mustard makers of Dijon was drawn up in 1390. The date, and use of the word 'mustard', must dispel the myth, beloved by Dijon, of the word's origin. For it had only been nine years since Charles VI had rewarded the city, and his uncle, Philip the Bold, for sending 1000 men to the ever-continuing fight against Flanders. The reward was a coat of arms with the motto *Mout me tarde*, I ardently desire, on a banner underneath. The story goes that the Dijonnaise were linguistically careless. The middle word *me* had appeared below the other two on the loop of the banner, and was subsequently dropped, producing a new motto – *Mout tarde*, much burning, not inappropriate to the town's main claim to fame. The more usual derivation is from the Latin, *must* (much) or *mustum* (the newly fermented wine juice) and *ardens* (burning). Or maybe the Celts gave us the word with their *mwstertt* (to give off a strong odour).

The specifications of the Ordinance were almost identical to the instructions given some thirteen and a half centuries earlier by Columella of Gades in his *De Re Rustica* (AD 42): 'Clean the mustard seed with great care, sift and swill with cold water . . . leave to soak in water for two hours then stir, and after squeezing the seeds in one's hands, throw them into a mortar . . . and crush with the pestle. When well ground, stir the paste towards the middle and flatten same with the hand. When well compressed, form grooves in the paste and pour nitrated water on hot coal previously placed in the grooves so as to rid the grain of all its bitterness and to preserve it from mould. Heat slightly so that the humidity disappears completely and pour strong white vinegar on the mustard stirring the mixture with the pestle and pass through a sieve.' The principles are still startlingly similar. The use of hot coals is especially interesting – for it is not so much bitterness that is removed by the heat as pungency. For all of Dijon's mustard starts life as '*extra forte*' (extra hot or strong). It is not extra pressings that make some mustards hot, but heating (for one tenth of a second at 130°C, on the pasteurization principle) that makes some mustards mild.

1407 (according to Garnier, *Essai sur l'Histoire de la Moutarde de Dijon*) saw a further edict: 'it was forbidden to use anything other than good mustard seed, and only to soak it in good vinegar from the vines, without adding sour wine (*vin aigre*) or the verjuice of apples.' Verjuice was traditionally taken to mean sour grape juice (i.e. from unripe grapes) but crab apple juice was often used instead, particularly where grapes were scarce. Interesting is the distinction between good wine vinegar, properly acetified, and wine that was sour simply

Mustard seller, 1586, France

through having gone bad. Despite the heavy penalties for using rotten vinegar, or wine, the rules continued to be broken. In 1443, there was an edict concerning the use of weights and measures in the selling of mustard, and a body of inspectors was set up.

Dijon's honour remained intact, despite the plethora of mustard sellers who had taken advantage of the new portable mill which appeared at the beginning of the century. This enabled many newcomers to enter the trade, primarily grocers, candlemakers (long associated in Paris with mustard making) and apothecaries (long associated in Dijon with mustard). It was an apothecary who was ordered 'to make mustard for the said King our sire and Madame the Queen' in 1477. The said King was Louix XI, and he had just annexed Burgundy into his kingdom. Legend has it that 'he was as devoted to mustard as much as to the leaden figure of the Virgin which decorated his velvet cap' and he undoubtedly had a good supply. For the apothecary had taken three days to grind 4 lb of mustard seed into mustard which filled two small casks.

In 1634, the vinegar and mustard makers decided to unite into one corporation in an attempt to regulate the profession. New rules covered the inspection of utensils and standards of hygiene; no master could have more than one shop and one apprentice at a time. Louis XIV granted them their own arms, azure with a funnel of silver, which were proudly displayed on banners and engraved on numerous seals.

Coat of arms of Moutardiers, 1634.
Granted in 1634 by Louis XIV

In 1712 even stricter statutes were drawn up – for the first time, the word *'moutardiers'* appears. Among the signatories was François Naïgeon, father of the founder of one of Dijon's greatest mustard houses.

François Naigeon had become a master vinegar maker in 1703 and soon became a major force in the mustard market. His goods were well known to Parisian gourmets: no doubt his passionate concern for quality played a large part in his meteoric rise. His son Jean-Baptiste (usually referred to simply as Jean Naigeon) instituted a small but revolutionary change in mustard making. In about 1756, the date usually given as the founding of the house, he decided to substitute verjuice for vinegar in the making of his mustard. Although verjuice had been known and used in Roman times, it had been ignored by the French mustard makers for centuries. Yet with Dijon surrounded by vineyards, what could be more logical? With such a choice to hand, Jean was able to specify which grape variety he wanted and exactly when they should be picked. Unripe grapes produce a very pure, sour juice, with no sugar or acetic acid present. Mustard made with verjuice is thus very fine, slightly less acidic or pungent than that made with vinegar. Naigeon's mustard was a roaring success. Imitations abounded but mustard from the house of Naigeon was, for many years, considered far and away the finest. Jean's son continued the business until 1808 when the firm was taken over by another Dijon mustard maker, Fremiet. Thereafter a succession of well-known Dijon names appeared over the doorway in Rue St Jean – Piron, Pierrot, Bizouard – until the firm was absorbed by Amora S.A. in 1977.

Dijon, of course, had many other mustard makers. In 1856 Denis Bornier was registered as a maker of the famous Dijon gingerbread, *pain d'épices*, which not unnaturally is spiced with mustard. Two years later he applied to the Mayor for permission to inscribe over his dooway *'Usine à vapeur, fabrique de chocolat de moutarde Bornier-Cery'* (his wife's name). He was jumping on the bandwagon created three years earlier by the invention of a man whose name today is synonymous with Dijon mustard. The words *'usine à vapeur'* (steam mill) give the game away.

Until 1853, mustard seed had always been ground in hand-operated mills. Then Maurice Grey, who in 1843 had taken over the firm of Demartelet (founded originally around 1769 by Forey), invented a new machine. It was simple but it could crush, grind to a fine powder, then sieve the seed virtually all in one operation. Whereas previously one man could manufacture 16–17 kg of mustard a day, now the same man could produce 50 kg in a day. Everyone was clamouring for the

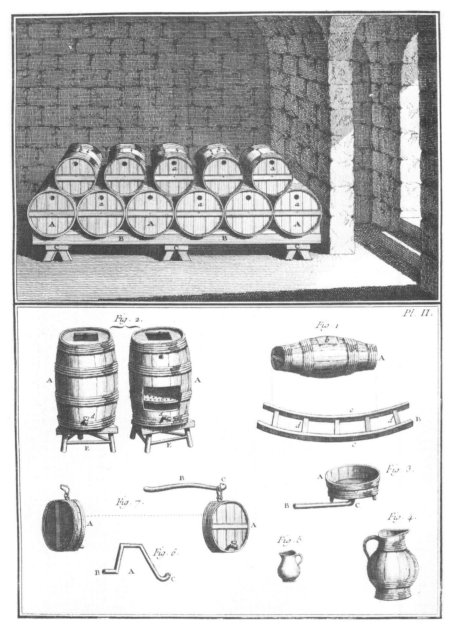

Techniques for vinegar and mustard making from
Encyclopaedia Panckouke (eighteenth century)

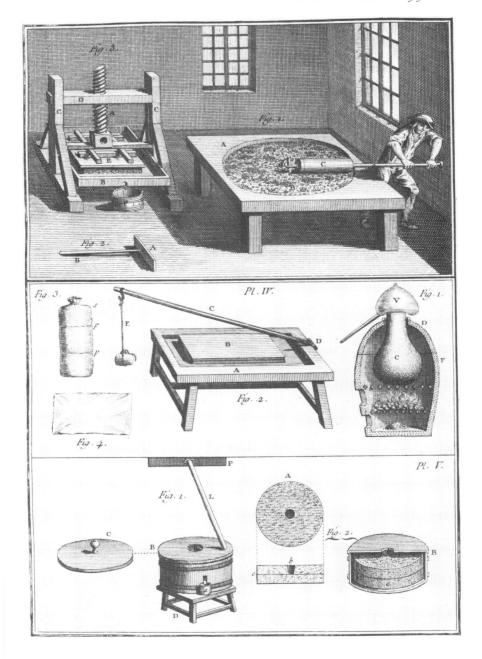

Mustard seller, eighteenth century (Nicholas de Larmessin)

new machine, advertising its proud possession not only above their doorways but also on their pots.

Maurice Grey was awarded two medals in 1855, one for his mustard, the other for his machine, and in 1860 he became the first Dijon mustard maker to be honoured by a royal appointment. In 1866 he was joined by Auguste Poupon. Although Grey obviously hoped his son, Anatole, would come into the business – he entitled a paper covering all aspects of mustard making, written in 1867, '*Moutarde, à mon fils*' (Mustard, to my son) – it was not to be, for Anatole was killed at the Battle of Champigny in 1870. The House of Grey became Grey-Poupon, and remained so until 1970 when it was taken over by S.E.G.M.A.* Maille. Happily the name Grey-Poupon is still recognized all over the world as Dijon mustard, and head of the ship is a direct descendant of Auguste, Henry Poupon.

Since Grey's heyday, in 1865, when there were thirty-nine mustard makers in Dijon, the industry has seen the decline, or the gobbling up, of many of the great houses. By 1911, there were only ten makers left in Dijon, four in the surrounding districts. The First World War saw the numbers diminish even further and by the early thirties firms like Amora were well on the way to becoming huge conglomerates.

In 1937 the regulations governing the making of mustard, and the seed to be used, finally became law. Specifically forbidden is the use of white seed – except in Alsace-Lorraine. Otherwise, only black or brown seed – or a mixture of the two – may be used, and the 'denomination of mustard from Dijon is reserved for mustard in paste made with crushed, and bolted or sifted seed'. Verjuice, which had been specified in the 1853 Declaration of the Academy of Dijon, is still permitted, but so, too, are wine and wine vinegar. Salt, spices and water can be added as well as sulphur dioxide to preserve the colour, but anything else – be it but a grain of white seed, a pinch of flour – and the paste can no longer be called mustard. It then has to be labelled 'condiment'. Seed selection is very carefully controlled. Cleared of all impurities and any bad grain, it is thoroughly washed and moistened, causing the grain to swell. It is then sent to the mill to be ground with the vinegar, verjuice or wine, salt and spices. The grinding is a fine art, the mills must be tuned with great precision so as to merely break the brown husks without crushing them so they can easily be sieved without leaving any bran to adulterate the bright yellow kernel. The paste is then pumped into huge oak casks and left to mature for five to eight days, vast wooden spatulas occasionally stirring the mixture.

* Société d'Exploitation des Grandes Marques Alimentaires

Grey Poupon jar 1875, and Grey Jar 1865: Post- and pre-merger

Only then is it ready to be bottled and labelled with those prized words '*Moutarde de Dijon*'. For Dijon was also granted in 1937 the right – like wines – to an Appellation Contrôlée. The mustard need not have come from the area of Dijon, it need only be made in the manner prescribed for it to be called Dijon mustard. Nonetheless nearly all the mustard so called is in fact from Dijon or its environs.

Sadly, today the makers are few. The Second World War saw the demise of most of the small family concerns. Now, despite an annual production of approximately 59,000 tonnes of mustard, 80 per cent of the market is controlled by Amora and S.E.G.M.A. (the latter a conglomeration of Maille/Grey Poupon and Parizot, another nineteenth-century Dijon maker) with Bocquet-Moutarde de France the biggest independent enterprise. For 85 per cent of the French, Dijon's mustard is their preferred variety, for the rest of the world, Dijon's name is synonymous with the finest mustard in the world. But for the exotic mustards, so favoured today, we must turn to Paris.

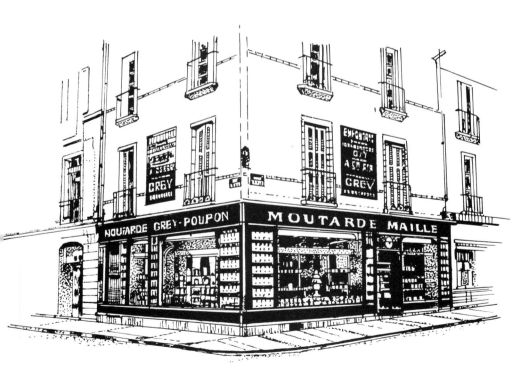

The Maille shop in Dijon today

Commercial mustard makers:
Paris and the Provinces

It is not such a bad trade, Savalette
and Le Comte have made a fortune . . .

Sebastien Mercier,
Le Tableau de Paris, 1782–1788

Long before those two gentlemen were making mustard their fortunes, the plant was providing a regular income for the monastery of the Abbey St-Germain-des-Prés at the time of Charlemagne the Great (*c.* AD 800). Some two hundred years later, a monk from the Benedictine Abbey de Saint-Gall also mentions mustard – as one of the food items figuring prominently on their table. Perhaps because the monasteries were such great consumers of mustard, the trade in its early years was always associated with the tallow makers. Then the '*vinaigriers*' entered the arena and in 1254 they too were permitted to make mustard. Yet mustard makers as such were not mentioned in The Book of Trades for that year. Officially they still fell under the aegis of the chandlers, although undoubtedly specialists were emerging – the tax register of 1292 lists ten '*moutardiers*'. In 1417, the *moutardiers* were included in the 15 Articles which detailed precisely how vinegar and sauce makers should run their business. At the end of the century, in 1494, they were at last formed into a Corporation, although adulterations persisted and Rabelais accused the mustard men of 'pissing in their pots'.

A new law in 1567 urged the mustard makers to insist on the cleanliness of their utensils. It was also forbidden for any one master to buy up all the mustard seed available in the market on any one day. The laws grew ever tighter and in 1658 Louis XIV drew up forty-three new articles: the mustard makers were now thoroughly protected. They, and only they, were allowed to sell mustard 'under pain of 100 pounds fine and seeing their illicit merchandise thrown into the river'. It was time for the fortunes to be made.

Savalette, an established maker of fine vinegars, decided in the middle of the century to launch a series of 'fine and aromatic mustards'. He was soon supplying Louis XIV and his court. The riches flowed in, and mustard became a profession 'with a house of its own'.

Around 1665, a group of gourmets and gastronomes formed themselves into the Société Vert-Pré, their ideals 'to renew the formulas of

Amora globe mustard pot, c. 1930

ancient French cuisine'. Among their products was mustard – a mustard which survived until 1960, when Amora absorbed the company. It was the eighteenth century, though, that was to become the age of new mustards, and rivalling mustard makers.

In 1742, M. Le Comte invented a new white vinegar, which earned him the appointment of 'Vinaigrier Ordinaire' to the King. His pupil Capitaine, who succeeded him in 1769, had on his list over 150 vinegars (for toilette, medicinal and gastronomic use) and more than thirty mustards, including, as he proudly boasted, 'that in powder from England'. Nonetheless, he was overshadowed by two even greater names: Maille and Bordin.

Antoine Maille had registered as a Master in 1742 and within five years was well established. He used sandstone vessels for distilling, thus avoiding the intrusive flavour of copper, and offered his clients – including Madame de Pompadour – nearly a hundred varieties of vinegar, both for the toilette and the table. His mustards numbered twenty-four and although not all were of his invention (capers and anchovies, for instance, had been launched by Le Comte), the quality was recognized as superb. Tarragon, red with three fruits, garlic, nasturtium, Chartreuse, lemon peel, lemon juice, yarrow,

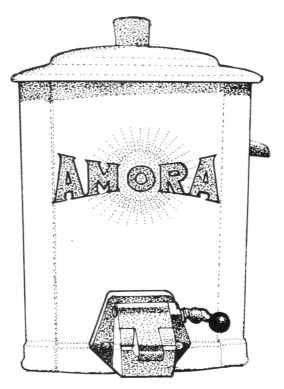

Amora bulk dispenser for shops, 1930s to 1960s.
These are still in use in parts of France today

mushrooms, truffles, six-berries, were among the most popular. In 1769, on the death of Le Comte, Maille took over as 'Vinegar-Distiller to the King and their Imperial Majesties'.

He had already amassed great riches, and soon put them to good use. He was a philanthropist and in 1771 gave enormous quantities of vinegar to the city of Moscow, where plague was raging. His reward was another title, Vinaigrier to Her Imperial Majesty, Catherine the Great. He was no less generous to his own countrymen. Every Monday morning, mustard was given away to the poor of Paris and outlying rural parishes – but to cure their chilblains.

The French Revolution, meanwhile, was about to cause upheaval in Paris, and in the life of Maille's successor, André-Arnoult Acloque. Born into the brewing business, he had made himself a small fortune with an establishment in the Paris suburbs. He also gained a less welcome reputation by defending the King when he was mobbed in

Mustard seller's costume, 1835

1792. In 1800 he bought the house of Maille, which he ran until his death two years later. In his short reign Acloque added many new mustards – chive, gherkin, shallot, morille (a type of mushroom), tomato, black (with olives), sweet mustard, green with fine herbs, and four-berries (good against chilblains and a 'superlative' condiment). Sadly, his son displayed not a jot of interest in mustard, and in 1819 signed a contract with the young Maille. Within the next seven years, Maille had recaptured the whole business.

François Bordin meanwhile had set up in Rue Simon le France, a 'wretched street, one of the most squalid quarters of Saint Martin' wrote Grimod de la Reynière. Here he flourished for twenty-three years, before moving 'to a magnificent locale in the Rue Saint Martin'. De la Reynière continues: 'It is there displayed with all pomp, this mustard of health and fragrance, which has earned such honour from the Louvre, and the Faculty – who have judged it for the last twenty-five years as favourable to the health as a mustard can be. The make of Bordin, one of the best and most celebrated of Paris, is now known to the two ends of Europe. The Russians eat his mustard like jam.'

In 1803 Bordin created a new mustard – Champagne – 'which has a flavour, a bouquet, an aroma easier to rejoice at than describe'. Two years later, he surpassed himself with his Moutarde Impériale, created in honour of Napoleon and 'superior to all others being made today, with much more aroma . . .' Despite the wonderful mustard, Napoleon ignored him. But royal patronage returned with Charles X, his successor Louis-Philippe, and the Emperor Napoleon III.

Together with Bordin, the house of Maille dominated the Paris market for most of the century, but in its closing years Maille began to decline. By 1930, the last direct descendant was dead. In 1963, the Dijon firms of Grey Poupon and André Ricard bought it out, forming, in 1970, the conglomeration of S.E.G.M.A. Maille. So the name lives, though with only eight of the original twenty-four mustards.

In the middle of the nineteenth century a Burgundian by the name of Bornibus decided to try his luck in the capital. He quickly made a spectacular name for himself, particularly for his so-called 'ladies' mustard', and he was a constant medal winner – thirty-five in 1890. His heirs kept up the tradition of fine mustards and today it is the only firm in Paris (as Grey Poupon in Dijon) still run by a direct descendant, Madame Hélène Boutet, who operates from the original premises at 60 Boulevard de la Villette.

Mustard making was not confined to Paris and Dijon. Saint-Maixent seems to have enjoyed early fame, and Orleans had its own

Bornibus jars 1950s and 1858–1930

corporation of Vinegar and Mustard Makers. Besançon produced a dry powder, which did not find much favour, and Angers made a mustard paste, sold in small barrels. Better were the mustards of Chalons – stronger than Dijon; Reims – highly thought of among connoisseurs; and Saint-Brieuc (in Brittany), created by Le Maout, who later did well in Paris.

Bornibus, maker of Moutarde des Dames

The town of Meaux produced a successful whole grain mustard, made by the monks since the early seventeenth century. In 1760, it was given to the Pommery family, who continued producing it according to the old formula, and in 1826 it received the accolade of Brillat-Savarin's recommendation. For that philosopher in the kitchen, Dijon's mustard did not take first place; '*Il n'est moutarde que de Meaux*' was his firm opinion.

In 1825 Louit was founded in Bordeaux. Their sensation came in 1845 with a new Moutarde Diaphane which soon sold a million pots a year. The firm was eventually absorbed by Amora. Bordeaux's success encouraged others. Small factories were set up in Avallon, Beaune, Brive, Cambrai, Coulommiers, Le Havre, Lille, Montmirail, Nancy, Nantes, Rouen, Strasbourg . . . It seemed as if all France was making its own mustard – except in the south, where garlic, pimentoes and pepper still took precedence.

Commercial mustard makers: England and the United States

He a good wit? Hang him baboon!
His wit is as thick as Tewkesbury
mustard!

Falstaff, *Henry IV, Part II*,
William Shakespeare

In medieval times, mustard making in England fell mainly within the province of the monasteries, with a few street-sellers in the large towns. Otherwise it tended to be made at home. In the sixteenth century one town suddenly emerged as a great mustard centre: Tewkesbury, in Gloucestershire. Its mustard was thick in texture, pungently hot in taste and came to be used, in all sorts of phrases, to mean one who was stupid and peppery.

By 1657, however, it was being highly praised. The herbalist Coles said, 'In Gloucestershire about Tewkesbury they grind mustard seed and make it up into balls which are brought to London and other remote places as being the best that the world affords.' Two factors gave Tewkesbury mustard its individuality: the infusion of horse-radish which gave added pungency, and the manner in which it was sold. The seed, once washed and pounded in a mortar, or with a large

THE NATIONAL CONDIMENT.

KEEN'S MUSTARD

MEDALS.
—o—
LONDON.
PARIS.
PHILADELPHIA.
MOSCOW.

1st PRIZE, SYDNEY, 1880.

SHAKSPERE

Shows that MUSTARD was in use
300 years ago.

KEEN'S MUSTARD

FACTORY ESTABLISHED.
A.D. 1742.

Was first Manufactured 125 years after
Shakspere's death.

Keen's advertisement 1880

cannon ball, was sifted; the flour was mixed with a cold infusion of horseradish and 'well beaten or stirred up for the space of at least an hour'. The mixture was then formed into large balls and dried. It was thus most convenient for transporting around the country, to sell at the local markets. The mustard ball could be kept until needed, when it would be reconstituted with vinegar, verjuice, cider, red wine, buttermilk or cherry juice, sometimes with honey or sugar added. It was extremely hot. Strangely, today in Tewkesbury there is no record of the business which made the town so famous: it must have been very much a cottage industry, and it vanished as dramatically as it had first appeared.

In 1720 'it occurred to an old woman of the name of Clements, resident at Durham, to grind the seed in a mill and to pass the meal through the various processes which are resorted to in making flour from wheat. The secret she kept for many years to herself, and in the period of her exclusive possession of it, supplied the principal parts of the kingdom, and in particular the metropolis, with this article; and George the First stamped it with fashion by his approval' (*The Gentlemen's Magazine*, September 1807).

Mrs Clements' mustard flour took England by storm, and competitors soon appeared. Within three years, the *London Journal* was carrying an advertisement: 'To ALL FAMILIES, etc. – The Royal Flower of Mustard Seed is now used and esteemed by most of the Quality and Gentry. It will keep good in the Flower as long as in the seed, and one spoonful of the Mustard made of it will go as far as three of that sold at chandlers' shops, and is much wholesomer.' Manufacturers continued to spring up throughout the century, and by the latter years Newcastle and Gateshead also boasted their own makers.

In Durham itself, with Mrs Clements presumably long since dead, the business seems to have been dominated by the Ainsley family. They claimed to have been established in 1692, and probably were – but as flour rather than mustard millers. By 1900, the only maker left was Simpson and Willan, who set up in 1888 and did not stay in business for long into the new century. In truth, Durham had enjoyed its heyday with Mrs Clements, for already in 1810 *Bailey's Agricultural Durham* was stating, 'This plant (mustard) was formerly much grown in this county, and *Durham Mustard* was proverbial for its excellence. At present a crop of mustard is rarely met with.' It was not to be met with again, and Durham's mustard, if it is remembered at all, lives on only in the phrase a 'Durham man': 'a knock-kneed man was so called, and was said to grind mustard between his knees', (Neasham's *North Country Sketches*). Mustard manufacturing had one more move to make – and this time it was not going to be ousted.

Before we turn to the Norfolk miller, we should perhaps remember the origins of a saying still in common use today – 'as keen as mustard'.

In 1742, in Garlick Hill, London, Messrs Keen & Sons set up in the mustard business. They were well placed to provide the city taverns with the condiment so necessary to the chop house customers and were hugely successful, their name quickly becoming synonymous with

Keen's mustard pot, 1870s, and mustard ointment, 1920s

mustard. A century later, despite the competition from Jeremiah Colman, Keen's (by now Keen Robinson & Belville) were still flourishing, and their product found great favour in Australia. In 1903 however, like so many of their French contemporaries, they were taken over. Mr Colman's competition had proved too much.

In 1804 Jeremiah Colman bought a windmill standing by Magdalen Gate in Norwich and set up in the business that he already knew – flour

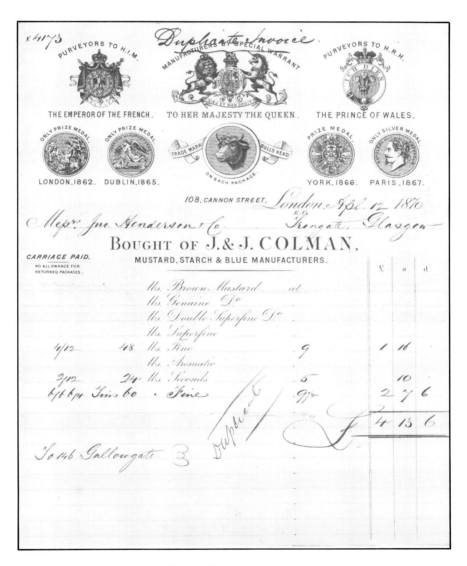

Colman's invoice, 1870

milling. Success brought expansion ten years later, when he took over a mill at Stoke Holy Cross, four miles to the south of the city.

Stoke Mill was a flour and mustard mill. Jeremiah, a cautious man, thought long and hard, and finally decided to continue making mustard. A wise decision: in 1856, the business had grown so much it had to move again. New premises were bought just outside Norwich, at Carrow on the River Wensum. As the factory expanded, so did the city for now Colman's works are officially in Norwich.

Although some of the process is still a tightly kept secret, the basic principles have not changed much. Fine quality seed (brown and white) – now all supplied by specially selected English growers – is thoroughly examined, tested for quality and cleaned. After drying, it is stored until needed, then blended so the quality of the final product is always constant.

Steel rollers crush the seed and steel sieves sift the flour. After a final blending of the brown and white flours it is ready to be put into the famous yellow labelled tins, themselves made in the adjoining building. The remaining husks have their oil extracted, then are dried and sold for animal feed.

It sounds simple, but Jeremiah spent a great deal of time and thought perfecting his mustard flour. The public responded magnificently; the big bull trademark and the name of Colman's were very quickly established. In 1866 Queen Victoria rewarded him with a royal appointment, the Prince of Wales following suit two years later and

Colman's covered box wagon, 1911

King Victor Emanuel of Italy added his seal of approval in 1869. Business expanded so quickly that often four trains were required to take away one day's production. The trains were Colman's own, with their emblem emblazoned on the sides of the cars. The army were supplied with a daily ration of mustard; Captain Scott took some to the Antarctic — efficacious against frost-bite; it was requisite in the luggage of every colonial; and a letter, from some far-flung part, with merely a drawing of a large bull's head above the word England, was safely delivered to Norwich.

No little part of this phenomenal success was due to marketing. In the early days, the advertisements were very simple – a mustard yellow background, with the words Colman's Mustard in huge letters, or perhaps just the lugubrious bull image.

Perhaps the most brilliant campaign was that thought up for Colman's by S H Benson, Ltd, the advertising agents, in 1926. Posters went up on all the London buses – 'Has Father Joined the Mustard Club?' Interest aroused, a 'prospectus' was published for the share issue. When a badge was offered, 2,000 applications were made: every day. Colman's had to open a special department with ten girls to deal with the influx. The success was beyond Benson's – and Colman's – wildest dreams. A card game was produced; eight Mustard Club songs were published; the club motto 'Mustard makyth Methuselahs' and the armorial bearings appeared all over the place on menus and postcards. The campaign continued for another seven years.

Today, the product that is so uniquely English mustard, with its bright yellow colour (turmeric added for vibrancy) and its pungent flavour (the careful blending of white and brown seeds) is still the favoured brand of some 85–90 per cent of the British market.

In the United States, they also have a bright yellow mustard but it is much milder in flavour. As recently as 1904, the Americans were not great mustard buyers. Despite R. T. French's claim, in 1885, to be 'the largest manufacturer of mustard in western New York State', sales were far from high. Francis French thought he knew the answer: 'a new kind of prepared mustard; one that is mild and has a true mustard flavour, and yet is light and creamy in consistency and color . . . It must be mild, for I believe that these hot mustards are used sparingly not because they are hot, but because people do not like them.'

French passed the problem over to his plant superintendent, George Dunn, who for some months experimented with different formulae. And then one day, Dunn came up with the solution. A cable was sent to Francis, 'Eureka!'. 'Eureka WHAT?' wired Francis in return – his specification long since forgotten. The excitement was a golden-yellow

Mustard Club poster, *Daily Mirror*, 29 October 1926

condiment, marketed as French's Cream Salad Brand – a little cream added to the mustard had changed its character dramatically, making it suitable especially as a salad dressing. It changed the company's fortune, and by 1915, sales topped one million dollars. In 1926 the family decided to sell out: Colman's was now the biggest manufacturer of mustard on both sides of the Atlantic.

Despite the continuing popularity of both the hot English and the mild American mustards, recent times have seen a revival of many small independent mustard makers in both countries.

In the United States, there are now over fifty brands of American 'speciality' mustards. Some are Dijon-style, others based on Colman's mustard flour, while Biggi sells mustards in the 'Russian style (hot and sweet), Chinese style (extra hot), English style (smooth and somewhat hot) and German style (hot, smooth and horseradishy)'. In Canada, Stone County produce the wonderful Honeycup Mustard – well worth looking for.

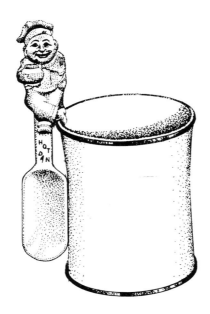

Hot Dan, the Mustard Man was the basis of French's
advertising during their growth in the early 1950s

In Britain, Gordons started by making a mustard using their English wine for flavouring and soon added to the range. Taylors, established in fact since the time of William IV, continued making their extra hot mustard while Wiltshire Tracklements became one of the success stories of the latter twentieth century, starting with a pot of home-made mustard on sale in the local pub. There is also, interestingly, a company – Boize – who have revived the ancient English tradition of flavouring their horseradish sauce with mustard.

Making mustard at home

For our ancestors, making mustard in the home was very much a labour of love, despite Hannah Woolley's simple-sounding instructions: 'Dry well your seed, then beat it little by little at a time in a Mortar, and sift it, then put the powder in a Gally Pot,* and wet it with vinegar very well, then put in a whole Onion pilled but not cut, a little Pepper beaten, a little Salt, and a lump of Stone sugar' (*The Queen-Like Closet*, 1670). Even with a quern (a pair of stones, one convex, the other concave, between which mustard seed was easily crushed, the 'flour' being pushed up the sides) rather than a mortar in the kitchen, this required patience, time and a strong wrist. The sifting especially was problematical – you really did have to grind the seed very fine to be able to sieve it satisfactorily.

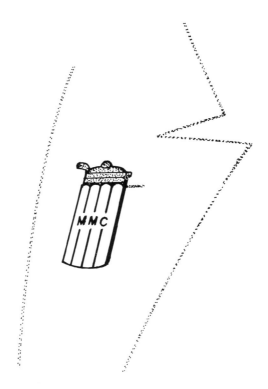

Mustard Club lapel badge, 1920s

* A small earthenware pot, much used by apothecaries for putting ointments in.

The technique for removing the husks

That magic innovation, the food processor, would have been a prized possession: with this, making mustard is easy. What you cannot do is grind the *dry* seed in the food processor. There is insufficient friction – they bounce around and ultimately change the container from transparent to opaque (sadly, proven . . .). So always soak the seed first, for *at least* 24–36 hours, checking from time to time to see if more liquid is needed to immerse the seed completely. Absorption capacity varies enormously depending on the age of the mustard seed – the longer it has been stored, the drier it will be. *Never* seal the jar when soaking mustard seed. It expands beyond belief and if sealed may well explode!

Vinegar is the age-old recommended liquid – and it will produce a milder mustard because the (dried) ground seeds release an enzyme (allyl senevol), some of which is dissipated in the soaking. If, however, further vinegar is used in the mixing, then the mustard can become quite pungent: again variation is enormous depending to a great extent on the vinegar used. Grape juice, 'must' (for the wine makers who wish to experiment with mustard) and water can also be used for the soaking, though water alone we found gives a rather bland flavour. It is more usual to add water as a 'mixer' to dilute a strong vinegar, despite John Evelyn's recommendation for 'water only, or the Broth of powder'd Beef' to be added to the 'stamp'd' seed. However, he then also added 'verjuice, Sugar, Claret-wine and Juice of Limon', thereby supplying flavour to this 'excellent sauce to any sort of Flesh or Fish'.

Once the seed is well soaked, it will break up quickly in the food processor – always use the metal blade. It then only remains to remove the husks (in Dijon, these are fed to the pigs: in a Bordeaux mustard, some of the crushed hulls are left in the mustard). This is a simple, although fairly time-consuming, procedure – and, like tying one's

Colman's Mustard Shop in Norwich opened in 1973,
the 150th anniversary of the company

shoelaces, far easier to do than describe (see illustration, p. 55). You will need a plastic spatula with a curved blade, and two conical sieves, both preferably metal; certainly, the final sieving *must* be through a metal sieve as the mesh has to be extremely fine and large nylon sieves are too coarse in texture.

Rotating the spatula with the tip in the palm of your hand, 'wind' it round and round the sieve, the curved part of the blade forcing the mustard paste through the mesh, the husks remaining behind. The process is repeated using a second, finer sieve to obtain a completely husk-free mustard, though it may occasionally be necessary to dilute the paste a little if it is too thick to sieve easily. Resist the temptation to dilute it too much, though, or you'll have a liquid on your hands. Home-made mustard does tend to be a little thinner than the commercially made product, since the centrifuges can remove all the husks with greater ease.

Your mustard is now ready for spicing. Here is where the fun begins, but do have some yoghurt at hand when tasting, also plain water biscuits and/or Cheddar cheese to give a bland background. Remember too Eliza Acton's advice. She was talking of the making of forcemeats but it applies equally well to the making of mustards and is as relevant now as in 1845: 'No particular herb or spice should be allowed to predominate powerfully in these compositions, but the

Taylor's of Newport Pagnell, founded in the reign
of William IV, is the only other independent mustard
maker in England dating from the nineteenth century

whole of the seasonings should be taken in such quantity only as will produce an agreeable savour when they are blended together' (*Modern Cookery for Private Families*).

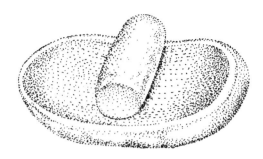

Saddle quern used for grinding mustard, *c.* 1500

Dijon Mustard

The result of *many* experiments, this produces a mild Dijon-style mustard – not quite so brightly yellow as Dijon's Dijon, but very good. The addition of the spices seems to darken the colour (though of course commercial Dijons also vary enormously – from a pale grey to lurid chrome yellow), and the seed itself obviously influences this. One can make a brighter, more pungent mustard by substituting cider or wine vinegar for grape juice and merely adding allspice, cinnamon, nutmeg and ground cloves, but the lack of herbs does make for a slightly less subtle mustard.

> *175 g/6 oz brown mustard*
> *seed*
> *300 ml/¹/₂ pint unsweetened*
> *grape juice*
> *3 cloves, ground in a spice*
> *grinder*
> *15 peppercorns, crushed in a*
> *mortar*
> *¹/₂ teaspoon ground ginger*

2 tablespoons dried chervil
½ teaspoon ground nutmeg
¼ teaspoon dried thyme
1 teaspoon ground cinnamon
2 garlic cloves, chopped
2 teaspoons dried tarragon
3 bay leaves
1 teaspoon Maldon salt

Soak the mustard seed in the grape juice, mixing in the herbs thoroughly. Leave for 36–48 hours, topping up with a little extra liquid if necessary – the seeds should be just covered. Cover the jar or bowl but don't seal tightly.

Place in the food processor and whizz for 3 minutes, using the metal blade, then leave to stand for 3 hours. Reprocess for 5 minutes. Pour into a conical strainer (mesh size approximately 15 per inch/6 per cm) and with a plastic spatula work the paste through the strainer. Transfer the paste to a finer strainer (mesh size approximately 30 per inch/12 per cm) and repeat the process.

Spoon the mustard into small jars and store, out of direct light, for at least 2 weeks before using, preferably a month. We have found the flavour good for up to 4–5 months, but without the colour-preserving sulphur dioxide it goes dark quite quickly. Small jars help to reduce the oxidation. Makes 300–450 ml/½–¾ pint, depending on the swelling powers of the seed, and the fineness of the sieve.

Now you have made your Dijon mustard, the world is your mustard pot, so to speak. You could, of course, cheat and use a bought Dijon to begin with.

To 300 ml/½ pint Dijon mustard, add for the following mustards:

Tarragon: 6–8 small sprigs (5 cm/2 in) fresh tarragon, finely chopped
Five-herb: 1 teaspoon each, finely chopped – parsley, chervil, tarragon, chives, shallots
Green pepper: 2–3 tablespoons green peppercorns, thoroughly drained from brine
Garlic-parsley: 2–3 garlic cloves, finely chopped, 2 tablespoons parsley, finely chopped
Three-fruits red: 3 tablespoons fresh tomato purée, 1 tablespoon strawberry purée, 1 teaspoon cassis (it may sound mad, but it's a traditional mustard and very good)
Mint: 2–3 tablespoons fresh mint, very finely chopped

Orange and clove: replace half the soaking liquid with concentrated frozen orange juice, add ½ teaspoon finely ground cloves

Paprika: another traditional mustard – 2–3 tablespoons sweet paprika, but do know your paprika (in Hungary, there are six strengths, few of them available outside that country. Frequently it's either very hot or very sweet!).

Other exotic combinations are often on sale, such as banana and pimento mustard, pineapple mustard, blueberry mustard. We leave you in the kitchen . . .

Anchovy Mustard

Excellent with steaks and fish, or in salad, cream or yoghurt dressings. You can use either home-made Dijon as the base or, for a punchier mustard, Dijon's extra strong.

>   *300 ml/½ pint Dijon mustard*
>   *15–20 anchovy fillets, drained and pounded*
>   *2 eggs*

Put the mustard, anchovy fillets and eggs into the food processor and blend, using the metal blade, for 1–1½ minutes. Very, very good. Makes about 400 ml/14 fl oz.

Dill Mustard

Excellent without the egg yolks – even better with them.

>   *75 ml/3 fl oz Dijon mustard*
>   *3 tablespoons sugar*
>   *4 teaspoons dried dillweed*
>   *1 teaspoon Maldon salt*
>   *freshly ground black pepper*
>   *1 teaspoon vinegar*
>   *2 egg yolks*

Put everything in the food processor and blend thoroughly. Can be used straight away, though it improves with a week's keeping. Makes about 2 small jars.

Type 1 A 1738-1775

Type 1 B 1775-1820

Type 2 A 1820-1830

Type 2 B Inscription manuscrite

Type 2 C Inscription au pochoir

Type 3 A 1810-1845
Type 3 B 1840-1850
Encadrement à la roulette

Type 4 A 1845-1885
Type 4 B 1845-1885
Encadrement à la roulette

Type 5 A 1850-1920
Type 5 B après 1900

Type 6 après 1908

Development of French jar shapes from 1738 to 1908.
The shapes developed as a result of the need to seal
the pots and of better pottery manufacturing techniques

Lenormand Mustard

The mustard maker's bible, *Manuel du Moutardier* by Julia de Fontenelle, still used in France today, was published in 1887 by Manuels-Roret. We found this mustard in it, remarkably similar to a Bordeaux despite a thorough sieving. Good with frankfurters and sausages of that ilk.

> *175 g/6 oz brown mustard*
>   *seed*
> *300 ml/½ pint red or white*
>   *wine or cider vinegar*
> *1 tablespoon fresh, chopped*
>   *parsley*
> *½ tablespoon celery seed*
> *1 tablespoon fresh, chopped*
>   *chervil*
> *1 tablespoon fresh, chopped*
>   *tarragon*
> *1 garlic clove, chopped*
> *3 anchovy fillets, drained but*
>   *not washed of their oil*
> *½ teaspoon Maldon salt*

Mix everything together and leave to soak for 36–48 hours, topping up with more vinegar as necessary to keep the seeds just immersed.

Place in a food processor and process in short, sharp bursts, using the metal blade, until the mixture turns the colour of coarse-grained mustard, i.e. brown with bright flecks of yellow. This will probably take about 2 minutes. Leave to rest for 2 hours, then reprocess for 4–5 minutes until the colour is more evenly yellow/brown. Sieve on the Dijon principle, using the larger meshed sieve first, then the very fine one. Put in small jars and store for 2–3 weeks before using. Makes about 2–3 small mustard jars.

Moutarde Soyer

As well as running (and redesigning) the Reform Club kitchens, writing books for the poor (and the rich), rushing out to Crimea to organize food for the Army, going to the opera and cooking dinner for his friends, Alexis Soyer also found time to invent, and patent, various sauces. His Aromatic Mustard was particularly popular: this recipe, published in the *Manuel du Moutardier* and attributed to Soyer, may, or may not, be the patented version. But it is good.

> *175 g/6 oz brown mustard*
>   *seed*
> *300 ml/½ pint white wine*
>   *vinegar*
> *4 teaspoons fresh, chopped*
>   *parsley*
> *2 teaspoons dried chervil*
> *4 teaspoons fresh chives,*
>   *chopped*
> *3 garlic cloves, chopped*
> *1 teaspoon celery seed*
> *¼ teaspoon four-spice*
>   *mixture (see below)*
> *½ teaspoon dried thyme*
> *½ teaspoon ground cinnamon*
> *1 teaspoon dried tarragon*
> *2 teaspoons Maldon salt*
> *2 tablespoons olive oil*

Combine all the ingredients except the oil, and leave to stand for 36–48 hours. Process in a food processor for 3 minutes, leave to rest for 3 hours, then whizz again for 4–5 minutes. Add the oil and blend for 1 minute, in short sharp bursts. Pass through two sieves as described for Dijon mustard, then bottle in small jars and keep for 1–2 weeks to mature. Makes 2–2½ small jars.

Note: Four-spice mixture is made with equal quantities of ground cinnamon, cloves, nutmeg and Jamaican pepper or allspice as it is now known.

Moutarde à l'Ancienne

Pommery's Moutarde de Meaux must be the most famous of the old coarse-grained mustards – mild, nutty and encased in lovely stoneware jars with red wax tops (now sadly often replaced by plastic). A good relation this, nice for cooking or as a table mustard.

75 g/3 oz brown mustard seed
175 ml/6 fl oz cider vinegar, or
   a mixture of white wine,
   water and vinegar
a good pinch of Maldon salt
freshly ground black pepper
1 teaspoon finely chopped
   fresh tarragon
1/2 teaspoon ground coriander
3 cardamom pods, seeds
   removed and ground
1/2 teaspoon sweet red pepper
   flakes, ground
pinch of ground bayleaf
1/4 teaspoon fresh thyme,
   finely chopped
1/2 teaspoon very finely
   chopped fresh fennel
2–3 pinches ground cinnamon
2–3 pinches ground cloves

Soak the seed in the vinegar for 36–48 hours. Put in the food processor, add salt and the spices, then blend for 1 minute. Leave for 2–3 hours, then blend for 1–2 minutes. Don't overprocess or you may break up too much of the mustard meal, releasing more volatile oil and making too pungent a mustard. The point of this one is a pleasantly nutty flavour without too much potency. Leave for 2–3 weeks before using – the longer it matures, the mellower it will be. Makes about 4–5 small jars.

Sesame Mustard

A beautiful mustard: not too strong and exquisitely nutty. Particularly good for bringing out the full flavour of chicken.

175 g/6 oz brown mustard seed
450 ml/3/4 pint unsweetened
   white grape juice
140 g/4 1/2 oz (white) sesame
   seed
1 teaspoon Maldon salt

Soak the mustard seed in 350 ml/12 fl oz of the grape juice for 36–48 hours. Add the remaining juice, the sesame seed and salt and leave for another 12 hours. Then whizz, briefly, to lightly break up the seeds and thoroughly blend. Add a little more grape juice if the mixture seems too thick. Leave for a week or two to mature. Makes about 6–8 small jars.

Roman Mustard

A coarse-grained mustard, based on Apicius's combination of pine kernels and almonds blended with mustard seed. Quite pungent, deliciously nutty . . .

> *275 g/10 oz brown mustard*
> *seed*
> *225 ml/8 fl oz red wine*
> *vinegar*
> *350 ml/12 fl oz red*
> *unsweetened grape juice*
> *3 teaspoons Maldon salt*
> *2 teaspoons cumin seeds,*
> *finely ground*
> *50 g/2 oz flaked almonds*
> *75 g/3 oz pine kernels,*
> *unroasted (roasted nuts give*
> *too overwhelming a*
> *flavour)*

Soak the mustard seed in the vinegar and grape juice, mixing in the salt and cumin seeds. Leave, covered but not sealed, for 36–48 hours. Put in the food processor and whizz for 1–2 minutes until coarsely ground, then add the almonds and pine kernels and run very briefly until they are completely broken up – don't overprocess. Makes about 700–800 ml/1 ¼–1 ⅓ pints.

Guinness Mustard

This is a stout mustard indeed – good at any barbecue, transforms bangers and mash.

*275 g/10 oz brown mustard
   seed
450 ml/3/4 pint Guinness
225 ml/8 fl oz red wine
   vinegar
1 teaspoon four-spice mixture
   (p. 63)
3 teaspoons Maldon salt
1 teaspoon black pepper,
   freshly ground*

Soak the seed in the Guinness and vinegar, having mixed in all the spices, for 36–48 hours. Place in the food processor and run briefly – just until the seed is coarsely ground and the whole nicely blended. Makes about 700 ml/1¼ pints.

Lemon Mustard

This is quite tangy, and good for cooking, but if you want to tone it down substitute unsweetened grape juice for the vinegar.

*40 g/1½ oz white mustard
   seed
40 g/1½ oz brown mustard
   seed
175 ml/6 fl oz cider vinegar
1 teaspoon Maldon salt
3 tablespoons lemon juice
grated zest of 1 small lemon
2 teaspoons clear honey
pinch of ground cinnamon*

Soak the mustard seed in the vinegar for 36–48 hours, adding a little extra vinegar if necessary. Blend in the food processor for 1 minute, add the remaining ingredients and leave to stand for 2 hours, then whizz again for 2–3 minutes. Pot up and leave for at least a month. Makes 4 small jars.

Tewkesbury Mustard

It is, of course, difficult to know exactly what the Tewkesbury mustard of our ancestors tasted like. This, though, makes an interestingly pungent mustard – good with roast beef, even better with the Yorkshire pudding and a dollop of rich gravy.

> *175 g/6 oz brown and white*
>   *mustard seed, roughly half*
>   *and half*
> *300 ml/½ pint cider vinegar*
> *¼ teaspoon Maldon salt*
> *freshly grated horseradish*

Soak the seed in the vinegar for 36–48 hours, adding extra vinegar if necessary to cover, then stir in the salt and blend in the food processor for 2 minutes. Leave for 2 hours. Add freshly grated horseradish – start with 1–2 tablespoons, but the quantity will depend on the pungency of the radish, the mustard seed and your tastes. Whizz again for 2 minutes, then taste – remembering that the mustard will mellow somewhat with time. Add extra horseradish if wished, whizz quickly just to blend in. Leave for at least 2 weeks. Makes 5–6 small mustard jars.

Hot Japanese Mustard

This is hot – be warned. In Japan, you are often given a small dish of made-up mustard, another of fresh grated horseradish, and chopsticks to mix the two together in the proportions you want. Based on that idea, this invention is particularly good for cooking.

> *75 g/3 oz brown mustard seed*
> *150 ml/¼ pint water*
> *1 teaspoon fresh grated*
>   *horseradish*
> *1 teaspoon Japanese plum*
>   *vinegar*

Soak the seed in water for 36–48 hours, then blend for 2 minutes in the processor. Leave for 1 hour, add the horseradish and vinegar and leave for another hour. Blend again very briefly. Pot up and let it mature for 2–3 weeks. Makes 3–4 small jars.

Matthew's Mustard

Matthew is eleven. He is an expert on mustard, with a fine palate, and this is the mustard with his seal of approval.

> *175 g/6 oz brown mustard*
> *seed*
> *225 ml/8 fl oz white grape*
> *juice*
> *125 ml/4 fl oz cider vinegar*
> *good pinch of four-spice*
> *mixture (p.63)*
> *¼ teaspoon Maldon salt*
> *thick honey*

Soak the seed and spices in the juice and vinegar for 36–48 hours. Blend for 2 minutes, then leave for 2–3 hours. Blend again for 1–5 minutes – the longer time will give a hotter mustard – then strain through a *coarse* sieve, just to remove the biggest hulls, still leaving the mustard slightly gritty. Or, for a really coarse-grained mustard, don't sieve at all.

Measure the volume of the mustard and melt half that volume of thick honey (runny honey gives too liquid a result). Pour into the mustard and mix well. Leave for a day then taste. If you would like the mustard sweeter, then melt a little more honey and add. The proportions vary between 1:2 and 2:3 of honey to mustard, depending on the seed, how long you have blended it, the sweetness of the honey, and your palate. Leave for a week. Makes 4–7 small jars, depending on the sieving and the amount of honey added.

Mostarda di Cremona (1)

Mostarda in Italian indicates their mustard-flavoured fruit relishes, *senapa* being the word for mustard. The Cremona relish is probably the most famous – and certainly the most readily obtained, both in Italy and abroad. Its traditional usage is as an accompaniment to roast eel, or *bollito misto*, that beautiful dish of boiled meats.

We give here two recipes out of the multitude available. The first, kindly sent to us by Enrico Dondi from Cremona (the family famous for their *mostardas*), dates from 1678 and is from *Practica de Speciali*, published in Venice and written by Father Domenico Avda, Capo Speciale dell'Archiopedale di Santo Spirito di Roma. It takes the form of a dialogue:

Q: How do you make Mostarda di Cremona?
A: Take a good quantity of black grapes, half a donkey panierful [these vary in size enormously, making a guess at quantity virtually impossible!], and make it into a pulp, then put it to cook in a zinc-lined pan that is completely dry, stir constantly with a stick – do not use a metal stick – take care that it does not burn. Cook until the grape skins come off.

Then with a mixer [what sort of contraption was this, in 1678?]

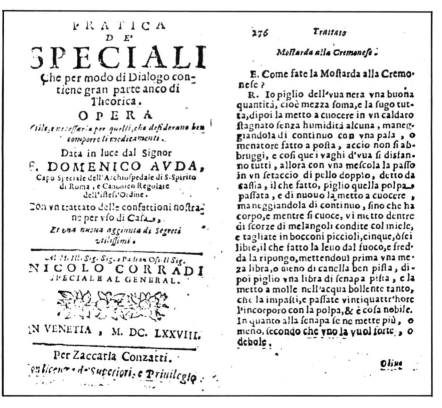

The original Mostarda di Cremona recipe, in the possession
of the Dondi family in Cremona, c. 1678

pass through a double-skinned strainer, then cook again, continuously stirring until pulp takes on body. While it is cooking add bitter orange peel, seasoned with honey and cut into small chunks 5–6 lbs, then take off stove and when cold put back on again adding half a pound of cinnamon well pestled. Take one pound of mustard ground, put it to soften with boiling water so it becomes a paste, after 24 hours add pulp and it becomes a noble thing. Add more or less mustard depending if you like it strong or weak.

> *1 kg/2¼lb grapes (seedless if*
> *you want to keep your*
> *sanity)*
> *mustard powder*
> *ground cinnamon*
> *zest of 1 Seville orange, all*
> *pith removed, very finely*
> *chopped*
> *3 tablespoons thick honey*

Put the honey in a small, heavy-based pan and melt gently, then add the chopped orange skin and simmer for 20 minutes, adding more honey if in danger of burning the pan. Remove the peel from the pan and leave to drain.

Meanwhile, wash the grapes, take off the stalks, and blanch the grapes in boiling water for 60 seconds. Then peel – the easiest way is to squeeze them as you open up the scar from the stalk: the skin should then easily slip away. Dragoon children or kind friends to help, and do the whole operation over a bowl to catch all the juices.

Using an enamel pan – the acidity of the grapes will turn aluminium (and the grapes) black – bring the fruit, with the juice, slowly to simmering point, then very gently continue to simmer until reduced to the consistency of marmalade, adding extra grape juice if absolutely necessary to prevent burning. Add the cinnamon and leave to cool, then stir in the crystallized orange zest.

Make the mustard into a paste with boiling water, then stir into the grapes once cooled. Reheat, stirring constantly, and simmer very gently until hot right through. Pot in sterilized jars and seal once cool. Makes about 4–5 small jars.

Mostarda di Cremona (2)

This is the modern recipe, using crystallized fruit. Fruits in all the *mostardas* vary enormously depending on what is in season, what looks good in the market, how you feel . . .

> 450 g/1 lb assorted
>   crystallized fruits (pear,
>   orange, cherry, pumpkin,
>   quince etc)
> 250 g/9 oz castor sugar
> 6 tablespoons brown mustard
>   seed
> pinch of Maldon salt
> 1/4 teaspoon dried red pepper
>   flakes

Dissolve the sugar in 150 ml/1/4 pint water, add the mustard seed, salt and pepper flakes and simmer gently for 10 minutes. Allow to cool, then stand for 24 hours. Return to the pan, bring to the boil, then strain through a metal strainer and again return to the pan with the crystallized fruit. Simmer for 10–15 minutes, gently, then remove the fruit to sterilized jars and pack tightly. Pour over the syrup, cool and then cover. If the sugar/mustard syrup crystallizes, it has been reduced too much so reboil with a little extra water added. Makes about 700 g/1 1/2 lb.

Mostarda di Venezia

This is traditionally made with quinces, although some recipes use a mixture of quince and pears. Since quinces can be hard to come by, and their flavour is very full, do this if necessary. But if you can get those sweet-smelling, golden fruit (and some enterprising greengrocers do stock them now, though only in season, in the early autumn) you will be rewarded. Keep them until the aroma is fully developed, then they are ready for use. Wipe off the soft down before peeling, and don't throw away peel and cores – they can be used to flavour apple pies, purées, jellies.

> 2 kg/4 1/4 lb quinces, or a
>   mixture of quince and pears

*juice and grated zest of 1
    lemon
200 g/7 oz castor sugar
4 tablespoons mustard
    powder*

Peel, core and chop the quinces, putting them into a saucepan with about 600 ml/1 pint water and the lemon zest and juice to prevent discolouration. Add enough water just to cover the fruit, stir in half the sugar and bring to a simmer. Cook until the fruit is soft (about 45 minutes for quinces, 5–10 minutes for pears). Remove from the pan with a slotted spoon and place in the food processor. Add the remaining sugar and the mustard, dissolved in a little boiling water to a paste, to the pan. Stir, then simmer gently until the liquid is reduced by about half and of a good syrupy consistency. Add a little to the fruit in

Eighteenth century Italian Mostarda di Fruita jar
from Palais des Ducs Museum, Dijon

the processor and blend. If the purée is too thick, add more liquid – the final consistency should be similar to apple sauce, and it will slightly thicken in the cooling. Bottle in sterilized jars, cool, then seal. Leave for 3–4 weeks. Makes about 1.4 kg/3 lbs.

Mostarda di Fruita

A cross between Mostarda di Venezia and Mostarda di Cremona. As with the Cremona relish, it is excellent with cold meats, spiced beef, tongue or a large ham on the bone.

> *500 g/18 oz quinces, prepared*
> *weight (approx. 1½ lb*
> *whole quinces)*
> *500 g/18 oz under-ripe pears,*
> *prepared weight (approx.*
> *1½ lb whole pears)*
> *150 g/5 oz pumpkin flesh from*
> *near the skin (start with a*
> *275 g/10 oz slice)*
> *200 g/7 oz dried figs, stalks*
> *removed*
> *juice and grated peel of 1*
> *lemon*
> *700 g/1½ lb castor sugar*
> *375 ml/13 fl oz white wine*
> *4 tablespoons mustard*
> *powder*

Peel and core the quinces and pears, chopping them into walnut-sized pieces and dropping them into a bowl acidulated with the lemon juice to prevent discolouration. Chop the pumpkin flesh into similar sized chunks; prick the figs with a skewer 10–12 times but don't cut them up. Put all the fruit into a large pan, just cover with fresh water, add 100 g/3½ oz sugar and the lemon peel and simmer gently until the fruit is slightly tender. Check regularly with a fork after about 5 minutes; the quince will take about 20 minutes, the rest of the fruit 5–10 minutes. Remove the fruit as it is cooked and leave to dry, discarding the water at the finish.

Mix about three-quarters of the wine with the remaining sugar and heat gently, stirring constantly to avoid burning. Add more wine if necessary and reduce until it is nicely thick, the consistency of golden syrup. Add the mustard, dissolved in a little boiling water to a paste. Stir well, then simmer for another minute.

Pack the fruit into jars and pour over the hot syrup. Leave to cool, then seal. Mature for at least a week; if possible, resist temptation for a month. Makes 1.8–2.3 kg/4–5 lbs.

Mostarda all'uso Toscano

Pellegrino Artusi was one of the most famous Italian cookery writers of the nineteenth century, elegantly combining the traditional with the imaginative. We have not found reference to a Tuscan *mostarda* elsewhere, but curiously it is not dissimilar to a *mostarda* found in Carpi, in the province of Modena, the other side of the Apennine Mountains.

> *350 g/12 oz*   } *seedless*
>   *black grapes*   } *if*
> *650 g/1 lb 6 oz*   } *possible*
>   *white grapes*
> *500 g/1 lb 2 oz apples,*
>   *pink-fleshed if possible*
> *1 large pear*
> *125 ml/4 fl oz white wine*
> *50 g/2 oz candied lemon peel,*
>   *very finely chopped*
> *25 g/1 oz mustard powder*
> *powdered cinnamon*

Peel, seed (if necessary) and mash the grapes with their juice. Peel, core and chop the apples and pear, then bring to the boil with the wine and simmer until the fruit is soft, 10–15 minutes. Add the grapes and continue simmering, stirring frequently, until the whole is a tender pulp.

Blend in the food processor, return to the heat and reduce until it is the consistency of jam. Leave to cool, stir in the mustard mixed with a little extra wine, and the candied peel. Pot in sterilized jars, sprinkle a little ground cinnamon on top and seal. Leave for at least 2 weeks. Makes 1.1–1.4 kg/2½–3 lbs.

Spicy Italian Vinegar with Mustard
(Aceto Picante Alla Senape)

A traditional Tuscan recipe – every family has its own variation. It is good as a sauce on its own, in salad dressings, and for making mustard. The quantities of herbs are for fresh ingredients. If you have to use dried, halve the amount, and in any case always use fresh parsley: dried is a travesty.

> 2 litres/3½ pints red wine
>   vinegar (white wine or cider
>   vinegar can be used, but the
>   red gives a lovely warm
>   colour)
> 2 teaspoons thyme
> 2 teaspoons marjoram
> 4 teaspoons oregano
> 4 teaspoons basil
> 4 teaspoons rosemary needles
>   stripped from the stalk
> 4 bay leaves
> good bunch of flat parsley,
>   finely chopped
> 10 garlic cloves, chopped
> 4 small onions, finely chopped
> 10 cloves
> 2 teaspoons black pepper
> 2 teaspoons freshly grated
>   nutmeg
> 2 teaspoons Maldon salt
> 150 ml/¼ pint olive oil
> 5 cinnamon sticks, totalling
>   about 37.5 cm/15 in in
>   length, broken into small
>   pieces
> 2 tablespoons mustard
>   powder

Put all the ingredients except the oil and mustard into a large jar. Seal and shake once a day for the first week, then twice a week for the next two weeks. After about three weeks remove the cinnamon bark, and add the olive oil and mustard powder. (Make sure all the cinnamon is removed – it doesn't soften and will cause havoc with the food processor.)

Blend in a food processor in small batches, for 2–3 minutes at a time. Strain through a fine meshed sieve and discard any small pieces of herbs and spices.

Return to the jar and leave for at least another week before using. It will separate naturally, so needs to be shaken before use. Makes about 2 litres/3 ½ pints.

Mrs Beeton's Horseradish Vinegar

Some of Isabella Beeton's recipes are distinctly odd: her 'Indian Mustard, an excellent Relish to Bread and Butter, or any cold Meat' is anything but. This horseradish vinegar, though, *is* excellent. We always make it up in the quantities she gave – and always seem to be needing more.

> *125 g/4 oz freshly grated*
> *horseradish*
> *1 small shallot, very finely*
> *chopped*
> *a pinch of cayenne pepper*
> *1.1 litres/2 pints red wine*
> *vinegar*

'Put all the ingredients into a bottle, which shake well every day for a fortnight. When it is thoroughly steeped, strain and bottle, and it will be fit for use immediately. This will be found an agreeable relish to cold beef, &c. *Seasonable.* – This vinegar should be made either in October or November, as horseradish is then in its highest perfection.' Makes about 1.1 litre/2 pints.

Tartar Mustard

Eliza Acton, from whom this recipe comes, states, 'This is an exceedingly pungent compound, but has many approvers.' Indeed so.

'Rub four ounces of the best Durham mustard very smooth with a full teaspoonful of salt, and wet it by degrees with strong horseradish vinegar, a dessertspoonful of cayenne, or of chili vinegar, and one or two of tarragon vinegar when its flavour is not disliked. A quarter-pint of vinegar poured boiling upon an ounce of scraped horseradish, and left for one night, closely covered, will be ready to use for this mustard, but it will be better for two or three days.

'Durham mustard, 4 oz [125 g]*; salt, large teaspoonful; cayenne or chili vinegar, 1 dessertspoonful [2 teaspoons]; horse-radish vinegar, quarter-pint [150 ml].'

English Mustard

Since (we feel) only a masochist would want to grind, by hand, in a mortar, so finely as to be able to sift it easily, the correct proportions of brown and white mustard seed (which are a closely guarded secret), we have spared you the intricacies of a recipe for making English mustard from scratch. Messrs Colman spend every day making, and marketing, various mustard powders – including one with no wheat flour for those on a gluten-free diet. But it is worth remembering their advice when wishing to turn mustard powder into mustard (and it is surprising how many think it unimportant): always use *cold* water. The reason for this is strictly chemical. The addition of cold water to ground mustard seed produces a chemical reaction between the enzyme myrosin and the glucosides sinigrin (in black mustard seed) and sinalbin (in white mustard seed). Acting as a catalyst, the water enables the myrosin to ferment the sinigrin, breaking it up into the essential oil of mustard (allyl isothiocyanate), potassium salt and sugar, producing a pungent odour and sharp taste. On the sinalbin, the myrosin acts to produce sulpho-cyanate of acrinyl, sulphate of sina-pine and sugar, unaromatic and less acrid in taste. The combination of all these is the clean, sharp taste of English mustard!

If you use tepid or boiling water, the formulae are lost. It is often said that it is the pungency that is destroyed: in fact, the burning sensation remains but with a slight bitterness and an absolute lack of any flavour. If you cook the mustard, the pungent overtones *are* lost, and very often any taste too though that will depend on the length of the cooking. In many cases, what happens is that the mustard vastly heightens the flavour of the base ingredient of the dish while leaving no trace of itself. But for the Englishman, and his roast beef, or slice of ham off the bone, the mustard must be mixed with cold water, left to stand for ten minutes, and then consumed.

* Use any good English mustard powder or mustard flour – and divide the quantities by four.

The Franklyn, a modern Chaucerian figure from a series
made by the Rye pottery

SAUCES

Woe was his cook but if his sauce were
poynaunt and sharpe . . .

The Franklyn, from the Prologue
to Chaucer's *Canterbury Tales*

The Franklyn, as a Knight of the Shire, was an important man, ever
prepared for a multitude of visitors, and his cook had to get things
right. In Chaucer's day, the palate demanded highly spiced and, to our
taste, somewhat sharp sauces. Vinegar was often used alone, particularly with salted fish; sweetly spiced with cinnamon and ginger it
would accompany roasted eels and lamprey, while with mustard and
sugar it was especially served with brawn. That particular trio crops
up in early manuscripts again and again (and again – in 1914 the *Daily
Mail* recommended 'the simplest sauce for boiled bacon – a teaspoon
of mustard and vinegar and pepper and sugar').

Most sauces went to the other extreme, being a complicated amal-
gam of many herbs and spices, and there were definite rules as to what
sauce went with what. Brawn, beef and salt mutton had mustard; lamb,
sucking pig, kid or fawn had ginger sauce; veal and bacon had verjuice
(crab apple). Besides these, there were other, more specialized sauces
such as chaudron for swan, camelyne for wild fowl, gauncel for goose,
peverade for venison, gelatine for water fowl and egurdouce for fish.

Many of these sauces were uncooked (unless they contained the
innards, blood or fat of the animal they were to accompany) and they
were usually very thick – almost a paste – and served on little saucers
beside the main dish. The Roman influence is easily discernible:
Apicius's recipes were mostly complex, with a multitude of herbs and
spices as well as dates, figs, nuts, honey, oil, must, broth, wine – and
mustard.

One must remember that in medieval days much meat was past its prime, or heavily salted. And, as there were no forks, dishes were either reduced to a pulp (no doubt losing much of their flavour) or had to be served in a form easily edible in one's fingers (and were therefore often rather tasteless and dry). Either way, a sharp sauce to enliven the dish must have been a welcome relief. The Harleian manuscript of 1450 has a sauce for roasted crane which minces the liver of the bird before mixing it with 'pouder' of ginger, vinegar and mustard. This principle remained a favourite for several decades, and in *Stere Hit Well*, the Pepysian Library manuscript 1047, there is a 'Sauce for a Pyke' almost identical in its making.

Meanwhile, in Paris, the *sauciers* had their own guilds, officially authorizing them to sell their sauces (as did the vinegar makers) on the streets. The narrow thoroughfares were thronged with men shouting out their wares, '*Sauce à la moutarde*', '*Sauce à l'aillée*', '*Sauce verte*'. It must have been very convenient for the cook – you could just pop outside when the vendors were in your street and buy not only mustard, vinegar or oil, but bread, flour, milk, butter, cheeses or pâtés. Often the children were sent on these errands: the Goodman of Paris wrote that the 'little children sang at night while going for wine or mustard'. By 1650, there were some 600 'walking *mustardiers*'. London too had her street peddlers, some selling sauces though more favoured actual provisions: garlic, interestingly, was widely sold.

The English sauces at this time were remarkably similar to the French. Both kitchens now saw a gradual change from the highly spiced, thick medieval sauce to smoother, subtler recipes, so that by the mid-seventeenth century many were merely unthickened gravies, judiciously flavoured with a few herbs and spices – though the permutations on this were enormous.

Vinegar however was still popular in England as a sauce: alone (particularly on salads), with mustard and also with horseradish. John Gerard's *Herball* of 1597 states: 'the horseradish, stamped with a little vinegar put thereto, is commonly used for sauce to eate fish with and such like meates as we do mustarde.' Horseradish and mustard were also associated together. Tewkesbury mustard was spiced with the root and Evelyn recommends steeping it in vinegar for a 'sallet' dressing (p.88) – though by now oil had made a comeback to the salad. For, despite the English predilection for vinegar alone, there is a recipe for 'salat' in the *Forme of Curye* which firmly states, after instructions to wash and pick over the herbs, 'pluk hem small with thyn hond and myng hem well with rawe oile. Lay on vynegar and salt and serve it forth.'

Mustard was also used in horseradish sauces, though to lightly colour rather than flavour them. Quite what effect it had in this recipe from *Dorset Dishes of the Eighteenth Century* is hard to imagine: 'Grate very fine 8 large sticks of horseradish and put into it three tablespoonfuls of white chile vinegar, a teaspoonful of mixed mustard and a gill of good cream, a gill of good white sauce seasoned with a little cayenne, some salt and very little white sugar. Then freeze the sauce as ice cream and serve.'

By this time, there was a clear division in sauce making. Catsups (from the Chinese *koe-chiap* meaning a relish or pickled fish sauce) were in fashion. Some included mustard, and many were combined in complicated mixtures. But also appearing were new recipes for very simple sauces. A mixture of butter, vinegar and mustard is frequently cited, not just for pork and fish dishes, but also for simpler fare such as 'sodde Eggs', hard-boiled eggs quartered, then fried in butter before being seasoned with vinegar and mustard.

From Germany, presumably with the Hanoverian Elector, had come sauces for brawn and boar's head which introduced as the sweet element port or redcurrant jelly. The variations on this were many, most notably the sauce we now consider indisputably English: Cumberland.

By the time of George IV, with Carême installed in the palm-tree-columned kitchens of Brighton Pavilion, an incredible number of sauces – taking days to make – were appearing on the royal table, including Sauce Ravigote à l'Ancienne: with onions, Chablis, consommé, lemon juice, garlic, shallot, gherkins, capers, herbs simmered, then added to a Sauce Espagnole, strained, *1 teaspoon* mustard added, strained again then a little butter added just before serving – one wonders whether the mustard would have been noticed by its absence.

More obviously noticeable was mustard's inclusion in the many salad dressings that abounded. Richard Dolby, who had made The Thatched House Tavern in St James's Street so fashionable a venue for the Regency bucks, created a dressing, clearly similar to a rémoulade (p.85); while Dr Kitchiner in his pompously titled *Apicius Redivivus, The Cook's Oracle* has a salad dressing which became popular as Dr Kitchiner's Salad Cream. A mixture of eggs (hard-boiled), cream, vinegar and mustard, this appears throughout the century in slightly varying guises to become universally known as English Salad Cream. Well made, it is very good, though the commercial travesties today do little to recommend its appearance on the table.

Mustard is used in these salad dressings, and often in mayonnaise, not just for its flavour. For one of mustard's great properties is that it acts as an emulsifier, thickening the sauce by 'holding' together the droplets of oil and vinegar. It is thus very useful in the making, too, of somewhat tricky sauces, such as hollandaise, since it minimizes the threat of curdling. Chemically, this is due to its absorption powers: the powdered seed absorbs up to one and a half times its own weight of oil, and twice of vinegar.

Today, once more, we have veered toward simpler sauces though with a certain amount of misplaced enthusiasm for odd combinations. There are some occasions when even mustard cannot come to the rescue, in spite of this suggestion in a recent American book: 'If lobster and blueberries or duck livers and kiwi fruit must be combined, mustard in a light cream sauce can give them togetherness.' This is to abuse both our digestions and mustard.

Punch cartoon, 28 June 1856. Gun toting was just as common in the United States in those days

Mustard Vinaigrette

The basic recipe for vinaigrette has hardly changed in 300 years. The English name – French dressing – recognizes the French influence in the addition of oil to the dressing. Previously, we had swamped our salads – and much else – with little but vinegar and sugar, much to the astonishment, and complaint, of foreign visitors. John Evelyn, with memories of vinegar and sugar being 'the constant vehicles', devised a perfect 'sallet dressing': 'Take of clear, and perfectly good *Oyl-Olive*, three Parts; of sharpest *Vinegar* (sweetest of all *Condiments* – for so some pronounce it, perhaps for that it incites Appetite, and causes Hunger, which is the best Sauce), *Limon*, or Juice of *Orange*, one Part, and therein let steep some Slices of *Horse-Radish*, with a little *Salt*; Some in a separate *Vinegar*, gently bruise a *Pod* of *Guinny-Pepper* [cayenne pepper], straining both the *Vinegars* apart, to make use of Either, or One alone, or of both, as they best like; then add as much *Tewkesbury*, or other dry *Mustard* grated, as will lie upon an Half-Crown Piece: Beat, and mingle all these very together; but pour not on the *Oyl* and *Vinegar*, ''till immediately before the *Sallet* is ready to be eaten: And then with the *Yolk* of two new-laid *Eggs* (boyl'd and prepar'd, as before is taught) squash, and bruise them all into mash with a Spoon; and lastly, pour it all upon the *Herbs*.'

With minor changes, that is the recipe we give here, and it is commonly used today. We do add sugar, despite Evelyn's comment that it 'is almost wholly banished from all, except the more effeminate palates', and, for this basic vinaigrette, we omit the egg yolks – though they make for a deliciously creamy dressing, the beginnings of a rémoulade in fact. Remembering his *Note*, 'That the *Liquids* may be made more, or less *Acid*, as is most agreeable to your Taste', you can of course change the proportions of oil to vinegar. Many writers recommend a one to five, or one to six ratio: much will depend on the vinegar, the mustard, the salad to be dressed. Your palate, of course, is the final arbiter.

> $^1/_2$ *teaspoon sugar*
> *1 teaspoon Dijon mustard*
> *1 tablespoon wine, cider or*
>   *Horseradish vinegar (p.76)*
> *3 tablespoons best olive oil*
> *Maldon salt*
> *freshly ground black pepper*

Mix the sugar, mustard and vinegar of your choice to a paste. Beat in the oil to make a thick liaison, then season – lightly – with salt and freshly ground black pepper. Taste and adjust the proportions, if wished, accordingly. Makes enough dressing for a salad for 4–6.

Yellow Sauce

In Spain, a dash of mustard powder is often added to vinaigrettes – one of the very few appearances of mustard in the Spanish kitchen. In this yellow sauce – Salsa Amarilla – it is blended with Madeira and stock, and is very reminiscent of Apicius with his 'wine, oil, broth, vinegar, mustard and pepper' combinations. We tried it with a good boiling fowl, cold pork and beef: excellent in all cases.

> *6 hard-boiled eggs*
> *2 tablespoons Madeira*
> *2 tablespoons extra virgin*
> *olive oil*
> *Maldon salt*
> *125 ml/4 fl oz good strong*
> *beef or chicken stock*
> *1 tablespoon wine vinegar*
> *1 teaspoon Dijon mustard*
> *½ teaspoon freshly ground*
> *white pepper*

Separate the egg whites from the yolks, pressing the former through a fine sieve and reserving. Mash the yolks, then stir in the Madeira to make a thick paste. Beat in the oil drop by drop, whisking well all the time, then add a good pinch of salt. Warm the stock until just beginning to melt and beat, slowly and thoroughly, into the mixture. Add the vinegar, mustard and pepper. In Spain they use mustard powder but the Dijon gives a smoother sauce. Lastly, stir in the egg whites. Makes about 300 ml/½ pint.

Sauce Rémoulade

There is a certain amount of entanglement historically between the Sauces Rémoulade and Tartare. Rémoulade was probably invented during the eighteenth century, along with so many other classic sauces. Certainly, Menon, the prolific French writer of the 1740s and 1750s, mentions it. His recipe is fairly simple, basically a vinaigrette with shallots, garlic, capers, anchovies, parsley and mustard added. By the nineteenth century, hard-boiled egg yolks – occasionally also a raw egg yolk – have made their appearance. At the close of the century, it seems firmly established that sheltering under the name of rémoulade are two, significantly different, versions of the sauce. The household recipe is based on hard-boiled egg yolks, with seasonings and oil added: the restaurant version has mayonnaise as the foundation – giving what many people today would recognize as Sauce Tartare. Curnonsky, in *Bons Plats, Bons Vins* (1949), gives both varieties of the rémoulade – though several pages apart and with no comment on either. To add to the confusion, his Sauce Tartare is very similar to the (household) rémoulade, but with an interesting note that the liaison will not hold very long so should be made at the last moment. If necessary though, one can substitute a raw egg yolk for one of the hard-boiled yolks 'but it is no longer a true sauce Tartare'. We have now come full circle to today's generally accepted method of making Sauce Rémoulade. It is creamier, less heavy and rich than the mayonnaise-based sauce (though both are indisputably good) and is often given as the alternative foundation to mayonnaise for making Sauce Tartare. So, if you should be given a sauce by another name that you thought was Tartare (or Rémoulade) it is perhaps comforting to know that neither you, nor the chef, has gone mad.

2 hard-boiled egg yolks
1 raw egg yolk
1 teaspoon wine or cider
    vinegar
1 teaspoon Dijon mustard
Maldon salt
freshly ground black pepper
150 ml/¼ pint best olive oil
1 teaspoon finely chopped
    tarragon

> *1 teaspoon finely snipped*
>   *chives*
> *1 teaspoon chervil*
> *1 teaspoon drained, chopped*
>   *capers*
> *1 teaspoon anchovy paste*

Mash the hard-boiled egg yolks with the vinegar to a smooth paste, then beat in the raw egg yolk. Add the mustard with a touch of salt and pepper, then whisk in the oil slowly, as when making mayonnaise. When it is thick and smooth, stir in the chopped herbs, capers and, finally, the anchovy paste. Serves 4.

Mustard Mayonnaise

Mayonnaise is perhaps the classic summer sauce. Thick, rich and gleaming golden yellow, home-made mayonnaise is instantly distinguishable from its commercial cousins. Sadly, its making seems to inspire terror in many, though with the electric blender – provided all the ingredients are at room temperature, and a stern patience is adhered to in the initial pouring of the oil – it is magically simple. Room temperature, incidentally, does not mean the kitchen in a New Orleans house on a June day – the oil should be clear but not hot: cooks in the tropics usually have to cool it a little on ice before proceeding. Should you want, however, to make the sauce on a cold winter's day, you may have to stand the oil – if it is at all cloudy – in a warm room for a few hours, or put it in a bowl of warm water, until it is crystal clear. If the bowl is very cold, rinse that in warm water too, then dry very thoroughly. With a mustard mayonnaise, of course, the problems are slightly eased by the fact that the mustard itself acts as an emulsifier.

> *2–3 egg yolks*
> *1 tablespoon Dijon mustard*
> *½ teaspoon Maldon salt*
> *1 teaspoon wine or cider*
>   *vinegar or juice of ½ lemon*
> *300 ml/½ pint olive oil*

Whisk the egg yolks thoroughly in a large bowl. Many advocate a wooden spoon for the beating but a whisk is easier and quite satisfactory. Add the mustard and salt and a *few* splashes of vinegar and whisk again. Then pour a few drops of oil into the bowl – it is best to have the oil in a jug for easy control. Whisking all the time, add a few more drops of oil only after the last have been absorbed by the eggs. As the liaison thickens you can pour the oil in a slow stream but in the beginning do go slowly. Whisk until really thick and the mayonnaise falls with a 'plop', then add a few more drops of vinegar (or lemon juice) to sharpen lightly. Should disaster strike and the sauce curdle, start again with another egg yolk in a clean bowl, adding the curdled mixture drop by drop as before. The mayonnaise will keep in an airtight jar in the fridge for 1–2 weeks, though if the sauce does not come to the top of the jar, you may have to skim off the surface skin. Until experience makes a confident 'mayonnaiser' of you, start with 3 egg yolks: after that you will find that you need only 2. You can also, of course, experiment with different mustards to vary the flavour subtly. Serves 6.

Avocado, Anchovy and Mustard Mayonnaise

A perfect combination: you can alter the balance of ingredients to taste, and according to the dish it is to accompany.

> *300 ml/½ pint mayonnaise*
> *(p.86, made* without *the*
> *mustard or with only ¼*
> *teaspoon added)*
> *1 medium-sized, ripe avocado*
> *1¼ anchovy fillets, drained*
> *and soaked in milk for 10*
> *minutes*
> *1 teaspoon Dijon mustard*

Mash the avocado thoroughly, pound the anchovy fillets, then stir into the mayonnaise and add the mustard. Beat or whisk very briskly to completely meld everything together. With these quantities, no flavour is too overpowering – if you want to heighten one of them, then add more avocado, anchovy or mustard, but don't overdo it: the harmony must not be too disturbed. Serves 6–8.

The Poet's Receipt for Salad

The Reverend Sydney Smith was a charmer. A great gourmet, a great wit, an intellectual, he was friend to the great. Banished to the country by the Church for his liberal views, he continued to amuse, to condole, to advise, in never-ending correspondence. His recipe for salad, delightfully written in verse, was well known amongst his friends but appeared for the first time in print in Eliza Acton's *Modern Cookery for Private Families*. She makes an interesting point: 'We could not venture to deviate by a word from the original, but we would suggest, that the mixture forms almost a substitute for salad, instead of a mere dressing.' Her 'suggestion' is certainly correct – it is a delicious potato salad (albeit mashed), and the last line of the poem, 'Fate cannot harm me – I have dined today', is surely indicative of this. The mistaken allusion to it as a dressing was obviously as prevalent in Miss Acton's time as it is today. Perhaps the confusion arose with the alternative version of the poem, which only differs in four lines and which appeared in Lady Holland's *Memoirs of the Reverend Sydney Smith*, published, ten years after Eliza Acton, in 1855. Perhaps he had taken to serving the potato salad on a bed of greenery. In any event, here is the salad (with both endings). Exceeding good, as Miss Acton would have said, with pickled herrings, or any smoked fish, or chicken.

> Two large potatoes, passed through kitchen sieve
> Unwonted softness to the salad give;
> Of mordent mustard, add a single spoon,
> Distrust the condiment which bites so soon;
> But deem it not, thou man of herbs, a fault,
> To add a double quantity of salt;
> Three times the spoon with oil of Lucca crown,
> And once with vinegar, procured from town;
> True flavour needs it, and your poet begs
> The pounded yellow of two well-boiled eggs;
> Let onion atoms lurk within the bowl,
> And, scarce suspected, animate the whole;
> And lastly, in the flavoured compound toss
> A magic teaspoon of anchovy sauce:
> Then, though green turtle fail, though venison's tough,
> And ham and turkey are not boiled enough,
> Serenely full, the epicure may say –
> Fate cannot harm me – I have dined today.

Lady Holland's version has four spoons of oil and two of vinegar, and continues after 'anchovy sauce':

Oh, green and glorious! Oh, herbaceous treat!
Twould tempt the dying anchorite to eat;
Back to the world he'd turn his fleeting soul,
And plunge his fingers in the salad-bowl!

Stick to the Acton quantities, using teaspoons for the mustard and salt (very scant for the salt), tablespoons for the oil and vinegar, and about half a small onion, *extremely* finely chopped. Serves 2.

Mustard Butter

Very simple, and keeps well in fridge or freezer. Cut in slices and serve on fish, steak, lamb cutlets, vegetables.

225 g/8 oz unsalted butter
2–3 tablespoons Dijon or
  other mustard of your
  choice
freshly ground white pepper
  (optional)
dash of lemon juice (optional)

Have the butter quite soft but not melting, then beat in the mustard, distributing it evenly throughout. Season with a grinding of white pepper and a splash of lemon juice if wished, then form into a 'sausage'. Chill until required, then cut into slices and put on your dish just before serving. Serves 8.

A particularly good variant of this is to fry 2–3 tablespoons black mustard seed in ½ tablespoon oil until they start to splutter (cover the pan or they will be all over the kitchen). Drain and mix into the butter. This gives a nutty butter rather than a mustardy one – you can, of course, add a bit of both seed and mustard for another variation.

Sauce Dijonnaise

There are countless sauces under the Dijon flag – all naturally with mustard in them. Here are two old classics, one cold (similar to, but much simpler than, a rémoulade) and one hot – a mousseline, akin to hollandaise but easier to make.

> 4 hard-boiled egg yolks
> 4 teaspoons Dijon mustard
> juice of 1 lemon
> 150–300 ml/¼–½ pint olive
>   oil
> Maldon salt
> freshly ground black pepper

Sieve the egg yolks, then mash to a paste with the mustard. Thin with lemon juice, briskly whisking, then add the oil, drop by drop at first, in a slow but steady stream as the sauce thickens. After adding the first quarter-pint, continue until the sauce is as thick as you like it, then season lightly with salt and freshly ground pepper. Serves 6.

Sauce Mousseline Dijonnaise

> 3 egg yolks
> juice of 1 lemon
> Maldon salt
> freshly ground black pepper
> 1 teaspoon cold water
> 175 g/6 oz unsalted butter
> 2 tablespoons Dijon mustard

Whisk the eggs in a bowl, add the lemon, salt, pepper and water and whisk again. Cut the butter into small pieces, put in the bowl with the mustard and place over a pan of simmering water. Now whisk constantly and at a steady pace until the whole is light, frothy and all the butter melted. Use a large bowl or it will splash all over you, the kitchen, the cooker. And be warned, it does take 15–20 minutes. Worth it. Serves 6.

Beurre Blanc à la Moutarde
White Butter with Mustard

One of the simplest – as far as ingredients are concerned – and subtlest of sauces. That 'Prince of Gastronomes', Curnonsky, said: 'It is a sauce of exquisite finesse and lightness, discreetly seasoned with Angevin shallots... Remember that the shallot must be, so to speak, volatilized in the vinegar, and that it should be no more than a remote presence. ... Many gastronomes hold that there is a sort of sleight of hand in making this sauce, ... see if you can give them the lie' (*A l'infortune de pot*, 1946). The trick – if there is one – in making this sauce successfully is not to let the butter actually melt – it must soften and appear to be *about* to melt, before the next piece is added. Then you will have the white creamy perfection that is *beurre blanc*. Bearing in mind the requisite remoteness of the shallots, it is an ideal sauce for spicing with mustard. A hint of mustard. A mild Dijon is good or, more delicately, very finely chopped mustard leaf seedlings. Here is Curnonsky's basic recipe.

> *4 shallots, very, very finely*
> *chopped*
> *125 ml/4 fl oz white wine*
> *vinegar*
> *250 g/9 oz unsalted butter, cut*
> *into small dice*
> *freshly ground black pepper*
> *Additional spicing: 1 scant*
> *teaspoon mild Dijon*
> *mustard, herb-flavoured if*
> *wished, or 2 tablespoons*
> *finely chopped mustard*
> *seedlings*

The shallots must be chopped so finely they are almost mashed. Place in a small saucepan – preferably heavy-bottomed as this will not transmit the heat so fiercely – with the wine vinegar. Cook gently until the shallots are quite soft, the vinegar almost completely evaporated.

Take the pan off the heat and whisk in the butter – piece by piece, adding each knob after the last has quite softened and almost melted – until the sauce is thick and creamy. That is the 'princely' method: many people find it easier to cool the shallot mixture, then whisk in the butter over a very low heat, lifting the pan off every few seconds – and instantly if the butter appears to be actually melting. Once it starts running, the sauce is lost, and you may well need to make it a few times to get it right. Try it in quarter-quantities at first, and remember the whole process should be quick – two minutes at the most. When it is ready, give 2–3 grindings of the pepper mill and stir in the mustard, or leaves, quickly. Serve at once, with fish, chicken or tiny, young, steamed vegetables. Serves 6.

Mustard Cream Sauce

Another supremely simple sauce, and one of the most sublime, perfect with practically anything.

> *125 g/4 oz unsalted butter*
> *125 ml/4 fl oz double cream*
> *dash of lemon juice*
> *1–2 teaspoons Dijon or other*
>   *mustard of your choice*

Melt the butter in a wide pan (this helps the quick thickening of the cream), when just about to sizzle pour in the cream, stir and bubble fairly hard for a minute or so until it has lightly thickened. Add a squeeze of lemon juice and stir in the mustard. Start with 1 teaspoon, then taste and add accordingly. Serve immediately with fish, flesh, fowl, vegetables. There are many variations – adding herbs, a combination of mustards, anchovies, a few soft roes, whatever is suited to your dish. The delicately green cream sauce from the Îles Chausey is a sophisticated variation with shallots and garlic sautéd in the butter, more mustard and a splash of vinegar instead of lemon, then cream and a couple of spoonfuls of finely chopped parsley and tarragon stirred in. Superb with cod, even more so with mackerel.

Sauce Messine

From Lorraine, this delicious concoction is perfect with the fine fat trout that hail from the River Moselle – or indeed any beautifully fresh fish.

> *few sprigs chervil, leaves very*
>   *finely chopped*
> *few sprigs parsley, very finely*
>   *chopped*

few sprigs tarragon, leaves
  stripped off the stalks and
  very finely chopped
2 tablespoons finely chopped
  shallots
1 tablespoon finely grated
  lemon peel
50 g/2 oz butter, softened
1 teaspoon flour
1½–2 teaspoons Dijon
  mustard
2 egg yolks
300 ml/½ pint single cream
juice of 1 small lemon

Mix the herbs, shallots and lemon peel together. Mash the butter and flour until the butter is quite soft, then add the mustard, mixing well, and blend in the egg yolks, lastly the cream. Put into a saucepan with the herb mixture and beat with the pan standing in another containing hot (not boiling) water. Stir continually until the sauce is thickening and the cream *almost* about to come to the boil. On no account must it ever actually boil or that lovely smooth velvetiness will be lost. Just before serving, squeeze in the lemon juice. Serves 4.

Coriander and Mustard Sauce

Coriander seeds are sweet and orangey, the leaves pungent and slightly peppery. Lovely together.

125 g/4 oz unsalted butter
1½ tablespoons coriander
  seeds, crushed (do not use
  pre-ground coriander: it is
  quite different)
125 ml/4 fl oz double cream
squeeze of orange juice or
  tangerine juice if possible
  (about 2 segments, crushed
  and sieved)
squeeze of lemon juice

1 teaspoon Dijon mustard
small bunch fresh coriander
    leaves, very finely chopped

Melt the butter, add the coriander seeds and cook gently until the aroma starts to give – about a minute, but watch the butter doesn't brown. Add the cream, bubble hard for 2–3 minutes until thickening, then add a squirt of orange juice, and lemon to sharpen. Finally stir in the mustard and, off the stove, the coriander leaves. For fish, chicken, lamb or veal. Serves 6.

Sauce Saint-Malo

Excellent with all kinds of fish, particularly shellfish.

75 g/3 oz unsalted butter
25 g/1 oz flour
400 ml/14 fl oz fish stock
2 shallots, very finely chopped
100 ml/3 1/2 fl oz dry white
    wine
3 anchovy fillets, soaked in
    milk, drained and pounded
1 tablespoon Dijon mustard

Melt 25 g/1 oz of the butter, sprinkle in the flour and stir thoroughly to make a smooth roux. Gradually add the fish stock, stirring all the time, until well amalgamated and the sauce starts to thin down. Keep stirring until it thickens again, then simmer on a very low heat for about 10 minutes.

Meanwhile, put the shallots and the wine in another pan and heat until the wine has completely reduced. Stir in the pounded anchovy fillets and the remaining butter and cook, still stirring, until all is well blended. Now sieve it into a bowl. Give the velouté sauce a stir, making sure there are no lumps, then – off the fire – whisk in the anchovy and shallot butter. Stir in the mustard and serve at once. Serves 4–6.

Russian Sauce

From Carême, probably one of the greatest exponents of sauce making, comes this simple sauce 'for large cuts of roast beef'.

> *1 slightly heaped tablespoon
>   unsalted butter*
> *1 slightly heaped tablespoon
>   flour*
> *350 ml/12 fl oz home-made
>   beef stock (or you could use
>   leftover gravy, slightly
>   thinned down)*
> *1 tablespoon finely chopped
>   parsley*
> *1 tablespoon finely chopped
>   chervil*
> *1 tablespoon finely chopped
>   tarragon*
> *1 teaspoon Dijon mustard*
> *½ teaspoon sugar*
> *pinch 'of fine pepper'*
> *juice of 1 small lemon*

Melt the butter in a pan and stir in the flour briskly to make a smooth roux. Cook gently for 4–5 minutes until it is lightly nutty brown, then very gradually pour in the stock, stirring all the time to prevent lumps. Cook for about 8 minutes, continually stirring, until it is just starting to thicken. Meanwhile, have another pan with boiling water at the ready. Put the chopped herbs into a sieve, dip into the water and blanch for 30 seconds. Shake off excess water and add the herbs to the velouté. Stir for another few minutes until the sauce thickens to about single cream consistency. Take off the heat, add the mustard, sugar, a grinding of black pepper and the strained juice of a lemon. Serves 4.

Note: There is another Russian sauce, mayonnaise-based, with sieved caviare and the coral and tomally of a lobster stirred in. Larousse states, 'Add mustard'; others omit it.

Sauce Robert

A sauce of great antiquity and, although the French may lay claim to it and say that it was named after their great Norman duke, it is, according to E. S. Dallas – who is usually very reliable – in fact English. 'The French had their *brouet de chevereuil*; and the English had their Roebroth and Roebrewert, for which there were a number of varying receipts. One of these receipts the French picked up; and with that glorious faculty of altering names which has never failed them since they appear in history, they thought its name must be the same as that of their famous Norman duke, and they called it Robert' (Kettner's *Book of the Table*, 1877). Its age is not in dispute: Taillevent, the great medieval chef, writes of it and by the sixteenth century it was so prevalent that Rabelais says it must accompany 'ducks, rabbits, roasts, fresh pork, poached eggs, salt hake, and a thousand other viands'. Today the sauce is usually an accompaniment to roast pork though it is excellent too with goose.

> *2 tablespoons unsalted butter*
> *3–4 large onions, very finely*
>   *chopped*
> *1 generous tablespoon flour*
> *300 ml/½ pint good light*
>   *stock*
> *splash of cider vinegar*
> *1 tablespoon Dijon mustard*
> *Maldon salt*
> *freshly ground white pepper*

Melt the butter, then add the onions (the amount varies enormously from authority to authority). Cook gently, stirring occasionally, until they are nicely golden, then sprinkle with the flour, stir and cook a few moments longer. Gradually pour in the stock (you can substitute a few tablespoons medium-dry white wine for some of the stock if you wish), stirring all the while, then simmer gently for a further 15 minutes. Add a splash of vinegar, then stir in the mustard. Lightly season and serve. Serves 4–6.

Horseradish Sauce

It seems to be an ancient English practice to stir a little mustard into horseradish sauce – not to season it, for it would be difficult to add to such a powerful flavour, but to colour it a gentle yellow: a sensible idea, for grated horseradish quickly discolours to grey or, even more unappetizingly, pale brown.

> *3–5 tablespoons grated*
> *horseradish (the lesser*
> *amount for the freshly*
> *pulled and grated root –*
> *well scrubbed and peeled, of*
> *course)*
> *1 tablespoon white wine or*
> *cider vinegar*
> *1 teaspoon castor sugar*
> *150 ml/¼ pint double cream,*
> *whipped to the soft peak*
> *stage*
> *1 teaspoon made English*
> *mustard*

Mix the grated root with the vinegar and sugar and leave for 5 minutes. Then stir into the cream, lightly but thoroughly, and lastly add the mustard. You can add a bit more if liked to heighten the colour. A must with roast beef – nice too with pork and chunky lamb chops. Serves 4–6.

Benton Sauce

Despite the title of her book, *A New System of Domestic Cookery* (published 1806), Maria Rundell is reflecting an age-old combination in this recipe for a sauce very similar to the medieval dipping sauces. It is very good.

> *50 g/2 oz fresh horseradish,*
> *very finely grated*
> *4 tablespoons wine or cider*
> *vinegar*

1 teaspoon made English
  mustard
2 teaspoons castor sugar

Grate the horseradish into the vinegar, add the mustard then the sugar. Whisk briskly until the sugar is dissolved then leave to stand for at least 2 hours. Particularly good as a piquant antidote to the richer cuts of pork. Serves 4.

Cumberland Sauce

One of the best of the English cold sauces – except that its origins are probably not English. Certainly it does not hail from the county of Cumberland. Legend has it that it was named after Ernest, Duke of Cumberland (brother of the Prince Regent, later the last Elector of Hanover). Undoubtedly, in Hanover we are nearer its true birthplace for it is very similar to a 'Hanoverian' sauce given by Elizabeth Ayrton for boar's head in *The Cookery of England* and to a sauce said by Soyer in his *Gastronomic Regenerator* to be the German accompaniment to the same dish (still made today in many Bavarian households).

2 Seville oranges (or 1 sweet
  orange and 1 large lemon)
6 tablespoons redcurrant jelly
1–1½ teaspoons Dijon
  mustard
Maldon salt
freshly ground black pepper
sprinkling of ground ginger
8 tablespoons port

Pare the rind from the oranges (or orange and lemon) being careful to keep them pith-free. Cut into matchstick strips and blanch in boiling water for 5 minutes. Drain and reserve.

  Meanwhile, melt the jelly, preferably in a bain-marie, add the mustard, stirring until smoothly amalgamated, then add the orange strips and strained juice, a good grinding of pepper, a little salt and a pinch of ground ginger. Stir for a further minute, pour in the port and cook for another 5 minutes. Pour into a small bowl and let cool – the sauce will thicken as it cools. It is not meant to be thickly set so *do not* add gelatine or cornflour as advocated in some recipes – this destroys the delicate texture and clear flavour. Serves 4.

Thomas Jefferson's Sauce for 'Stew Made of Cold Meat'

Before leaving Washington for Monticello, Jefferson always sent ahead of him a list of provisions to be put in store. Mustard makes frequent appearances, on one occasion '6 bottles of mustard' being called for. However, Jefferson knew when little was best: its contribution here is small in amount, significant in flavour. A sauce good for leftover game and roast beef, preferably fairly rare to begin with so as not to be thoroughly overdone in the recooking.

40 g/1 ½ oz unsalted butter
2 tablespoons walnut ketchup
2 tablespoons redcurrant jelly
1 teaspoon Dijon mustard
¼ teaspoon freshly ground
   black pepper
Maldon salt

Heat the butter, ketchup and jelly with 2 tablespoons water, stirring until the jelly is melted and the sauce nicely blended. Add the mustard, pepper and salt to taste and simmer gently. Lay your slices of meat in the sauce and cook for 2–3 minutes to heat through. Serves 2.

'Sauce for A Mawlerd (Rosted)'

Among the papers in Samuel Pepys' library was the manuscript *Stere Hit Well*, dating it seems from the late fifteenth century and mainly concerned with cookery. This sauce for roast duck is an exemplary lesson in how to make perfect gravy – before cornflour and other sundry devices arrived on the culinary scene, with such devastating results. It can be applied to almost any joint, with the substitution of an appropriate liquid for ale (wine, port, cider, brandy or other liqueur, even orange, apple or grape juice) and a mustard suitable to the meat being roasted.

Take onyons And mense them Wele
Put sum yn thy mawlerd so have yᵉ Sele [good luck]
And mynce mo[re] Onyons I the[e] ken [tell]
With the grece of the malwerd seth [boil] hit then
Put ale musterd And hony ther to
Boyle all to gedy tyll hit be enowe.

> *2 medium onions*
> *1 tablespoon of fat from the*
>   *roasting juices*
> *3–4 tablespoons ale or other*
>   *alcohol or fruit juice*
> *1 teaspoon Dijon mustard (or*
>   *mustard of your choice)*
> *1–2 teaspoons clear honey*
> *Maldon salt (optional)*
> *freshly ground black pepper*

Chop one onion coarsely and put in, or under the joint (good luck is always welcome – and so is the flavour the onion gives to the meat), then roast in the usual manner. When the meat is done, strain off the pan juices, putting one tablespoon of fat in a small pan, skimming off the rest.

Grate an onion into the hot fat and cook for 5 minutes until softened. Mix in the mustard, then stir in the ale and the honey. Bring to the boil, add the reserved, skimmed meat juices, then cook, stirring, for 2–3 minutes until the honey is dissolved. Season with salt if necessary, and a good grinding of black pepper, then taste. Depending on the ale used, you may need a little more honey. If port, or a sweetish liqueur or fruit juice was the liquid, it may need a little sharpening – a squeeze of lemon should be sufficient. Serve very hot. Serves 4–6.

Ambrose Heath's Sauce for Goose or Duck

Very simple, very good.

> *2 tablespoons made mustard*
> *the juice of 1 lemon*
> *2 tablespoons port*
> *sprinkling of cayenne pepper*

Whisk everything together in a small saucepan, bring to the boil and serve hot. Serves 2–3.

Seville Mustard Sauce

If you are an habitual maker of fine sauces – Espagnole or demi-glace, for example – they will give a fine base for this. For most of us lesser mortals, a good, strongly reduced chicken or beef stock, or even leftover gravies from such joints, will do admirably.

> *300 ml/½ pint good chicken*
>   *or beef gravy (not a stock*
>   *cube in sight) or 600 ml/1*
>   *pint chicken or beef stock*
>   *reduced by half*
> *1 Seville orange*
> *1 tablespoon brandy, whisky,*
>   *kirsch, etc or red or port*
>   *wine*
> *1 teaspoon Dijon mustard*
> *½ teaspoon Matthew's*
>   *mustard (p.68)*
> *pinch of cayenne*

Bring the gravy or stock to a simmer. Meanwhile, peel the orange (no pith to be taken with the zest), cut into matchsticks and blanch for 2 minutes in boiling water. Drain and chop finely, add to the gravy, then squeeze in the juice through a strainer. Add the alcohol and boil for 1 minute, then turn off the heat and stir in the mustards. Stir for a good minute before adding a dusting of cayenne. Serve in a hot sauceboat with steak, chicken breasts or legs. Oddly enough, it is good with pork too. Serves 3–4.

Mustard and Ginger Sour Cream Sauce

Sharp, with a nice bite, and good with cold fish, chicken or lobster.

> *150 ml/¼ pint sour cream*
> *5 cm/2 inch piece fresh root*
>   *ginger, peeled and grated*

1–2 teaspoons Dijon mustard
1–2 tablespoons olive oil
juice of 1 lemon
freshly ground white pepper
freshly ground allspice
few sprigs salad burnet, very
finely chopped (optional)

Chill the sour cream. Add the ginger and mustard (start with 1 teaspoon and adjust to taste). Stir in the oil, half the lemon juice and a generous grinding each of white pepper and allspice. Taste, adding more oil or lemon accordingly, then stir in the salad burnet just before serving. If you can't beg, borrow or steal some of this heavenly herb, don't try and substitute anything else. Nothing tastes the same. Serves 6.

Orange, Mustard and Yoghurt Sauce

Very refreshing, with a hint of piquancy. Particularly good with smoked chicken or turkey: or thin it down with extra orange, add some olive oil and use as a salad dressing.

1 sweet orange
1 teaspoon Matthew's
mustard (p.68)
150 ml/¼ pint thick natural
yoghurt
splash of Spicy Italian vinegar
(p.75)
3–4 cardamom pods, seeds
removed and crushed
sprinkling of cinnamon

Very finely grate about a quarter of the orange zest into a bowl. Squeeze the juice, strain and add with the mustard. Stir in the yogurt, add a dash of vinegar, then sprinkle over the cardamom seeds and a touch of cinnamon. Chill lightly. Serves 4–6.

Very Superior Bread Sauce

Very unorthodox but very good. Like many inventions, it happened by accident.

> *25 g/1 oz butter*
> *3–4 spring onion bulbs, finely*
>   *chopped*
> *2 garlic cloves, thinly sliced*
> *1 heaped tablespoon flour*
> *1 heaped teaspoon mustard*
>   *powder*
> *600 ml/1 pint milk*
> *3–4 slices wholemeal bread*
> *Maldon salt*
> *freshly ground black and*
>   *white peppers*
> *freshly grated nutmeg*
> *freshly ground allspice*
> *pinch of cinnamon*

Melt the butter, add the onions and garlic and sweat gently for 5 minutes to soften but not colour. Sprinkle in the flour and mustard powder, stir to make a thin, smooth paste, then gradually pour in about half the milk. Stir for 5–7 minutes until it begins to thicken, then break the bread into small pieces and whisk in. Simmer, very gently, for 20 minutes, checking occasionally and adding a little milk if need be to prevent sticking. Then add another 150 ml/¼ pint of milk and simmer for a further hour, adding the remaining milk little by little as it is absorbed. The end result should be thick and creamy. Season with a little salt, fairly generously with the peppers, nutmeg and allspice. Serves 4–6.

Devil Chantilly

A slight adaptation of a recipe from Nancy Shaw's *Food For the Greedy* (published 1936) – a must for the bookshelves, and worth the search.

*1 ½ teaspoons Matthew's
    mustard (p.68)
1 teaspoon Spicy Italian
    vinegar (p.75)
1 teaspoon anchovy sauce or
    ½ teaspoon anchovy paste
½ teaspoon Maldon salt
¼ teaspoon freshly, and
    coarsely, ground white
    pepper
½ teaspoon Worcestershire
    sauce
150 ml/¼ pint double cream*

Mix the mustard, vinegar, anchovy sauce or paste, salt, pepper and Worcestershire sauce together – thoroughly. Whip the cream until soft peaks form, then fold the mustard mixture into the cream. Chill before serving. A little grated lemon peel is a nice addition. Serves 4.

Gubbins Sauce

The Victorian author, Edward Spencer, adopted the charming alias of Nathaniel Gubbins for his weekly humorous column in the *Daily Express* during the late nineteenth and early twentieth century. The name – and the sauce – reek of the British Empire in its heyday.

> . . . invaluable, especially for the sluggard. The legs and wings of fowl, turkey, pheasant, partridge or moor-hen should only be used. Have these scored across with a sharp knife, and divided at the joints. And when your grill is taken, 'hot as hot', but *not burnt*, from the fire, have poured over it the following sauce. Be very particular that your cook pours it over the grill just before it is served up. And it is of the most vital importance that the sauce should be made, and well mixed, on a plate *over hot water* – for instance, a slop-basin should be filled with boiling water and a plate placed atop.
>
> Melt on the plate a lump of butter the size of a large walnut. Stir into it, when melted, two teaspoons of made mustard, then a dessertspoonful of vinegar, half that quantity of tarragon vinegar, and half a tablespoonful of cream – Devonshire or English. Season with salt, black pepper and cayenne, according to the (presumed)

tastes and requirements of the breakfasters. (*Cakes and Ale*, Edward Spencer, 1897)

Delicious at any meal, with any sort of grilled meat – particularly tiny lamb cutlets. A double boiler for the making is easier than a plate, an ounce of butter about the right amount, and, to our tastes, a tablespoon of cream to smooth the edges. Serves 2.

Alice B. Toklas's Devil Sauce

It is the eccentricity, plus of course the anecdotes about Alice Toklas and Gertrude Stein's years in France, combined with the sharp commonsense that one expects to come out of a French kitchen, that makes her *Cook Book* such irresistible reading. A very devilish sauce this (we cut the cayenne by half), which she served with some thoroughly devilled smelts.

>   *300 ml/½ pint dry white wine*
>   *1 tablespoon white wine*
>   *vinegar*
>   *1 tablespoon chopped shallots*
>   *¼ teaspoon black pepper*
>   *225 ml/8 fl oz tomato juice (or*
>   *1½ tablespoons tomato*
>   *purée mixed into 200 ml/7 fl*
>   *oz good chicken stock)*
>   *1¼ tablespoons butter,*
>   *softened*
>   *1¼ tablespoons flour*
>   *1 tablespoon English mustard*
>   *powder*
>   *1 tablespoon Dijon mustard*
>   *½ tablespoon anchovy paste*
>   *⅛ teaspoon cayenne pepper*
>   *(or less)*
>   *2–3 saffron filaments, crushed*
>   *in 1 tablespoon boiling*
>   *water*

Put 50 ml/2 fl oz wine in a pan with the vinegar, shallot and black pepper: simmer over a low heat, until reduced by half. Add the tomato juice and remaining wine and bring to the boil. Mash the flour and butter to a smooth paste, then stir into the simmering sauce, little by little, until the sauce thickens, being careful to prevent lumps forming. Mix the powdered mustard with the Dijon and the anchovy paste, stir in the cayenne and the saffron with its soaking water. Whisk into the sauce thoroughly, then simmer very gently for 10 minutes. Strain into a warmed sauceboat and serve immediately. Serves 6.

Glazes

There are many glazes with mustard for all varieties of meat. Sugar and mustard for ham is perhaps the best known: below are a few variations to start the experimental ball rolling.

For ham or gammon joints:
> 2 tablespoons Dijon mustard
> 2 tablespoons brown sugar
> 4 tablespoons cream

Mix all together and smear over the joint – increase the quantities proportionately for a large ham.

For pork:
> 2 tablespoons Matthew's
>   mustard (p.68)
> 1 tablespoon Dijon mustard
> 1 tablespoon soy sauce
> 1 tablespoon olive oil

For lamb:
> 2 tablespoons redcurrant jelly
>   (even better, crab apple
>   jelly)
> 1 tablespoon Roman mustard
>   (p.65)
> 1 tablespoon olive oil
> 2 tablespoons red wine

For beef:
> 2 tablespoons Anchovy
>   mustard (p.60)

1 tablespoon Worcestershire
 sauce
2 tablespoons port
2 tablespoons olive oil

For chicken:
 1 tablespoon Lemon mustard
  (p.66)
 1 tablespoon lemon juice
 1–2 garlic cloves, crushed
 2 tablespoons apply jelly
 1–2 tablespoons olive oil

The variations on these are infinite: marmalade is good with pork (English mustard, ginger wine and oil), mint jelly with lamb (Dijon mustard, Calvados and oil). You can spice it up, or down; you can add herbs, alcohol or sauce seasonings (Harvey's, Tabasco, chilli, etc) to suit your mood, the dish – and your store-cupboard.

Devilled Glaze:
 2 tablespoons Dijon mustard
 2 tablespoons black treacle
 2 tablespoons brown sugar
 3 tablespoons soy sauce
 2 teaspoons anchovy paste
 cayenne pepper

Dip the spoon in a flavourless oil before measuring out the treacle, which will then fall easily off the spoon. Add 1 tablespoon boiling water, then mix in the remaining ingredients. Divinely good for grilled chicken wings.

2

SOUPS

Soup of the Evening,
     Beautiful Soup

Alice's Adventures in Wonderland
Lewis Carroll

Mustard has been used as an ingredient in soup for a long time. Theophrastus, a Greek scholar (372–287 BC) who did much research on plants, heavily praised it and grew it especially 'to use in soups'. It would seem to be the leaves he used rather than the seed, at that stage often finely ground and sprinkled on foods much as we do pepper today. At any rate, the combination had been discovered – and appreciated.

It appears next in fourteenth-century France, specifically as 'mustard soup'. Taillevent and the Goodman of Paris have almost identical recipes, only the last sentence differing slightly. It may have been a very old and well-known recipe, for the soup is a primitive one – basically an oil, water and wine bouillon, seasoned with mustard, then poured over a thick 'mess' of crumbled 'crisped bread'.

When the idea reached England, we don't know, but Michael Smith has two fine soups in his *English Cookery*. One is a delightfully simple concoction of chicken stock and cream; the other, a lovely earthy purée of mushrooms. Research turned up one or two other interesting recipes – Jerusalem artichokes and mustard, modernized with yoghurt to give lightness and a tang, while several cooks seem to have appreciated the virtues of mustard with ham stocks. Really surprising, though, and particularly pleasing, were the kitchen experiments. Day after day, as the wooden spoons stirred, so did the telephone wires buzz. Mustard was good in soup. English mustard, Dijon mustard, mustard seed, mustard oil, mustard greens . . . We had to stop. But the way was clear. Add a little mustard, and there was beautiful soup.

Cream of Onion and Mustard Soup

Classic French onion soup needs no addition: deeply brown and sweet, it is earthy and satisfying. Creamy onion soup is altogether different. Delicate and pale, it takes to spicings of all sorts.

SERVES 4–6
2 very large onions, finely
chopped
2 tablespoons unsalted butter
25 cm/1 inch piece fresh root
ginger, peeled and grated
1 teaspoon sugar
freshly grated nutmeg
1.5 litres/2½ pints good
chicken stock
8–10 sprigs fresh mint,
preferably eau-de-Cologne
juice of ½ large lemon
Maldon or sea salt
freshly ground white pepper
150 ml/¼ pint double cream
1 tablespoon Dijon mustard

Sweat the onions with the butter in a small, deep pan – a butter paper placed on top of the onions helps keep them elegantly pale. Cover tightly and leave over the gentlest of heats for 20–30 minutes. They should be very soft and creamy coloured.

Stir in the ginger, sugar, a generous grating of nutmeg, and half a ladleful of stock, then simmer, covered, for another 5 minutes. Liquidize, with half the remaining stock, to a fine purée.

Pour the rest of the stock into a large pan, and gradually add the purée, whisking briskly all the while. Chop the mint very finely and add, with the lemon juice, to the soup. Bring to bubbling point, season with salt and a good grinding of white pepper, then stir in the cream. Let the soup be very hot but not quite boiling, then stir in the mustard and serve immediately with warm crusty bread.

Red Pepper Soup

Strangely, the Aztec kitchen did not have soup. But once the Spanish arrived and made the introduction, it was quickly welcomed, and Mexican inventiveness soon produced a host of brightly coloured, exotically flavoured dishes. A great favourite is Elizabeth Lambert Ortiz' classic Sopa de Pimientos Morrones (to be found in her lovely book, *Latin American Cooking*). The idea that it might combine with a jar of mustard with green peppers was a good one.

SERVES 6
1 large onion, finely chopped
2 tablespoons olive oil
3–4 large red peppers
1 litre/1 ¾ pints good chicken
 stock
Maldon or sea salt
freshly ground black pepper
1 mace blade, crumbled
300 ml/½ pint natural
 yoghurt
1–2 tablespoons mustard with
 green peppers
handful finely chopped fresh
 coriander leaves

Heat the onion very gently in the oil until well softened but hardly coloured. Meanwhile, split the peppers in half, remove the seeds and put under a very hot grill until the skin is quite charred. When they are really blackened, wrap in a damp cloth and leave for 5 minutes. Then peel off the skins, rubbing any charred flesh clean under warm running water. Chop the peppers and purée with the onions.

Return to the pan, and whisk in the stock. Season lightly, add the mace and bring to the boil before simmering, covered, for about 20 minutes. Taste, adding more salt and pepper if need be, then mix the yoghurt with the mustard, and beat into the soup, off the heat. Serve sprinkled with the chopped coriander. An excellent luncheon soup, especially chilled.

Fennel Soup with Cinnamon Sticks

We tend to think of fennel as an odd, foreign vegetable. Yet it was one of the nine holy herbs in Anglo-Saxon times and one of the four 'hot' herbs of the medieval garden, where it was much grown by monks. A good blend with mustard, too.

SERVES 4
2 large bulbs of Florence
    fennel, finely sliced, and
    green fronds reserved, finely
    chopped
3 tablespoons olive oil
1 litre/1¾ pints veal or good
    chicken stock
½ teaspoon ground cinnamon
50 ml/2 fl oz crème fraîche
50 ml/2 fl oz double cream
1 tablespoon Roman mustard
    (p.65)
Maldon or sea salt
freshly ground black pepper
4 cinnamon sticks

Warm the oil in a large pan, then add the fennel and sauté gently for about 10 minutes, turning occasionally. Add the chicken stock and ground cinnamon, bring almost to the boil, then simmer very gently, covered, for 30 minutes until the fennel is soft.

Liquidize and return the soup to the heat, bringing it very slowly to simmering point. Whisk the crème fraîche, double cream and mustard together, then beat in all but 30 ml/2 tablespoons. Add salt and black pepper, then whisk the soup until lightly frothy.

Pour into warmed soup bowls, drizzle a little of the reserved cream/mustard mixture over each, garnish with the chopped fronds, and pop in a cinnamon stick, for each person to stir and flavour their soup. Warmed sesame bread and chilled butter make a particularly good accompaniment.

Pumpkin and Prawn Soup

In America pumpkin means pumpkin pie and Thanksgiving, in England we hollow them out for Hallowe'en, and in the Middle East they eat many a bowl of the nutty seeds. From the Caribbean comes perhaps the best way of dealing with this giant. Squash soups of all sorts are popular there, but pumpkin has the sweetest, fullest flavour. We added the mustard and prawns. And, if they haven't all been nibbled away, add a garnish of the seeds to heighten the pumpkin taste.

SERVES 6
1 kg/2¼ lb pumpkin
450 g/1 lb unshelled, boiled
    prawns
½ lemon
3 sprigs parsley
1 mace blade
1 small onion, unpeeled and
    cut in half
2 tablespoons unsalted butter
2 large onions, finely chopped
1 large garlic clove, crushed
2 tablespoons mustard
    powder
Maldon or sea salt
freshly ground black and
    white pepper
lemon juice (optional)
150 ml/¼ pint single cream
mustard and cress, to garnish

If you want the seeds (which you should), start the day before. Scrape them out of the pumpkin (wrap that in clingfilm and keep chilled), then wash them very thoroughly of all fibres, dry and lay out on a baking sheet. Leave them for at least 12, preferably 24 hours in a very low oven. When they are quite dry and slightly shrivelled, rub off the casings and lightly toast them. They can be stored in an airtight jar.

Peel the prawns, putting the heads, shells and roes, if any, into a large pan with the half lemon, parsley, mace blade and small onion. Cover with 1.1 litres/2 pints cold water and bring to the boil, then simmer, uncovered, for about 30–45 minutes. Strain and reserve the stock.

Sweat the chopped onions and garlic clove in the butter until nicely softened, then sprinkle over the mustard powder. Stir and cook for a further few minutes, while peeling and chopping the pumpkin. Add that to the pan and turn around until lightly golden all over, then pour in the stock. Simmer for 30 minutes until the pumpkin is tender, then liquidize.

Return the purée to the pan, add the prawns and a good seasoning of salt, black and white peppers, then simmer for 10 minutes.

Taste, and add a little lemon juice if the flavour needs heightening – this will depend on your pumpkin, for even home-grown ones vary in their intensity of taste. Stir in the cream and garnish with some chopped mustard and cress. Serve hot but not blazingly so – this is a subtle soup and excessive heat kills it.

Gammon and Gruyère Soup

Two classic combinations – ham and cheese, gammon stock and mustard – marry here to give a soup that can be as gutsy or as delicate as you wish. For a starter, light but with some substance, everything should be very finely chopped. For a warming supper soup, the ham can be left quite chunky and beaten egg whisked in at the finish. Either way it is very good.

SERVES 4–6
1 gammon knuckle, soaked in
* cold water for 1 hour*
1 tablespoon sunflower oil
3 shallots, finely chopped
1 leek, finely sliced
1 carrot, finely sliced
* lengthways*
1 onion skin
2 cloves
1 tablespoon brown mustard
* seed*
1 small sprig fresh sage
300 ml/1/2 pint dry white wine
* or dry cider*

1 tablespoon walnut ketchup
freshly ground green pepper
  (green peppercorns are
  available now freeze-dried –
  corns in brine are not
  suitable. Use black if
  necessary.)
lime juice
1 tablespoon Dijon mustard
2 large eggs, beaten (optional)
handful of fresh parsley, very
  finely chopped
125 g/4 oz Gruyère cheese,
  minutely diced

Place the gammon knuckle in a pan of fresh cold water and bring to a lively simmer, then let it bubble for 5 minutes before discarding the water. Keep the knuckle aside and heat the oil in the pan, add the mustard seeds and leave for a minute until they start to pop. Add the shallots, leek and carrot and sauté gently for 5 minutes, then add the onion skin, cloves, sage and white wine. Cook on a fierce heat for 2 minutes, then pour in 1.1 litres/2 pints cold water and immerse the knuckle. Bring the liquid to the boil quickly, then simmer, very gently, for about an hour, with the pan half-covered.

Remove the knuckle and strain the stock – preferably into a tall jug. Stand this in a basin of cold water to speed up the cooling process, and the fat can then easily be skimmed off the top. (Or start the day before, chilling the stock overnight, if you wish.) Skin and defat the knuckle, cut off all the meat and chop either very finely or coarsely as you prefer.

Return the stock and the meat to the pan and heat until simmering. Season with the walnut ketchup, a good grinding of pepper (it shouldn't need salt, but check), and a squeezing of lime juice, then take a small ladleful of stock and mix with the mustard in a bowl.

If you want a 'supper' soup, let the liquid boil hard for 30 seconds, then drop in the beaten eggs, whisking briskly as you pour. Turn off the heat, add the parsley, tip in the cheese, and stir in the mustard/stock mixture. Serve at once. If you're not adding the eggs, then simply stir in the parsley and cheese, stirring for about 20 seconds, then add the mustard and again, serve immediately. Melba toast or crusty bread and chilled butter to accompany.

Mushroom and Blood Orange Soup

Mushrooms and mustard are good together. This clear soup is lightly sweetened with the deep red juice of a blood orange. Or you can blend it to give a fine tweedy texture – ideal when the night is cold, and one's spirits are down.

SERVES 6
*350 g/12 oz small button
  mushrooms, wiped with a
  damp cloth*
75 g/3 oz unsalted butter
*3 tablespoons dry Madeira or
  dry sherry*
freshly ground allspice
1.1 litres/2 pints chicken stock
juice of 1½ blood oranges
1½ teaspoons Dijon mustard

Cut the mushrooms in half through the stalk, then slice crossways very finely. Melt the butter in a wide pan until frothy and slightly 'nutty', then add the mushrooms and cook for 2–3 minutes, stirring, adding extra butter if need be. Pour in the Madeira and bubble for a minute over a high heat, then grind over lots of allspice. Pour in the stock and bring quickly to the boil. Add salt to taste – pepper, for once, is superfluous.

Mix the orange juice with the mustard, then, with the pan off the heat, briskly whisk into the soup. Serve with thin, thin slices of good wholemeal bread.

Stilton and Almond Soup

Stilton makes wonderful soup – even stale end pieces, provided you soak them in a little milk first. And it combines well with nuts of all sorts. We have made this with walnuts and hazelnuts as well as almonds – these give the most delicate flavour, hazels being slightly sweeter and walnuts intensely nutty.

SERVES 4
75 g/3 oz Stilton, crumbled

125 g/4 oz flaked almonds
1 lime
freshly grated nutmeg
1.1 litres/2 pints chicken stock
75 ml/3 fl oz Greek yoghurt,
    thinned with a little milk to
    single cream consistency
Maldon or sea salt
freshly ground black pepper
1 tablespoon Matthew's
    mustard (p.68)

Put the Stilton with three-quarters of the almonds in a blender. Grate the lime zest and reserve, then squeeze the juice into the blender, and add 300 ml/½ pint of the stock. Liquidize to a thick purée, add another 300 ml/½ pint stock and blend again, then transfer to a pan and gradually beat in the rest of the stock over a low heat.

Simmer for 5–10 minutes and toast the remaining almonds meanwhile until deeply golden. Stir the yoghurt into the soup, then season – lightly with salt, well with pepper. Take a ladleful out of the pan and mix in a bowl with the mustard, then pour back into the soup. Mix well and serve at once, garnished with grated lime zest and toasted almonds. Good with very hot, crusty rolls.

Fish Soup

Fish soups are strangely neglected in England, which is a pity for they are very good and infinitely versatile. For a heartier dish you could add a couple of red mullet, quickly sautéd in mustard oil, then roughly chopped, and perhaps a few prawns. Variations are endless, depending only on your tastes – and what happens to looks good on the fishmonger's slab.

SERVES 4–5
350 g/12 oz cod fillet
1.1 litres/2 pints veal stock or
    light beef broth
1 teaspoon brown mustard seed
freshly grated nutmeg
pinch of cayenne pepper

2 teaspoons lemon juice
150 ml/¼ pint medium dry
 white wine
1 box mustard and cress
1 teaspoon arrowroot
Maldon or sea salt
croûtons (preferably fried in
 mustard oil), to serve

Bring the stock to the boil, then turn to a low simmer, add the fish and poach for 3–4 minutes until beginning to firm up, then remove from the stock, skin and flake it, taking out as many bones as possible.

Add the mustard seed, a generous grating of nutmeg and a pinch (or two) of cayenne pepper to the stock and simmer for 15 minutes before returning the fish to the pan. Simmer for another 2–3 minutes, then add the lemon juice, white wine and the mustard and cress, finely chopped. Cook for no more than 3 minutes, raising the heat slightly so the stock is not quite boiling.

Mix the arrowroot with a little cold water, stir into the soup and whisk lightly until it is slightly thickened. Season with salt to taste, then serve immediately, with the croûtons in a bowl on the table.

Deep-fried Greens Soup

Deep-fried seaweed has long been a favourite on Chinese menus. When we discovered that the 'seaweed' was not seaweed at all but *bak choi*, often called mustard greens, the dish became a firm favourite at home too. Spring greens, cabbage or even broccoli leaves are all good substitutes. Fine shredding is of the essence, and mustard oil for that extra 'bite' – almost imperceptible, until you taste the greens cooked in another oil. As a vegetable, they can accompany chicken, pork or fish. Alone they make an unusual starter, especially with prawn crackers – also fried in mustard oil. Dropped into boiling hot consommé, they make a wonderfully sizzling soup.

SERVES 4–6
1.5 litres/2½ pints good beef
 consommé
150 ml/¼ pint dry sherry
lemon juice

freshly ground white pepper
mustard oil, for deep-frying
1 small head fresh spring
    greens or about 150 g/5 oz
    bak choi, *shredded as finely*
    as possible (preferably using
    the slicing blade in a food
    processor)
1 fat garlic clove, very finely
    chopped

Pour the consommé into a large pan with the sherry, a good squeeze of lemon juice and a generous grinding of white pepper. Bring to the boil, then simmer gently.

In another large, deep pan heat a good 25 mm/1 inch of mustard oil until nearly smoking. Standing well back from the pan, tip in the shredded greens – they will splutter enormously for a few seconds. Once the sizzling has died down, you can stir the greens, with a chopstick ideally, until they are deeply brown all over. Watch carefully, for the dividing line between nicely charred and inedibly burnt is very fine – about 2–2½ minutes usually does them perfectly. Then immediately remove with a large slotted spoon and pile on to a dish.

Quickly pour about a tablespoon of the hot oil into a small pan, add the garlic and stir-fry for a minute until crispy and golden, then scatter over the greens. Bring the soup to the boil, pour into individual soup plates and drop a good handful of greens into the centre of each. Eat instantly.

Note: Once the oil has cooled, strain it through muslin then pour into a clean bottle and keep for re-use.

3

STARTERS

Now good digestion wait on appetite,
  And health on both.

Macbeth, William Shakespeare

Perhaps mustard should have been on Macbeth's table as an aid to both appetite and digestion. A touch of it in sauces, in marinades, or as a condiment will increase the salivation rate as much as eightfold. This not only sets in motion the digestive processes (to give good and efficient appetite) but it also heightens the awareness of the taste buds to such an extent that it brings out the flavour of all foods subsequently eaten at the same meal – whether or not they also contain mustard.

So what more ideal place in a meal for mustard, than at the beginning? History shows that it used to be so – after the first remove, soup, came brawn with mustard sauce as the second remove. The brawn could be any cold cooked meat, not necessarily brawn as we know it today, but the point was that it always appeared before the main set pieces were put on the table. Certainly Gerard knew that 'mustard makes an excellent sauce good to be eaten with gross meats, whether fish or flesh, because it doth help indigestion, warmeth the stomach and provoketh appetite.' And it is interesting that until the introduction of the Russian service by Carême in the nineteenth century, all the main dishes, roast fish and meats, were placed on the table simultaneously after the second remove of brawn and mustard sauce had been served *alone.* With the new order of service, the meal became a matter of courses. The idea of having ten or more set pieces on the table all at once disappeared very rapidly – and so did mustard's place at the start of the meal. Even with the advent of salads and cold starters, an idea which came from America at the beginning of this century, mustard did not regain its former position, although the dishes involved were admirably suited to the spice.

A few isolated exceptions exist of course: Scandinavia has her Gravlax with mustard and dill sauce (p.140) – although often it is served as a dish on its own for festive occasions rather than as a mere introduction. Burgundy has a wider repertoire, principally involving eggs, to give some beautiful and stimulating appetizers. And yet the scope is so much greater. Simple salads, such as finely sliced sweet tomatoes and shredded raw leeks, are enhanced with a mustard vinaigrette; a plate of charcuterie will often benefit from an accompaniment of mustard (Germany knows this, and rarely will cold meats arrive without their mild and sweet mustard pot), while crudités, the classic pre-dinner nibble, definitely need a spicy dip.

Pasta takes to mustard very nicely – ribbons or bows in a plain mustard cream sauce, perhaps with a little tuna or salmon (smoked or fresh), make a good beginning to a light meal.

Britain has many traditional supper dishes that, in smaller portions, make unusually good beginnings: little cheese soufflés, small strips of Welsh Rabbit among others. Even the classic smoked salmon is enhanced by a little mustard – as one wartime airman, stuck in Scotland and utterly fed up with the prize fish in all its forms, discovered. It became a habit he adhered to for the rest of his life. Lunching at Wilton's in London one day, he asked for the mustard. 'With smoked salmon!' exclaimed the horrified waiter. 'You bring the mustard, I'm paying the bill.' The Colman's was brought.

The potential is vast but suit your starter to the menu. If the next course is delicate, keep the mustard touch light. With gutsier dishes to follow, one can be bolder, but never forget that fine dividing line between a mild stimulation and highlighting of flavours, and mustard's more powerful role as irritant.

Soufflé Omelette
with Mustard and Tomato Sauce

In Burgundy, where they may be said to know about mustard, omelettes flavoured with the condiment are a favourite: sometimes as a light lunch with a good, well-dressed green salad, and often as a starter, to whet one's taste buds for the many courses to follow.

SERVES 2
2 large, ripe but firm tomatoes
3 large eggs

1 large egg white
Maldon salt
freshly ground black pepper
40–50 g/ 1 ½–2 oz unsalted
   butter
4 tablespoons double cream
1 teaspoon Dijon mustard
lemon juice

Blanch the tomatoes in boiling water, then peel. Chop one very finely, discarding the seeds and juices. Liquidize and then sieve the other to make a smooth purée.

Beat the eggs until frothy, season with salt and pepper, then whisk the white until stiff and fold lightly but thoroughly into the eggs. Melt a knob of butter in a heavy frying pan over a high heat and when sizzling pour in the eggs. Put the remaining butter in another pan, ideally wide and shallow. Melt quickly, add the tomato purée, and whisk it once or twice, then leave to simmer. By this time the bottom of the omelette should have started to set. Lift the edges up gently with a palette knife and swirl the unset eggs to the edge of the pan. Scatter over the chopped tomato, and keep swirling the eggs until they are almost completely set, just slightly moist in the middle still. Fold in half and slide on to a hot plate. Now you have to work fast, adding the cream to the sauce and bubbling over a fierce heat for about 30 seconds, whisking briskly. Stir in the mustard and a squeeze of lemon juice, pour over the omelette and serve at once. Since omelettes have to be quickly made, and instantly eaten, this is probably best for you and one other. Or just pamper yourself.

Mustard Kipper Salad

Kippers are something one should be pedantic about. Buy the best and buy them whole. Frozen or canned fillets are useless. Mallaig, Loch Fyne and Isle of Man are the place names to look out for, and are worth the search. Particularly when, as here, you are serving the kippers raw.

SERVES 6–8
2 large kippers
about 150 ml/ ¼ pint yoghurt,
   depending on thickness

½–1 teaspoon lemon mustard
  (p.66)
1 small, sweet onion, very
  finely chopped
fresh dillweed, very finely
  chopped
lemon juice
freshly ground white pepper

Skin the kippers, cut off the heads and tails, then pull out the large bone, bringing out as many side bones as possible with it. Now comes the boring bit – using tweezers if you wish, pull out *all* the small bones remaining in the kipper. It is tedious, it is time-consuming, but it must be done. Chop the kipper flesh fairly finely, put in a bowl and add the remaining ingredients. Half a dozen sprigs of dill should be enough (at a pinch dried will do, about 1 teaspoon) and be sure to snip it finely – it's surprising how like a fish bone a long piece can seem. Add just enough mustard and lemon to taste, chill for about 20 minutes, then serve surrounded by triangles of bread fried until crisp in butter. An excellent dish.

Chicken Wings with Mustard and Lime

In the Middle Eastern kitchen chicken wings are always cut off, to be cooked separately in a variety of ways, then served as a *mezze*. It is a habit worth copying. The wings are too good not to enjoy on their own – and the mustard seeds add a nutty dimension to the traditional Arab marinade of lime or lemon juice.

SERVES 3–6
6 chicken wings
juice of 2–3 limes
1 garlic clove, very finely
  chopped
3 tablespoons brown mustard
  seed
3 tablespoons mustard oil
pinch of sugar (optional)
25 mm/1 inch piece ginger
  root, very finely chopped

Marinate the wings in a shallow bowl with the lime juice and garlic clove. Turn several times and leave for at least 30 minutes and up to 6 hours.

Place the chicken, with the marinade, in a pan, preferably in one layer, then add a little water to just cover. Simmer very gently, uncovered, for about 20–30 minutes until the meat is tender. Meanwhile, fry the mustard seeds in the oil until they start to splutter. Remove them, add the ginger to the pan and fry for about a minute until golden and crispy. Keep aside with the mustard seeds.

Turn the heat up under the chicken, taste the sauce, adding a pinch of sugar if needed, and cook fiercely for a minute to lightly reduce the cooking juices. Stir in the mustard seeds and ginger, then pile into a dish and serve with warm bread to mop up the juices.

Smoked Salmon, Avocado and Mozzarella Salad

A simple variation on that Italian classic, tomato and mozzarella salad. The sauce is also excellent served with plain smoked salmon if one is feeling extravagant.

SERVES 6
1 small crisp lettuce, such as
    Cos or Romaine, finely
    shredded
225 g/8 oz smoked salmon,
    cut into 6 thin slices
250 g/9 oz mozzarella cheese,
    finely sliced
3 small avocados
freshly ground black pepper
cayenne pepper
For the dressing
lemon juice
2 tablespoons Matthew's
    mustard (p.68)
150 ml/¼ pint olive oil
3 thin spring onions, green
    tops only, very finely
    snipped

small posy fresh dillweed, very
*   finely snipped*
2–3 drops Tabasco sauce

Divide the shredded lettuce between six plates. Lay the salmon down one side of each, then the slices of cheese in the middle. Leave the avocado until just before serving or it will discolour.

    To make the dressing, stir the juice of half a lemon into the mustard, then gradually add the oil, whisking constantly until it is thick and well emulsified. Beat in the chopped onion and dillweed, then taste and add extra lemon if needed, before stirring in a few drops of Tabasco – there should be a bite not searing hotness. At the last minute, cut the avocados in half, peel and stone them, then slice very finely. Arrange the slices on the plates, then grind over a little black pepper – not too finely – and sprinkle a pinch of cayenne on the salmon. Pour over the dressing and serve with thin, thin slices of brown bread, lightly buttered.

Smoked Haddock with Horseradish Dressing

Among the many things Colman's Mustard Club produced was a highly entertaining little booklet, *Mustard Uses Mustered*, written by the founder, Baron de Beef. Full of fascinating snippets of information, it includes a suggestion for mock smoked salmon sandwiches: mustard-buttered brown bread enveloping thin slices of smoked haddock fillet. An intriguing thought – but why not? Raw kipper is good, smoked salmon, of course, very good; and we decided that smoked haddock is excellent. Particularly with this Victorian-inspired dressing in which the mustard acts as a flavour enhancer for the horseradish rather than exuding its own taste.

SERVES 6
3 tail pieces smoked haddock
*   fillet, about 175 g/6 oz each*
*   in weight*
For the dressing
4 tablespoons freshly grated
*   horseradish*
juice of 2 oranges
6 tablespoons olive oil

6 tablespoons fresh
  breadcrumbs, soaked in
  water
2 tablespoons milk
1 teaspoon Dijon mustard
pinch of salt
pinch of sugar

Blend the horseradish and orange juice together, add the oil and blend again. Squeeze the breadcrumbs of as much water as possible, then heat, very gently, with the milk, stirring frequently until the mixture is quite dry without being browned. Cool slightly, then add to the dressing with the mustard, salt and sugar and blend well. Pour into a bowl.

Slice the haddock very thinly, on the diagonal as one would smoked salmon. You won't get such long slices as the flesh of haddock is coarser grained, but this doesn't matter as long as the pieces are small and neat. Arrange on individual serving plates and accompany with the sauce and thin brown bread and butter – rye bread is good.

Devilled Ham Paste

The travesties produced under the label 'paste' make many shudder. Serve them up as 'pâté' and you have welcome thanks. Which, as Elizabeth David says, is both 'comical and misleading'. Fish and meat pastes are not only delicious but have a perfectly respectable heritage in the English kitchen. Pâtés are equally good but quite different – the raw ingredients are mixed together *before* cooking. So let's be proud of our traditions and serve such dishes as Potted Beef, Sardine Butter and Ham Paste under their rightful titles.

SERVES 4–6
175 g/6 oz ham, off the bone,
  chopped coarsely
125 g/4 oz curd cheese
juice of ¹/₂ blood orange
1 teaspoon lemon mustard
  (p.66)
¹/₄–¹/₂ tablespoon Matthew's
  mustard (p.68)

¼ teaspoon coriander seeds
cayenne pepper
clarified butter

Chop the ham in a food processor until quite fine, then add the remaining ingredients except the coriander seeds, cayenne and butter. Dry fry the coriander for a minute or so until the aroma is pungent, then crush lightly in a mortar and pestle and add to the ham. Whizz until the mixture is quite pasty. Taste, adding extra Matthew's mustard if need be, and a pinch of cayenne: blend again. Pack into a small pot, pressing well down to exclude all air, then cover with melted clarified butter and chill until ready to serve. Provided you have put a good layer of butter on – at least 15 mm/½ inch – it will keep for 2–3 days. Serve with Melba toast or crunchy warm bread.

Potted Smoked Oysters

Cans of smoked oysters are a wonderful store-cupboard standby – extremely versatile and ridiculously cheap.

SERVES 4–6
175 g/6 oz canned smoked
   oysters, drained and rinsed
175 g/6 oz fromage blanc
1–2 tablespoons Matthew's
   mustard (p.68)
cayenne pepper
small posy salad burnet, very
   finely chopped
lemon juice
clarified butter

Chop the oysters coarsely, then combine in a food processor with the remaining ingredients except the lemon juice and butter. Taste, adding extra mustard if necessary and a squeeze of lemon if the flavours need sharpening. Pack into small pots and cover well with clarified butter, then chill for up to 48 hours. Serve with Melba toast and lemon wedges.

Mustard and Ginger Crab

A small but rich starter. If you can use fresh crab so much the better –
but don't be tempted by canned artichoke hearts. They're only slightly
less trouble, for a vastly inferior taste.

SERVES 6
6 small artichokes
225 g/8 oz white crabmeat,
flaked
2 tablespoons grated fresh
ginger
1 small garlic clove, finely
chopped then lightly
crushed
3 tablespoons double cream
3 tablespoons light
mayonnaise
few drops soy sauce
squeeze of lemon juice
½–1 tablespoon
coarse-grained mustard
Maldon salt
freshly ground black pepper
mustard vinaigrette (p.83)
mustard and cress

Break off the artichoke stalks and discard. Cook the artichokes in a
large pan of boiling water until a leaf at the bottom will pull off easily
and the little 'half-moon' of flesh is tender. Drain and cool, then peel
off the leaves (keep for soup or a starter the next day) and scrape out
the hairy chokes to leave the hearts. Trim their bottoms if necessary so
they stand upright, then marinate in the mustard vinaigrette while
preparing the crab.

Combine the flesh in a bowl with the remaining ingredients except
the mustard and cress, mixing thoroughly and adjusting the balance of
flavours to taste. Drain the artichoke hearts, put on individual plates,
and pile a little crab on top of each. Surround with chopped mustard
and cress and serve, lightly chilled, with brown bread and butter.

Mustard Crumbles

Sweet crumbles are a classic of the English kitchen – yet rarely does a savoury crumble feature. One day, at Rudland and Stubbs in Smithfield market, there appeared on the menu fish crumble. We have added a mustard sauce and spiced the crumble.

SERVES 6
350 g/12 oz fish, a
  combination of smoked and
  plain haddock is good
125 g/4 oz potted shrimps
700 ml/1¼ pints milk
60 g/2½ oz unsalted butter
scant 4 tablespoons flour
1 teaspoon Dijon mustard
2–3 tablespoons double
  cream
freshly ground white pepper
Maldon salt (optional)
For the crumble
150 g/5 oz flour, half and half
  wholemeal to white
75 g/3 oz unsalted butter,
  chilled, then cut into small
  pieces
2 teaspoons coarse-grained
  mustard powder (now
  marketed by several firms)
Maldon salt

Cook the fish in the milk for 10 minutes, then stir in the potted shrimps (butter and all). As soon as the butter has melted, remove the fish and shrimps. Skin, bone and flake the fish then mix with the shrimps in a bowl. Keep aside.

Strain the milk and keep warm. For the sauce, melt the butter, then stir in the flour and cook for 2 minutes, stirring vigorously to make a smooth roux. Off the heat, gradually add the milk, constantly stirring to avoid lumps. Return to the heat and bring to a bubble, gently and still stirring all the while, until the sauce has thickened. Add the Dijon mustard, then pour half to three-quarters over the fish, mixing well.

The fish should be generously coated without swimming in sauce. Pile into small ovenproof dishes.

Mix the flour with the mustard powder and a pinch of salt then rub in the butter until the mixture resembles fine breadcrumbs – or simply whizz in a food processor for a couple of minutes. Sprinkle over the fish and bake in the oven at 200°C/400°F/Gas Mark 6 for 25–35 minutes until the crumble is golden and lightly crisp on top. Mix the remaining sauce with the cream, heat (stirring to prevent lumps) until bubbling then pour into a small jug and serve with the crumbles.

Mustard Prawn Puffs

Beignets – little deep-fried choux pastry puffs – terrify many home cooks. But they are not difficult to make: speed and good elbow power are the main requisites. Let imagination do the rest, for many ingredients can be folded into your basic choux mixture to give these wonderfully airy *bonnes bouches*.

MAKES ABOUT 35
75 g/3 oz unsalted butter
125 g/4 oz flour
3 large eggs
½ teaspoon mustard powder
275 g/10 oz boiled prawns
   (generous half-pint)
tarragon mustard
½ firm but ripe avocado
3 spring onions, green tops
   only, very finely snipped
peanut oil, for deep-frying
Maldon salt
lemon juice
a big bunch of parsley, very
   finely chopped

Put 225 ml/8 fl oz cold water into a smallish pan with the butter and bring to the boil. Take the pan off the heat and throw in all the flour at once, then beat quickly and vigorously until you have a thick, very glossy paste. Cover and chill for an hour. Beat in the eggs one at a time, whisking extremely hard between each addition. The glossier the mixture looks, the better. Sprinkle in the mustard powder and a squeeze of lemon juice. Peel the prawns (keep the shells for stock), then chop them finely and mix with a little tarragon mustard, about a teaspoonful. Peel the avocado and chop into tiny dice, mix with the prawns then carefully fold into the paste. Finally add the chopped green onion tops.

Fill a large pan about one-third full of oil and heat until a cube of stale bread turns gold in 60 seconds (180°C/350°F for those equipped with a fat thermometer). Taking up a tablespoon of batter at a time, smoothing the top with another spoon, drop it gently into the pan and cook, five or six at a time so they have room to swirl around, for 4–5 minutes until beautifully golden and puffed up. Drain well on absorbent paper, cook the rest the same way, then pile on to a bed of chopped parsley. Sprinkle with a little lemon juice and Maldon salt and eat instantly.

4

FISH

And they gave him a piece of broiled fish and
of an honeycomb.

St Luke, 24:42

What a wonderful image that verse conjures up – a fish fresh from the
sea that morning, grilled no doubt with the local olive oil, perhaps a
squeeze of fresh lemon, followed with newly baked bread and honey
made from the powerful thyme that covers the hillsides around
Jerusalem. Mustard undoubtedly was not there for, despite the
parable of the mustard seed, it is doubtful whether the plant Christ
referred to was *Brassica nigra* – botanists have been arguing for
centuries over that. Mrs Grieve in her *Modern Herbal* suggests that it
was confused with a type of tree, abundant by the Sea of Galilee,
similar in looks to the mustard plant, possibly *Salvadora persicoria*.
Other scholars have simply stated there was a confusion in the
translation from the early Greek. Whichever, it seems certain that it
was not mustard.

Many early writings suggest fish as a partner to mustard, and it was
a common idea in medieval times. Just how widely mustard was used
with fish we can clearly see from the papers of Isabella of Portugal.
Married to Philip the Good, Duke of Burgundy, she kept a comprehen-
sive domestic record from the year of her marriage, 1430, until three
years before her retirement from court in 1457. In particular it covers,
in detail, the foods bought on a daily basis, and notes whether it was a
fast day or not and when a banquet was given. Fascinatingly, while it
clearly shows a greater consumption of mustard on both such days,
this was highest on fast days, when fish was the prime dish. The
expenditure on vinegar and verjuice too (both of course used in the
making of mustard) was also greater. Undoubtedly, piquant sauces, in

great variety, were used to render changes in the menu, for even though there was a wide selection of fish available – bream, mackerel, salmon, carp, shrimp (also much favoured on meat-eating days), mussels, perch and herrings – with three fast days every week, much ingenuity was needed to avoid a dull diet. Saffron, cumin, caraway and pepper were all bought in greater quantity besides mustard. Sadly, the Duchess's papers relate only to expenditure – would that she had had her chef record his transformations of the ingredients so carefully listed.

Today, we have a much smaller repertoire, though in Dijon they still serve salmon with mustard – deliciously combined in Le Toison d'Or restaurant where the fish is pasted with mustard and served on a tomato and cheese sauce. Sweden has her Gravlax, and herrings are traditionally served in Britain with a mustard sauce. But there it seems to stop. (Salt fish, since antiquity a natural partner to mustard – and one of the few dishes where mustard is recommended in the Middle Eastern kitchen, by Al-Baghdadi in the thirteenth century – has almost entirely disappeared from the modern table.) The field is wide open for experimentation.

Fresh tuna would be nicely enlivened by a little mustard, though again that is not a new idea. The Romans knew it well, and it has been suggested that mustard was an ingredient in the fermented sauce, *garum*, highly prized – and expensive – at the close of the Roman Empire. (This included pickled tuna intestines, possibly also anchovies, though the exact recipe is unknown.) We do know that mustard was popular with shellfish, both for poaching and in sauces. Apicius has a sauce for spiny lobster with chopped sautéd onions, pepper, lovage, caraway, cumin, figdates, honey, vinegar, wine, broth, oil, reduced must, and, 'while boiling add mustard'! Raw smoked fish proved a highly successful partner, and Japan serves a hot, hot mustard dip with raw fish.

Of all the ingredients we tried with mustard, fish, perhaps, has the most potential. The variety of fish is so endless, and our stock of old recipes so small. But whatever fish you are cooking – with or without mustard – you cannot fail to thank mustard afterwards: a spoonful mixed with cold water as a rinse for the pots, pans and plates will dispel any unpleasant fishy odours.

Marinated Haddock Fillet with Orange and Mustard

Blood orange juice is the secret to this very simple but elegant and delicious dish. Buy plenty of the oranges in season, and freeze the juice in ice cube containers for use throughout the summer.

SERVES 4–6
700 g/1½ lb haddock fillet,
   skinned
juice of 1 large lemon
juice of 2 blood oranges
4 tablespoons butter
125 ml/4 fl oz double cream
Maldon salt
freshly ground black pepper
1 tablespoon Dijon mustard

Put the fish in a shallow dish and pour over the lemon and orange juices. Leave for at least 30 minutes, preferably 2–3 hours, turning once or twice. (Unless the kitchen is very hot it is best not to chill the fish while marinating as this dulls the flavours.)

Melt the butter in a large frying pan. Take the fish out of the marinade and pat lightly dry then add to the pan and sauté for 2–3 minutes. Turn and sauté the other side for 1–2 minutes – the fish should be just done right through but not overcooked. Remove and keep on a warmed serving platter.

Add the marinade to the pan and bubble for 2½–3 minutes, then stir in the cream and boil hard for a further 2–3 minutes, until lightly thickened. Season, not too heavily, with salt and pepper, then stir in the mustard and cook for another 30 seconds. Pour immediately over the fish and serve. Good with thin, steamed leeks for dipping, on the asparagus principle, into the sauce. For a summer extravaganza, the recipe is gorgeous with fillets of fresh salmon. And asparagus, of course.

Mackerel in Black Treacle and Mustard

Victor Gordon's unusual and stimulating *English Cookbook* provided the inspiration for this unlikely combination. While we were trying his recipe for *Blackerel*, improvisation was necessary due to an unusually empty store-cupboard. Of mustard there was no lack. The end result was dark, spicy – and very good.

SERVES 4
*4 mackerel, very fresh, cleaned
    and split*
200 ml/7 fl oz cider vinegar
1 teaspoon brown mustard seed
*1/4 teaspoon black
    peppercorns*
2 cloves
*25 mm/1 inch piece cinnamon
    bark*
*4 spring onions, finely
    chopped*
1 tablespoon mustard oil
*1 tablespoon unsalted butter,
    plus extra for finishing the
    sauce*
1 large onion, finely chopped
*1 tablespoon soft, dark brown
    sugar*
150 ml/1/4 pint fish stock
1 tablespoon black treacle
1/2 teaspoon walnut ketchup
pinch of cayenne pepper
pinch of ground ginger
*1/4 teaspoon powdered
    mustard*
lime juice
*1–2 tablespoons chopped
    walnuts*
finely chopped parsley

Simmer the vinegar for 5 minutes with the mustard seed, black peppercorns, cloves and cinnamon bark. Cool until barely tepid, then pour over the fish in a shallow dish, sprinkle on the chopped spring onion and leave for at least 2 hours, turning occasionally. (If you have some home-made pickled walnuts, use their vinegar as does the original recipe. Do not use vinegar from bought pickled walnuts as this tends to be malt vinegar and is far too overpowering.)

Remove the fish from the marinade and pat dry. To make the sauce, melt the mustard oil and butter until foaming, then add the chopped onion and cook until soft and darkly coloured, about 15 minutes. Stir in the sugar and caramelize over a gentle heat, then pour in half the marinade and bubble hard for 2–3 minutes. Add the rest of the marinade, the fish stock and the treacle. Stir well, then lower the heat again, add the walnut ketchup and simmer while cooking the fish.

Mix together the cayenne pepper, ground ginger and powdered mustard, then sprinkle on both sides of each mackerel. Put under a medium hot grill, flesh side upwards, and cook for about 15 minutes, until quite blackened – but not burnt.

Turn the heat up under the sauce, whisk in a small knob of butter to gloss and lightly thicken then add a squirt of fresh lime juice. Serve the fish sprinkled with chopped walnuts and lots of parsley with the sauce handed round separately. A good green salad and crusty bread, to mop up the sauce, are the only accompaniments needed.

Mackerel Stewed with Wine

'No red wine with fish' is one of those taboos made to be broken. In the Loire, for instance, freshly caught salmon are delectably cooked in the local red wine (and incidentally, fresh mint – another English rule quietly ignored!). Mackerel, with its strong flavour, is a good candidate for unconventional treatment and we idly wondered whether red wine and mustard would make up a happy trio. Of course, it had already been done – by Eliza Acton. As she herself wrote, very good. One can do no better than reproduce her recipe.

SERVES 2
Work very smoothly together a large teaspoonful of flour with two ounces of butter, put them into a stewpan, and stir or shake them round over the fire until the butter is dissolved; add a quarter of a teaspoonful of mace, twice as much salt, and some cayenne; pour in by slow degrees three glasses of claret; and when the sauce boils, lay in a couple of fine mackerel well cleaned, and wiped quite dry; stew them very softly from fifteen to twenty minutes, and turn them when half done; lift them out, and dish them carefully; stir a teaspoonful of made mustard to the sauce, give it a boil, and pour it over the fish. When more convenient, substitute port wine and a little lemon-juice for the claret.

Mackerel, 2: flour, 1 teaspoonful; butter, 2 oz [50 g]; seasoning of salt, mace, and cayenne; claret, 3 wine-glassesful [300 ml/½ pint]; made mustard, 1 teaspoonful: 15 to 20 minutes.

Note: Made mustard refers to freshly made powdered English mustard, but Dijon mustard can be used with equal success.

Herrings in Oatmeal with Mustard

Herrings, being one of the oily fish, have always called for a mustard accompaniment though occasionally freshly grated horseradish root was used instead. Salted herrings, despite being a winter staple for the poor (especially in the North), were also considered a delicacy and often replaced the 'brawn' course of a great feast on 'lean' days. This is beautifully illustrated in a fascinating document written in the 1420s by a Master Chiquart, cook to Amadeus VIII, Count-Duke of Savoy. For the banquet celebrating the marriage of his master to Marie, daughter of the Duke of Burgundy, which took place on a 'lean' day, he instructed: 'Get big salt fish such as salt mullets . . . with several other salt fish . . . then, with this, get herrings and set them out in another fine dish by themselves; for all that has just been mentioned there is no other sauce needed but mustard.' It is still the finest sauce, and the traditional Scottish method of dipping the fish in oatmeal adds a welcome texture.

> SERVES 6
> *6 plump fresh herrings, filleted*
> *75 g/3 oz medium-coarse*
> *oatmeal*
> *75 g/3 oz unsalted butter*
> *Maldon or sea salt*
> *freshly ground white pepper*
> For the sauce
> *1 tablespoon lemon juice*
> *75 g/3 oz unsalted butter, cut*
> *into small pieces*
> *1–2 teaspoons Dijon mustard*

Rinse the herrings quickly, then dry well. Be careful not to dislodge the roes – or, if that's impossible, keep them whole and cook separately.

Cover the fish all over with oatmeal, pressing well in. Melt the butter and when it is foaming add the herrings (you'll probably have to use two frying pans, otherwise use a large roasting pan over two hot-plates). Cook for 3–5 minutes each side until crispy and browned, then transfer on to hot serving plates, and keep warm.

For the sauce, bubble the lemon juice in a small pan until reduced by half, then add a piece of butter. Whisking constantly over a medium heat, add more butter once the first piece has melted. The sauce should be pale in colour and creamy in consistency. Never stop whisking; if it should become too hot and seem in danger of curdling, lift the pan high off the heat until cooled slightly. (It's a good idea to have a bowl of iced water by the cooker, into which you can dip the bottom of the pan and quickly reduce the temperature.) As soon as the last piece of butter has melted, whisk in the mustard, pour the sauce into a jug and serve immediately.

Note: Traditionally, in Scotland, they use bacon fat to fry the fish. Delicious if you have some.

Cod Steaks with Walnut and Mustard Sauce

In the Middle East, nut sauces of all kinds are popular. Walnuts are favoured for fish, and they marry well with mustard to make a fine sauce for cod steaks – firm in flesh but often bland in flavour. If you can buy inshore cod, do. The difference in taste is startling.

SERVES 4
4 cod steaks
300 ml/½ pint dry white wine
2 parsley sprigs
6 white peppercorns, lightly
*   crushed*
1 thyme sprig
1 bay leaf
5 cm/2 inch piece lemon zest,
*   or Seville orange zest*
finely chopped parsley
1 lime, cut into quarters
For the sauce
175 g/6 oz walnuts

juice of 1–2 limes
3–4 tablespoons olive oil
1 teaspoon Dijon or Roman
  mustard (pp.58 and 65)
Maldon or sea salt

Put the wine, parsley sprigs, peppercorns, thyme, bay leaf and lemon or orange zest into a pan with 300 ml/½ pint water. Bring quickly to the boil, then simmer gently for 25 minutes. Leave to cool.

Place the cod steaks in a wide shallow pan, cover with the cooled bouillon, then bring slowly to the boil. Just before it boils, turn the heat very low and cook the steaks, the liquid barely bubbling, for about 15 minutes until they are just done. Take off the heat and leave them to cool in the stock. When they are tepid, transfer to a serving plate and cover loosely with foil. Do not chill unless you absolutely have to – in which case bring to room temperature before serving.

Return the stock to the heat and bubble furiously until it has reduced to no more than 3–4 tablespoons.

Make the sauce by grinding the nuts, in a coffee grinder in small batches, to a fine powder. Whisk with the lime juice, then add the oil, a little at a time, to make a thick emulsion. Stir in the mustard, then a little salt and finally some of the reduced stock to thin the sauce down slightly and soften the flavour. How much you add is very much a matter of taste – and mood. Serve the fish, sprinkled thickly with chopped parsley, accompanied by lime quarters, and let people help themselves to sauce.

Times-*baked Trout*

One of the finest ways to cook trout, or indeed any whole fish, keeping it moist and succulent, firm yet tender. Beloved of Victorian anglers, the method was no surprise to M. Henry Poupon, President of S.E.G.M.A. Maille. For French fishermen, he said, it was the only way to cook trout. *We* use *The Times*, one whole sheet being just the right size to envelop one fish. For lovers of pink trout, the choice of newspaper needs no comment . . . By one of those curious quirks of coincidence, the greatest users of mustard also happen to be readers of those venerable organs.

SERVES 6
6 fresh trout, cleaned, heads
   and tails left on
6 tablespoons Roman mustard
   (p.65)
50 g/2 oz pine nuts
Maldon or sea salt
freshly ground black pepper
6 pages of The Times

Wipe the trout with a damp cloth. Mix the mustard with the pine nuts, lightly crushing a few of the nuts to release their oil. Season lightly with salt and black pepper, then spread the paste thickly on the inside of each fish. Skewer the fish closed with cocktail sticks then wrap each in a sheet of newspaper, turning down the ends to make a neat parcel. Soak under the cold tap until quite wet, then bake in the oven at 180°C/350°F/Gas Mark 4 for 10–25 minutes, until the paper is almost dried out. The discrepancy in time depends on the size of your fish and on your oven – convector ovens dry the paper more quickly. Fish over 700 g/1½ lb will probably need about 30–35 minutes, while a really big one (say 1.5 kg/generous 3 lb) will need an hour. To serve hot, peel the paper off – the skin should come cleanly, too, to give you a perfectly done trout. Cold, it is equally delicious: simply leave to cool in the paper, then peel away. Small new potatoes and *fresh* peas or baby broad beans complete the perfect summer dish.

Mustard and Honeyed Salmon Fillet

In medieval times, fish was often cooked with sweetness and spices: reminiscent of Apicius in ancient Rome with his blend of herbs, honey, nuts, raisins and mustard. For salmon, it would be too much of a good thing, but mustard and honey give a delicate sweet-sharp flavour.

SERVES 4–6
1.1–1.4 kg/2½–3 lb salmon,
   skinned and boned to leave
   2 large fillets
4 tablespoons clear honey
125 g/4 oz unsalted butter,
   softened

4 tablespoons Five-herb
 mustard (p.59)
Maldon or sea salt
freshly ground white pepper
4 × 5 cm/2 inch very thin
 slices of fresh, peeled ginger
lemon wedges, to serve

Lightly season the salmon with salt and freshly ground pepper. Heat the honey until runny, then brush all over the salmon, on both sides, being careful when turning the fillets.

Mash the butter with the mustard, then spread the paste over the fish, again on all sides, putting a thicker layer in the middle to sandwich the fillets together. Place the fish on a large sheet of foil, then tuck two of the slices of ginger underneath the fish, and put two on the top. Fold the foil into a loose parcel, sealing the edges tightly, and cook in the oven at 220°C/425°F/Gas Mark 7 for about 20 minutes until the fish is just done. Transfer to a serving dish, in the foil, unwrapping at the table so everyone can enjoy the wonderful smell. Have lemon wedges on the table, and lots of good bread to mop up the buttery juices. A herb salad, delicately dressed, and as good a white wine as one can afford are the only other requisites.

Gravlax with Mustard Sauce

One of the world's great classics, hailing from Scandinavia where it is traditionally served on Walpurgis Night (30 April) to herald the arrival of spring and the return of the salmon. It is an ideal way to treat a tailpiece – though these are no longer the bargain they once were. Kinder on the purse, and equally good for the dish, is Canadian frozen salmon. Herrings, and kippers particularly, also benefit wonderfully from being 'buried' in the pickle (*gravlax* literally means 'grave salmon'), thus obliging us with a year-round treat. The principle is the same but you will need four small herrings or two large kippers.

SERVES 6–8
700–900 g/1 ¹/2–2 lb tailpiece
 salmon
1 ¹/2 tablespoons Maldon salt,
 lightly crushed

1 tablespoon sugar
1 tablespoon black
  peppercorns, crushed
small posy fresh dillweed,
  finely chopped
For the sauce
3 tablespoons Dijon mustard
1½ tablespoons castor sugar
1 tablespoon white wine
  vinegar
100 ml/3½ fl oz peanut oil
100 ml/3½ fl oz soured cream
small posy fresh dillweed,
  finely chopped
Maldon salt
freshly ground white pepper

First, bone the salmon. Cover the fish with a tea towel, roll it gently on a hard surface to loosen up the bones; then insert a thin-bladed knife between the bone and the flesh, at the wide end, and push the knife right along the spine, before easing it down to the side, pressing as close to the bone as possible. Slit through the skin (this stays on during the pickling process), and repeat the operation on the other side of the spine, then turn the fish over and repeat again. Now you can lift off the flesh in to two kite-shaped pieces. The whole process takes little longer than reading how to do it!

Mix together the salt, sugar and crushed peppercorns, then sprinkle a good layer of dill in the bottom of a dish into which the fish will fit snugly. Add a layer of the salt/sugar mixture, put in the fish, skin side down. Scatter over a layer of dillweed and pickle mixture. Place the second piece of fish, flesh side down, on top, again covering with dill, salt and sugar.

Cover with kitchen foil and a heavy weight (a couple of large tins are fine). Chill for at least 24 hours, not more than 5 days, then slice the fish, very thinly on the diagonal (like smoked salmon), and serve with lightly buttered rye bread and the mustard sauce.

This takes minutes to make but the flavour is vastly improved if it is left to stand for 2–3 hours. Whisk the mustard and sugar together, beat in the vinegar, then add the oil, whisking very briskly. It thickens quickly to a very solid vinaigrette – indeed many books suggest a vinaigrette-type sauce, and some a mayonnaise, but in Norway they serve a soured cream sauce, which is perhaps the nicest. So, add the soured cream, then the dill and season to taste with salt and pepper. Serve chilled.

Monkfish with Mustard Seeds and Lime

Monkfish used to be one of those glorious finds at the fishmonger that was delicious – and cheap. Now *nouvelle cuisine* has turned it into a star fish, at twice the price. Still, it is exquisite in flavour and there is little wastage. Milky in colour, rather solid in texture, it is one of the few fish where bigger is better – the large steaks across the middle or a good-sized tailpiece are the prime parts. Tailpieces in particular are easy to fillet, and attractive to serve.

SERVES 6
1.1–1.4 kg/2½–3 lb tailpiece monkfish
2 tablespoons mustard oil
3 tablespoons brown mustard seed
2 tablespoons flour
75 g/3 oz unsalted butter
2 tablespoons sunflower oil
Maldon salt
freshly ground black pepper
3 tablespoons cognac
juice of 2–3 limes
125 ml/4 fl oz fish stock
¼ teaspoon Dijon mustard

Monkfish is usually sold skinned, so it merely needs filleting by slipping a long, thin-bladed knife in beside the central cartilaginous bone at the thicker end of the tailpiece, then gently cutting through the flesh to the sides down to the tip. Repeat on the other side of the bone, separating the top fillet from the bone as you do so. Lift off the top piece, then remove the bone from the bottom – you should now have two neat triangles of fish which can be sliced lengthways into three long, narrow fillets.

Heat the mustard oil in a small, deep pan until nearly smoking, then add the mustard seeds and cook, covered, for about a minute until they start to pop. Drain, discarding the oil. Mix the seeds with the flour, then coat the fillets lightly. Melt the butter with the sunflower oil; when just starting to sizzle add the fish and cook for 3–4 minutes on both sides until just cooked through. Sprinkle with a little salt and black pepper, then flame with the cognac (a slight warming in a ladle helps ensure quick ignition). Remove the fish and keep warm on a serving platter. Add the juice of 2 limes and bubble the sauce hard, then add the fish stock and return to the boil. Taste, adding the extra lime juice if necessary, then reduce slightly until lightly glazed. Stir in the mustard, pour over the fish and serve at once.

Roast Turbot with Mustard, Coriander and Cider

Rarely does one see turbot at the fishmonger's nowadays, especially whole turbot. Yet our ancestors knew it well. Those extravagantly huge, diamond-shaped copper pans that adorn country house kitchen walls were specifically for the monster fish – often up to 3 feet in length, and weighing in at 20 kg/45 lb. With its large, flattened snout and knobbly-skinned back it is a daunting creature to look at, but its flesh is sweet, firm, very white – and superb in flavour. Hannah Glasse in the *Art of Cookery made Plain and Easy* (1747) bakes turbot with fresh horseradish. That led the way to mustard. Thankfully, the more manageable chicken turbot – a modest 1–1.8 kg/2¼–4 lb in size – is equally good in flavour.

SERVES 6
1 chicken turbot, about 1.6
  kg/3½ lb, cleaned but left
  whole
50 g/2 oz butter, plus extra for
  greasing
1–2 tablespoons Dijon
  mustard
1 tablespoon coriander seeds
Maldon or sea salt
freshly ground black pepper
freshly grated nutmeg
600 ml/1 pint dry cider
lemon juice
small posy fresh coriander
  leaves, finely chopped
1 teaspoon arrowroot
½–1 teaspoon Dijon mustard,
  to finish the sauce

Make a slight incision on the dark side of the fish from head to tail down the centre bone to prevent the fish curling up during cooking, then lay it in a large, well-buttered roasting pan and rub the mustard well into the top side of the turbot. Sprinkle over the coriander seeds, a little salt, lots of black pepper and nutmeg. Flake the butter all over the fish, then pour in the cider around the sides, drizzling just a tablespoon or two over the flesh.

Cook in the oven at 170°C/325°F/Gas Mark 3 for 40–50 minutes until the flesh is white and firm when tested with the tip of a knife. Very carefully lift out on to a warmed serving dish and rest in the turned-off oven while finishing the sauce.

Pour the cooking liquor into a small pan, reduce by fast boiling by about a third, then add a squirt of lemon juice, the fresh coriander leaves and the arrowroot mixed with a little water. Stir over a medium-low heat until slightly thickened, add the mustard, just to sharpen the sauce – it should not be overtly mustard in taste. Pour into a gravy boat and serve at once with the roast fish.

Mustard Grilled Lobster

Despite Apicius, lobster with mustard is not a combination that instantly springs to mind. And indeed, cold with a mustard mayonnaise it was horrid – that elusively beautiful flavour killed in an instant. Hot, with a mustard cream sauce, or as spiced soup, it was less than delightful. Then that gem of a book, *The Gentle Art of Cookery* by Mrs Leyel, gave it to us: 'Open a lobster and break its claws. Sprinkle it when open with dry mustard, pepper and salt, and cover with little pieces of butter.' One of the best ways of cooking the noble crustacean. For the lobster's sake, blanch it first. Death is instantaneous, and it is easier to scoop out the flesh. Ready cooked lobster is not suitable for the recipe since the extra grilling will toughen and dry it out.

SERVES 2
1 live lobster, about 700 g/1½
    lb in weight
50 g/2 oz unsalted butter, plus
    extra for greasing
dried, home-made
    breadcrumbs
½ teaspoon mustard powder

Maldon salt
freshly ground black pepper
For the sauce
25 g/1 oz unsalted butter
lemon juice
small bunch parsley, finely
  chopped
Maldon salt
freshly ground white pepper
½ teaspoon English mustard

Bring a large pan of lightly salted water to a rapid boil, then plunge in the lobster, head first. Boil for 1 minute, then lower the heat and simmer for 5 minutes – this will almost cook the lobster (normally you would allow 5 minutes to the pound). Take out and leave until just cool enough to handle.

Lie the lobster on its back and, with a sharp blow of a cleaver or large-bladed knife, divide it into two lengthways. Remove the stomach (a little dark sac confusingly near the head), then scoop out the body meat, discarding the dark vein running through the lobster. Do not discard the soft, creamy greenish meat – this is the liver (tomalley) and extremely delicious. Neither should you discard the other delicacy – the roe, or coral, present under the tail in a female lobster. Put them into separate bowls and keep aside. Now crack the large claws and carefully pull out the flesh – try and keep the pink tip intact if you can. Clean the shells and dry them, then lightly grease the insides with butter. Sprinkle with breadcrumbs, shaking off the excess, and refill with the meat, cut into chunks, leaving a gap in the middle to pile in the liver and roe.

Sprinkle with the powdered mustard, a little salt and black pepper, dot with the butter, and put under a fierce grill for 4–5 minutes. Quickly melt the butter for the sauce, whisk in the juice of a small lemon, the parsley, a little salt and pepper and then, off the heat, beat in the mustard. Serve at once with the lobster, accompanied by thinly sliced brown bread. Delicious. The sauce, incidentally, is also extremely good with tiny new potatoes – preferably steamed.

5

CHICKEN AND TURKEY

And when we meet, with champagne and a chicken, at last.

Lady Mary Wortley Montagu, *The Lover*

Chicken was, until recently, a luxury. It appeared late as a food in the Western world, and seems first to have been appreciated by the islanders of Cos around the third century BC. Before that the birds were apparently kept only for their eggs. The Romans learnt quickly from the Greeks and by 175 BC it was frequently being mentioned in the records of Pompeii.

The Middle Ages continued to regard it highly, and we learn from Isabella of Portugal that fowls formed the greatest expense when her kitchen was preparing for a banquet. By the eighteenth century, when Lady Mary Wortley Montagu was writing, chicken was the epitome of a luxurious dinner for the lovers.

Today we are more blasé about chicken, now one of the cheapest of meats. This is a shame, for it is also one of the healthiest to eat. We should treat it with respect and enjoy it, for a little judicious cooking – and mustard – can work wonders on even the cheapest frozen varieties. We experimented by smearing them all over with a little Dijon mustard before roasting in a chicken brick. Every time there were comments on how intense the chicken flavour was – not a hint of the little hot seed, merely a return to the forgotten taste of chickens reared freely in the fresh air.

When we went to Colman's at Norwich, John Hemingway – who knows more about mustard than man has forgotten – told us an enchanting story of some delicious chicken once served in Nyasaland. The hostess enquired the recipe of the cook, to be told that he had merely used a little of the special poultry spice she had given him. Puzzled, she trooped her guests to the kitchen where the proud cook delightedly pointed to a packet of Poultry Mustard. This was one of Colman's most successful lines at the beginning of this century – but for feeding to the chickens. One teaspoon per six chickens mixed in with their morning mash proved startlingly efficacious in improving their egg-laying capabilities, their strength of fertilization and their general stamina.

Interestingly, we found few recipes in the ancients for chicken with mustard. Apicius has two, then there is silence until we reach Taillevent, chef (legend has it) to Charles VI in the late fourteenth century. According to Dumas, the King, after a hard day fighting the English, arrived in the little village of Sainte-Menehould. Devastated, with only half a dozen houses still standing, it could offer neither much food, nor people to cook it. However, four pig's trotters and three chickens were found and a toolmaker's wife was asked to cook them. She did not let her King down: the birds were roasted, the trotters grilled. Both had a rolling in breadcrumbs and *fines herbes* and were served with mustard. Only the bones were left by the royal party – and the King thereafter often requested Chicken à la Sainte-Menehould. To this day, those words on a menu indicate that method of cooking, more usually with pigs' feet than chicken, and the mustard will often appear in the form of a piquant sauce.

If you're lacking stuffing ingredients for your chicken, a little mustard mixed with sautéd onions, breadcrumbs and fresh herbs brings out the flavours wonderfully – you can add fried mustard seeds for extra nuttiness. A tasteless gravy is vastly improved by an added spoonful of the condiment: bubble the sauce hard for a minute or two to reduce the taste of the mustard.

Turkey, which can be uninspiring, took on new dimensions when spiced with mustard and one of the simplest and most delicious dishes we had was leftover turkey breast, steamed to heat it through, then covered lightly with the supremely easy cream and mustard sauce (p.92). Cold, both turkey and chicken are lifted with a mayonnaise flavoured with anchovy, avocado and mustard (p.87) – again the mustard not intruding itself but enhancing a peculiarly delicate and subtle combination of tastes. And if cold leftovers are not enticing, one can mince the flesh, mix it with herbs, a little egg white, a few mustard seeds (fried until beginning to splutter) and breadcrumbs, then form it into small balls. Fried until golden and crispy, they can be accompanied by a mustard sauce of your choice. They are also excellent on a bed of mixed salad leaves with a mustard vinaigrette poured over them the instant they come out of the pan. It is not difficult, with mustard, to restore chicken to a place of honour at the table.

Chicken Dijon with Spice and Wine

Dijon chicken, chicken Dijonnaise, Chicken Dijon – there must be as many names, and dishes, as there are mustards. This recipe comes from the Maille leaflet: superbly simple, and supremely delicious.

SERVES 6
1.1 kg/2½ lb chicken pieces
25 g/1 oz unsalted butter
sea salt
freshly ground black pepper
1 garlic clove, crushed
1 bay leaf
¼ teaspoon dried marjoram
¼ teaspoon dried thyme
175 ml/6 fl oz chicken stock
175 ml/6 fl oz dry white wine
12 small onions, peeled but
  left whole
12 whole baby carrots
400 g/14 oz canned artichoke
  hearts
5 tablespoons Maille Dijon
  mustard with white wine
1 tablespoon cornflour

Lightly brown the chicken pieces in butter in a large flameproof casserole, sprinkle with a little salt and pepper, then add the garlic, bay leaf, marjoram, thyme, chicken stock and wine. Bring to a gentle simmer, cover and cook for 35 minutes, stirring occasionally.

Add the onions, carrots and drained artichokes and cook, covered, for a further 10–15 minutes until the vegetables are tender.

Transfer the chicken and vegetables to a warmed serving platter and keep warm in a low oven. Stir the mustard into the cooking liquid and bring to the boil. Mix the cornflour with a little cold water, add to the pan and stir until lightly thickened. Pour the sauce over the chicken and serve immediately.

Maille received a Royal appointment to Queen Victoria
in 1866 and to King Edward VII in 1903

Chicken Legs Dijonnaise

Another variation of Chicken Dijonnaise simply makes a mustard butter which is spread all over the chicken – under the skin. It is a particularly good method for grilling chicken legs; spicy and succulent, they are delicious hot, even better cold. Ideal picnic food, although they have been known to disappear at Saturday breakfast.

SERVES 6
6 chicken legs
Maldon salt
finely ground black pepper
a few tarragon sprigs, very
  finely chopped
1–2 tablespoons Dijon
  mustard
75 g/3 oz unsalted butter,
  softened
juice of 1 large lemon

Carefully using a long, thin-bladed knife, slip it under the skin and loosen all around the leg joints. Mix some salt with a good grinding of black pepper and the chopped tarragon and rub all over each leg. Leave for 30 minutes.

Mash the mustard and the butter together, then beat in the lemon juice. Spread a little of the paste – about 2 teaspoons – between the skin and the flesh of each leg, then cook under a medium grill for 15–20 minutes, turning once. Raise the heat and grill for a further 5–10 minutes (depending on the size of the legs) until deeply golden and crispy.

Steamed Chicken Breasts with Nettle Mustard Sauce

Nettles have long been known for their goodness and were a prized first sign of spring in the Victorian market place. Today, they cost nothing and are widely ignored. Delicious in soups, and this delicate sauce.

SERVES 6
6 chicken breasts, skinned and
off the bone
juice of 1 large lemon
50 g/2 oz unsalted butter
2–3 garlic cloves
3 cloves
6 shallots, finely chopped
600 ml/1 pint nettle tops,
young top sprigs only,
gathered wearing rubber
gloves
200 ml/7 fl oz good chicken
stock
Maldon salt
freshly ground white pepper
2 teaspoons Dijon mustard or
1–2 teaspoons lemon
mustard

Put the chicken on a flat dish and squeeze the lemon juice over both sides. Leave for 30 minutes. Place the breasts in a steamer, or colander, fanned out with the thickest ends in the middle, and put over a pan of gently simmering water. Cover and cook for 5–7 minutes each side, until just done in the middle. Once cooked, keep warm in the steamer – off the heat.

Meanwhile make the sauce. Melt half the butter in a large pan, add the garlic and the cloves and cook gently for 2–3 minutes then add the shallots and sweat for a further 5–6 minutes. Wash the nettle tops (still wearing rubber gloves – the sting disappears only with cooking), rinse, shake dry and add to the pan with 6–7 tablespoons of stock. Stir, then cook until the nettles are dark green and limp, about 8 minutes.

Purée the nettles with the rest of the stock, return to the pan, add salt and pepper and bring to a simmer. Whisk in the remaining butter to thicken and gloss the sauce, then stir in the mustard. Whisk for a further minute, then pour a little sauce on to serving plates. Place the breasts on top, drizzle over a little more sauce and serve immediately.

Chicken Breasts
with Tomato, Mustard and Yoghurt Sauce

Tomato and mustard is a particularly good combination. Fresh tomatoes give a sweeter, subtler taste, though the canned plum variety are a good substitute – add a pinch of vanilla sugar to counteract their extra acidity. A similar, though much richer, sauce is served by John Tovey at Miller Howe, with pork chops. Based on reduced cream, lightly flavoured with tomato purée and English mustard, it is very good indeed but chicken is, perhaps, more suited to the delicacy of this recipe.

SERVES 6
6 chicken breasts, skinned and
boned
freshly ground black pepper
700 g/1½ lb fresh tomatoes
1½ teaspoons Moutarde
Soyer (p.62)
1½ teaspoons Maille Dijon
mustard
300 ml/½ pint natural
yoghurt
Maldon salt
¾ teaspoon cornflour
handful finely chopped fresh
chervil, or parsley

Sprinkle the meat with freshly ground black pepper on both sides, then leave. Bring a large pan of water to the boil, drop in the tomatoes and blanch for 3–4 minutes. Take out, cool slightly, then peel and blend to a purée. Strain into a pan, stir in the mustards and put over a very gentle heat.

Meanwhile, stabilize the yoghurt (to prevent a curdled-looking sauce): whisk it in a large shallow saucepan until smooth and fairly liquid, then add the cornflour, mixed with a little water to form a thin paste, and about ¼ teaspoon salt. Place on a low heat and bring to the boil, stirring all the time with a wooden spoon *in the same direction.* When it is just about to boil, turn the heat to the lowest possible and simmer for 10 minutes until thick and smooth. *Do not cover* the pan since steam – even one tiny droplet – will undo your good work and instantly destabilize the yoghurt. It can now be cooked with impunity. Incidentally, if you make your own yoghurt from salted goat's milk, it can be used as it is since it won't curdle. Keep an eye on the tomato mixture during the stabilization process and turn off the heat if it is reducing too rapidly. About a quarter is right – and the flavours of the mustards should have melded almost completely. You are aiming for a very fresh tomato taste – with just a hint, rather than an awareness, of mustard.

Once the yoghurt has started to simmer, you can steam the chicken. Lay the pieces in a colander or steamer over a pan of barely simmering water and steam for about 12 minutes, turning once, until just cooked through to the middle. Keep warm in the steamer, covered, but off the heat, while finishing the sauce.

Whisk the yoghurt into the tomato, check the seasoning, adjusting if necessary, blend thoroughly and bring to a bubble. Put the chicken on to warmed individual plates, spoon some sauce around or over each breast and sprinkle with lots of chopped chervil.

Stir-Fry Chicken with Mustard Seeds, Satsumas and Watercress

China's rare use of mustard in the kitchen nearly always combines it with chicken. This Chinese-inspired dish is simple, quick and very good.

SERVES 2

2 *chicken breasts, boned and skinned*
1 *egg white*
3 *tablespoons peanut oil*
1/2 *tablespoon brown mustard seed*
2 *garlic cloves, finely chopped*
2 *spring onions, bulbs quartered, green tops finely sliced on the diagonal*
4–5 *raspings of dried root ginger (not ground ginger)*

pinch of ground cinnamon
150 ml/¼ pint home-made
  chicken stock
2 satsumas
1 tablespoon English mustard
  powder
1 teaspoon powdered
  arrowroot
Maldon salt
1 bunch watercress, finely
  chopped

Cut the chicken breasts into long strips, then into small pieces. Lightly beat the egg white and mix into the chicken. Chill for 20 minutes.

Heat 1 tablespoon of the oil, in a wok for preference but otherwise in a heavy-based pan (in which case you may need a little more oil for the second frying, but keep it to the minimum). Add the mustard seeds and stir fry until they start popping, about a minute. Remove the seeds and drain. Wipe the pan, add another tablespoon of oil, heat, then stir in the garlic and chopped spring onion and sauté for 4–5 minutes, stirring constantly. Remove from the pan and keep aside.

Wipe the pan clean again, then add the remaining oil. When just beginning to smoke, add the chicken and stir constantly for 2–3 minutes until opaque and firming up. Sprinkle over the ginger and cinnamon, add the reserved mustard seeds and the onion mixture and pour on the stock. Grate in a little satsuma zest, then peel the satsumas, divide one into segments, add to the pan, then blend the other and strain the juice into a small jug.

While the cooking juices are coming to the boil, mix 2 tablespoons of the satsuma juice with the mustard to form a thin paste, then pour the remaining juice into the pan. Simmer for 3–4 minutes longer, then mix the arrowroot with a little water and stir into the chicken. Stir for another minute or so until the sauce is very lightly thickened. Season lightly with salt then pile on to a shallow dish. Sprinkle over the chopped watercress and eat at once, dipping every third mouthful or so into the hot mustard.

Grilled Poussin
with Tarragon Mustard Shallot Sauce

Outstanding among many memorable lunches in Lyons was a simple yet spectacularly delicious young plump chicken smothered in a mustardy onion purée, crisped in breadcrumbs and served with a piquant reduction of shallots and vinegar. Adapted, and simplified, the recipe is perfect for poussin.

SERVES 2
1 poussin, about 450 g/1 lb in
  weight
50 g/2 oz unsalted butter
1 tablespoon Dijon mustard
1 tablespoon finely chopped
  fresh tarragon
Maldon salt
freshly ground black pepper
8 shallots, finely chopped
3 tablespoons Spicy Italian
  vinegar (p.75)
1 bunch watercress

Ask the butcher to split the poussin down the back, or do it yourself with a heavy sharp cleaver, then flatten each half with a good blow with the side of the cleaver.

Melt the butter, stir in the mustard and tarragon then brush each half-poussin (skin side) liberally with the mixture. Season, lightly with salt, generously with pepper, and cook under a medium grill for about 10–12 minutes until they begin to turn colour. Turn the poussin over, brush with more butter and cook for 5 minutes, then turn again, baste, and cook under a fierce heat for 4–5 minutes until the skin is really crisp, the poussin cooked through. Keep warm in a low oven, covered in foil.

Scrape up the cooking juices from the grill pan, add to the melted butter remaining in the saucepan, then stir in the shallots and sweat for 5 minutes. Pour in the vinegar and cook, over a high heat, uncovered, until the vinegar has reduced to a bare tablespoon and the shallots are mushy – the sauce should taste lightly sharp but not biting. Serve at once with each poussin half laid on a bed of chopped watercress.

Garlic Mustard Chicken in a Brick

The best way to roast a chicken is in that old Roman invention, the chicken brick. Also in this day of low-fat diets, it is the obvious answer – the method needs no fat for basting, yet gives a crispy skinned, succulent joint. Not only chickens can go into the brick – lamb, pork, pheasants, partridge all emerge perfectly cooked (though the dry game birds do need added butter). This dish evolved with the arrival of the new season's garlic. We had no lamb, the chicken was already in its brick. So, shortly afterwards, was the garlic.

SERVES 5–6
1 fresh chicken, about 1.6
kg/3 ½ lb dressed weight
4–5 heads of garlic
Maldon salt
freshly ground black pepper
2 tablespoons Dijon mustard
3 tablespoons medium dry
white wine

Rinse the chicken and pat dry inside and out, then place in the brick. Peel the garlic – do try and buy heads of a good size; ideally each clove should be the size of a hazelnut. Not only will the taste be better – the peeling won't drive you insane. Bring a pan of water to the boil, throw in the garlic and blanch for 1 minute. Drain and add to the chicken brick – tuck some cloves down the sides, scatter the rest all over.

Sprinkle the chicken lightly with salt, generously with freshly ground black pepper, then mix the mustard with the wine and pour over.

Cover the brick, and cook in the oven at 200°C/400°F/Gas Mark 6 for about 1½ hours until the chicken is beautifully golden and the aroma of the garlic tantalizing. Transfer the bird to a warmed serving platter, cover and keep warm.

Strain the cooking juices into a tall jug and put the garlic in a blender. After a minute or so, all the fat will have risen to the top of the jug and can be easily spooned off. Add a couple of tablespoons of the juices to the garlic and blend to a thick purée. Thin with a little more gravy if wished but this sauce should be thick – akin to bread sauce. Reheat if necessary then pile into a small bowl. Bring the gravy to the boil, add a little hot water (not too much; the taste should be concentrated) and a sprinkling of pepper, then pour into a gravy boat and serve at once with the chicken, garlic sauce, roast potatoes and a good green salad. Any other vegetable is superfluous.

The original prototype Dunhill lighter
in 1923 was a Colman's mustard tin

Smoked Chicken
with Mustard Vinegar and Dill Dressing

Home-smoked chicken is excellent. If you haven't a home-smoker, do, please indulge. The expense is not vast: the results are incomparable. Poultry, lamb, fish and cheese are given a new look – and taste. This dish, the chicken mixed with frizzy endive, a few nasturtium leaves and flowers, fresh herbs and the blue bonnets of borage, is one of the finest summer suppers.

SERVES 6–8
2 small chickens, split into
    quarters
1 large head frizzy endive,
    washed and shredded by
    hand
a handful small nasturtium
    leaves, finely chopped
6–8 nasturtium flowers, taken
    off the stalks, finely
    chopped
2–3 sprigs lovage, coarsely
    chopped
2–3 sprigs lemon balm, finely
    chopped
2 sprigs summer savory,
    finely chopped
2–3 sprigs golden marjoram,
    finely chopped
2 dozen borage flowers, pulled
    off the calyx
For the dressing
1 hard-boiled egg yolk
1 egg yolk
1 teaspoon Dijon mustard
2 tablespoons Spicy Italian
    vinegar (p.75)
about 150 ml/¼ pint extra
    virgin olive oil
good handful fresh dill, finely
    chopped

Always use your smoker outside. Apart from the fire hazard, the smell, delicious wafting on the open air, is less so in the confines of the kitchen. Place the chicken pieces, skin side up, in the smoking compartment (having fuelled the smoker according to the maker's instructions) and smoke for 20–30 minutes. Remove from the smoker and cool slightly, then take all the meat off the bones and chop into bite-sized pieces.

Mix the chicken with the endive and herbs, keeping the flowers aside.

To make the dressing, mash the hard-boiled egg yolk with the raw egg, then beat in the mustard and vinegar. Gradually add the oil, drop by drop at first (as if making mayonnaise), then in a slow trickle, whisking well all the while. Stop when it is very thick and the taste suits you. Beat in the dill and pour over the salad. Toss very thoroughly until everything is gleaming. With so many herbs, extra seasoning is almost superfluous but have salt and pepper mills on the table with good crusty bread and chilled unsalted butter.

Turkey Breasts with Vinegar, Mustard and Garlic

Turkey can be very dull. But, married to this ancient Burgundian sauce – sweet-sour in flavour and a relic from the Roman occupation – it takes on new dimensions. Traditionally, this was a sauce for chicken, turkeys being unknown in Europe until the sixteenth century. Brought over from Central America by the Spanish conquistadores, they soon became popular on the Continent. For preference, buy a hen, and one that has enjoyed a free life, ranging around the farmyard. Its fullness of flavour is so different from that of mass-produced frozen creatures that even the most ardent turkey-hater has to admit it is good.

SERVES 6–8
*1.4 kg/3 lb boned turkey
  breast
1 tablespoon peanut oil
60 g/2½ oz unsalted butter
6 fat garlic cloves, unpeeled
Maldon salt
freshly ground black pepper
150 ml/¼ pint red wine
  vinegar
200 ml/7 fl oz dry white
  Burgundy, or other good
  wine
1–1½ tablespoons Dijon
  mustard
1 generous tablespoon tomato
  purée
1 tablespoon brandy
2–3 tablespoons double
  cream
finely chopped parsley*

Cut the turkey breast, slightly on the diagonal, into 6–8 long escalopes. Put between 2 sheets of greaseproof paper or clingfilm and batter *lightly* to flatten.

Heat the oil with 50 g/2 oz butter in a very large frying pan or roasting tin. When just beginning to bubble, add the breasts, and the garlic, and sauté gently for 9–12 minutes, turning the meat once, until cooked through and lightly golden. Transfer the escalopes to a warmed serving dish, cover with foil and keep warm over a steamer.

Drain off nearly all the fat; peel the garlic. Pour the vinegar into the pan, scraping up the sediments, bubble for 30 seconds, then pour in the wine, adding the mustard and tomato purée stirred together. Whisk lightly, add the garlic and simmer for 3–4 minutes until the vinegar fumes have been driven off. Add the brandy, cream, the rest of the butter and a little parsley. Stir vigorously, mashing the garlic lightly, until the sauce has thickened a little, season, then simmer gently for another 2–3 minutes. Pour over the turkey, sprinkle generously with the remaining chopped parsley and serve at once.

Honey and Mustard Roast Turkey Breasts

Apicius would undoubtedly have approved today's penchant for the honey–mustard combination. Pine nuts – another Roman favourite – add a sweet nuttiness, while the lemon zest prevents sweetness from turning into sickliness. The obvious choice of honey is rape-seed, pale and thick with a delicate flavour. Mustard honey, though good, is rare and it crystallizes very easily. It may also have a slightly bitter aroma (which does not however affect the flavour).

SERVES 6–8
2 × 700 g/1½ lb turkey
    breasts, boned but not
    skinned
50 g/2 oz unsalted butter, plus
    extra for greasing
3 tablespoons coarse-grained
    mustard
2 tablespoons rape-seed or
    clover honey
grated zest of ½ lemon
25 g/1 oz pine nuts

Maldon salt
freshly ground black pepper

Put the turkey breasts, flesh side down, on a lightly greased foil-lined roasting tin. Melt the butter, mustard and honey until runny then paint the skins of the breasts liberally with the mixture. Sprinkle over the lemon zest, pine nuts, a little salt and lots of black pepper, then cover the tin with foil and cook in the oven at 180°C/350°F/Gas Mark 5 for 1¼–1½ hours, basting frequently, until nicely golden and the flesh is cooked through.

Serve at once with the juices poured over. Accompaniments should be simple and beautifully fresh.

Devilled Turkey Drumsticks

Devilling, so beloved of the Victorians, is a method particularly suited to turkey: the meat is gutsy enough to withstand the treatment, and even the most frozen of creatures is vastly improved by the spiciness. For a spectacular picnic centrepiece, paint a whole capon, trebling the quantities of glaze.

SERVES 6
6 medium-sized turkey
    drumsticks
2 crushed garlic cloves
6 tablespoons Dijon mustard
3 tablespoons olive oil
3 teaspoons cayenne pepper
7.5 cm/3 inches fresh root
    ginger, peeled and grated
1 teaspoon soft brown sugar
few dashes Worcestershire
    sauce
Maldon salt
freshly ground white pepper

Score the drumsticks deeply in several places, then mix the garlic with the mustard, oil, cayenne, grated ginger, sugar and Worcestershire sauce. Season lightly with salt and pepper then paint each drumstick, liberally and evenly, with the paste. Chill for at least 12 hours, bringing to room temperature before cooking.

Heat the grill to very hot, then turn it low and cook the drumsticks for about 1¼ hours, turning frequently and basting with any juices which have poured off them, until they are very dark and the meat is cooked through.

Turn the grill to high and cook for 3–4 minutes, turning them round, just to warm through thoroughly and crisp up the skin. Either serve at once with sautéd potatoes or leave to cool, when they are almost more delicious.

Stuffed Turkey Legs

Perhaps one of the best of the turkey variations, certainly the most elegant – and turkey shows its advantage here over chicken in that the legs are large enough to make boning them simple.

SERVES 4–6
3 large turkey drumsticks
6 slices streaky bacon
4 tablespoons mustard oil
For the stuffing
125 g/4 oz Parma ham, finely
  chopped
50 g/2 oz fresh breadcrumbs
25 g/1 oz freshly grated
  Parmesan
2 tablespoons Moutarde Soyer
  (p.62)
2 mace blades, crumbled
5 tablespoons finely chopped
  parsley
2 eggs, beaten
Maldon salt
freshly ground black pepper

If you don't have an obliging butcher, chop off the small knobbly end of each drumstick with a sharp cleaver, then – using a very sharp knife, with great care – make a slit through the skin and flesh down one side of each drumstick right through to the bone. Slip the knife between the flesh and bone all the way round, then pull out the bones. Lay each piece of turkey (rectangular shaped, slightly tapered at one end), skin side down, on a clean work surface.

Mix the stuffing ingredients, except the seasoning, in a bowl, then spread a little down the centre of each piece of meat, leaving a small gap at each end. Season lightly with salt, generously with pepper, then fold the pieces into sausage shapes. Flatten the bacon with the back of a knife, then wrap around each sausage, sealing the join and covering the ends – unless you buy home-butchered cured bacon, you'll need two slices per parcel. Tie round with string to secure the sausages then plump them lightly by squeezing between the palms of the hands.

Heat the oil in a flameproof casserole until nearly smoking, then sear the sausages on all sides, turning them gently. Transfer to the oven, at 180°C/350°F/Gas Mark 4, and cook for about 40–50 minutes until cooked through. Pierce gently with a sharp knife through to the turkey flesh – the juices should run clear. Remove from the oven and cool slightly for about 5 minutes, then cut away the string, carefully remove the bacon and slice thickly. Also delicious cold.

6

GAME

Cold stomachs must be quickened; therefore I commend
the use of mustard with Duck, Widgin, Teal, and all
water Fowl; sugar and mustard with red Deer, Crane,
Shovelar and Bustard.

Thomas Muffett, 1655

When that gem emerged from the piles of research, it threw our plans
for game awry. Game is probably man's oldest form of meat and, since
prehistoric man was aware of mustard seed, the combination of game
and mustard is likely to be an old one. But more recent tradition has
little mustard with game – *lapin moutarde* perhaps being the obvious
exception. Rabbit with mustard, in many guises, is indeed good and
we played with a few other game recipes, with pleasing results. But it
was not a partnership that we intended to feature heavily, until we
read Dr Muffett's *Health Improvements*.

He instructs that: 'temperate meats speedy of digestion', 'Mutton,
Lamb, Veal, Kid, Hen, Capon, Pullet, Chicken, Rabbet, Partridge, and
Pheasant', should all have 'mustard and greenswace' without which
they 'would soon corrupt in our stomachs'. Apicius had already shown
the way, for he has sauces, with mustard, for nearly all those species of
game singled out by Dr Muffett. With the Roman influence so heavy in
our kitchens even in the Middle Ages, was it likely that a whole area of
cooking would really just have vanished? The answer, of course, was
that it didn't.

We knew from the Harleian manuscript that roasted crane had a
sauce of the liver minced 'with pouder of ginger, vinegar and mustard'.
Then for pheasant, 'his sauce is to be sugar and mustard', also for
partridge and coney. Venison, too, was rubbed with powder of ginger,
or mustard, to stave off 'highness' in hot weather, prior to soaking in

brine or milk (a good tip if venison appears to be too high for your liking). For the Elizabethans mustard and vinegar sauce was a prerequisite with stubble goose (one fattened for the last few weeks of its life on the stubble, and eaten at Michaelmas). Though long domesticated, goose was formerly considered game. Hannah Glasse has A Hare Civet, with 'mustard and a little Elder Vinegar'. And so it went on. Mustard, vinegar and sugar were the predominant features, giving a sharp, sweet/sour flavour redolent of the Roman sauces. Often added to these were fruits: pears, grapes, nuts and quince jam in the case of goose. The stuffing was roasted with the bird then removed and made into the sauce (a Sauce Madame). A 'gauncil' or thick flour-based garlic sauce was also often served with goose, a relic of centuries past, though by 1615 the garlic seems to have been dropped. The sweet-sour balance was still prevalent however.

Venison was the game most highly prized by all, from kings to peasant poacher, and was served at all the great feasts. The best cuts appeared on the banqueting table, the 'umbels' (innards) going into pies for the servants' hall. But mustard is not mentioned in the many references to venison sauces – perhaps because the venison had been rubbed with mustard before cooking, perhaps because mustard sauce (considered the 'best' sauce for everything) was anyway on the table. One must remember that the term 'mustard sauce' indicated 'a sharp biting sauce made of small seed, bruised and mixed with vinegar': much as we know the condiment today. Since Dr Muffett particularly included red Deer to be accompanied by sugar and mustard, it seems unlikely that the combination was rare. Certainly, we had found that game and mustard were more than passing acquaintances.

Lapin Moutarde

As this is one of the classics of the French kitchen, every family has its own special recipe, but the basic components are always the same: a young rabbit, plenty of mustard (Dijon of course), cream and fresh herbs. It is simple, and quite excellent. Interestingly, the Romans (once again) knew the problems of rabbit breeding. The animals were firmly kept in *leporaria* or hare gardens, and when the Romans conquered England, they brought their rabbits with them. So well were they confined that the rabbit disappeared from the British diet along with the colonizers, and only reappeared at the end of the twelfth century, from France. Over the next 300 years large colonies of wild rabbits were established. These are gamier in flavour, though they do need to be young. Stick to the old definition of rabbit, a coney less than a year, and you will have excellent eating.

SERVES 4
1 young rabbit or 4 rabbit
  hind legs
2 tablespoons unsalted butter
1 tablespoon olive oil
Maldon salt
freshly ground black pepper
4–6 tablespoons Dijon
  mustard
6 shallots, finely chopped
225 g/8 oz button
  mushrooms, finely sliced
4 tablespoons Armagnac or
  good brandy
300 ml/½ pint double cream
good posy parsley, very finely
  chopped, or a mixture of
  fresh chervil and chives

If using a whole rabbit, cut into joints, the two back legs, saddle split in half, and the two front legs. Melt the butter with the oil in a pan large enough, if possible, to take the rabbit pieces in one layer. Add the joints and brown lightly, then remove from the pan. Sprinkle with salt, and a good grinding of black pepper, then smear them all over with the mustard.

Add the shallots to the pan and sauté for 5 minutes, then stir in the mushrooms. Put the rabbit joints on top of the vegetables, pour over the brandy and set alight (warming the brandy first speeds the process). When the flames have died down, stir in the cream and bring to bubbling point. Cover the pan and simmer very gently for 25–30 minutes until the sauce is very thick and the meat tender. Add a little more salt and pepper if necessary then scatter over the parsley. Let it bubble, without stirring, for another 2 minutes, then serve.

Fried Rabbit with Mustard

Although Eliza Acton wrote in the 1840s, many of her ideas are extraordinarily up-to-date. Consider this, from her recipe for fried rabbit: 'Dish the rabbit, pour the sauce *under* it, and serve it quickly.' The original dish had no mustard, and is very good. The addition is excellent – we hope she would approve.

SERVES 4
4 rabbit hind legs
1 large egg, beaten, or 2 egg
    whites, lightly whisked
home-made breadcrumbs, 3
    days old and finely ground
1 tablespoon mustard powder
Maldon salt
freshly ground white pepper
75 g/3 oz unsalted butter
300 ml/½ pint rabbit or
    partridge stock, or
    home-made chicken stock
    (not a cube)
2–3 strips lemon zest
1 chicken liver, or rabbit liver
    if possible
1 teaspoon flour
2 tablespoons double cream
    (optional)
lemon juice
1 teaspoon lemon mustard
    (p.66)

Put the joints into a pan of boiling water, unsalted, and cook for 5 minutes, drain and cool. Dip them into the beaten egg, then into the breadcrumbs previously mixed with the mustard powder. Press the crumbs well in, then season lightly with salt and pepper. Melt 50 g/2 oz of the butter in a large frying pan. When it is bubbling add the pieces and gently fry for about 15 minutes, turning them two or three times.

Meanwhile, simmer the stock with the lemon zest, add the liver for 5 minutes, remove and mash thoroughly. Mix it with the remaining butter and the flour to a thick paste, then add, little by little, to the stock, whisking constantly, until the sauce thickens. Stir in the cream if wished, a squeeze of lemon juice and the mustard. Let it bubble for a minute. When the rabbit is nicely browned and cooked through, put on a serving dish, 'pour the sauce under it' and serve at once.

Roasted Hare
with Mustard, Allspice and Soured Cream

Hare, though highly prized by the Romans, was slightly lower on the medieval scale than coney or rabbits. Both these appeared often on festive menus which hare rarely did, though it figured prominently on the list of household provisions in the 1450s. By the time Henry VIII had gained the throne both were common man's hunting – the hare usually with greyhounds and often in the snows, when its tracks easily led its hunters straight home. Indeed, for a time, Henry had to ban hare (and rabbit) hunting, so devastated were their numbers. Today, hare has rightfully regained its prestige.

SERVES 4
1 young hare, with liver
    reserved for the stuffing
4 large bacon rashers
125 g/4 oz butter, melted
1 heaped tablespoon flour
1 teaspoon Dijon mustard
150 ml/¼ pint soured cream
freshly ground allspice (not
    pre-ground)
For the marinade
300 ml/½ pint red wine
3 tablespoons olive oil
1 sprig lemon thyme
Maldon salt
freshly ground black pepper
For the stuffing
1 tablespoon brown mustard
    seed
175 g/6 oz canned whole
    chestnuts, drained and
    chopped
50 g/2 oz sultanas

50 g/2 oz pine nuts
5 tablespoons home-made
  fresh breadcrumbs
1 tablespoon white wine
  vinegar
2 tablespoons white wine
1 large egg, beaten

Always make sure you buy a young hare for roasting – easily distinguishable by its short neck, long joints and thin saddle. Its ears are soft and will easily tear while its older cousin will have a clearly marked cleft in the lip. The darker the meat, the longer has been the hanging – ideally 4–5 days. All hare has a bluish, thin membrane which must be removed. Fiddly rather than difficult, this is most easily accomplished by sliding a long, thin-bladed knife underneath the membrane (which is transparent), loosening it then peeling it away. Now you can put your hare in a large dish and cover with the marinade ingredients. Leave for at least 24 hours and up to 3 days – not only to tenderize but also to give flavour.

Combine all the stuffing ingredients, not forgetting to cut out any yellowish bits from the liver before chopping it finely, then season generously with black pepper and allspice. Remove the hare from the marinade (reserving the liquid), and pat dry. Place the stuffing under the front and back legs. Lay in a roasting tin then mix the mustard into the soured cream and grind in a little more allspice. Smear half the paste over the hare then cover with the bacon. Pour over the melted butter and cook in the oven, covered with foil, at 180°C/350°F/Gas Mark 4 for 1½ hours, basting every 20 minutes or so. Remove the foil, dust the hare with the flour (an ancient technique called 'frothing' which facilitates the browning of the joint) and return to the oven, uncovered, for 15 minutes. Transfer the hare to a warmed serving platter, carve into joints and keep warm while finishing the sauce.

Pour the cooking juices into a pan, add the marinade and bring to the boil. Whisk in the soured cream, boil hard for a minute, adjust the seasoning if necessary, then serve at once with a little sauce poured over the joints, the rest poured into a hot sauceboat.

Civet of Hare in Vinegar and Mustard

'Harys in Cyvye' was a common medieval recipe and made its appearance again in sixteenth-century England from France where it always remained popular. It is ideal for the older hare as the long gentle stewing ensures tenderness. The ancient marinade of wine and vinegar also helps break down tough sinews – and adds a piquant flavour.

SERVES 4
1 hare, jointed, bluish
   membranes removed (see
   previous recipe)
450 ml/¾ pint white wine
   (medium-dry)
150 ml/¼ pint white wine
   vinegar
6 cloves
2 bay leaves
2 sprigs parsley
2 sprigs thyme
2 tablespoons olive oil
4 shallots, finely chopped
1 tablespoon flour
Maldon salt
freshly ground black pepper
10 cm/4 inch strip of orange
   peel
225 g/8 oz tiny button
   mushrooms, wiped with a
   damp cloth and left whole
1–2 teaspoons Matthew's
   mustard (p.68)
25 g/1 oz unsalted butter

Put the wine, vinegar, herbs and spices into a large pan, add about 200 ml/7 fl oz water and bring to the boil. Simmer for 5 minutes, then cool and pour over the hare. Leave for 24 hours, turning the joints three or four times.

Drain the hare, patting it quite dry, and strain the marinade. Heat the oil in a large heavy-based pan, add the shallots and sweat for 5 minutes, then add the hare and brown the joints lightly. Sprinkle on the flour, stir for a minute or so, then season, lightly with salt, generously with pepper, add the orange peel and pour in the strained marinade. Bring to the boil then turn the heat to the lowest possible, cover the pan and simmer very gently for 3 hours until the flesh is meltingly tender. Add the mushrooms and cook, uncovered, for a further 15 minutes. Remove the hare and pile on to a warmed serving dish. Reduce the sauce by rapid boiling for 2 minutes, then add the mustard, adjust the seasoning if necessary and whisk in the butter to lightly glaze. Pour over the hare and serve with good crusty bread to mop up the juices.

Braised Wild Duck with Mustard and Coriander

Wild duck, a rarity today, was well known to prehistoric man, providing a large part of his winter diet since it is conveniently at its best after the first frost until Candlemas (2 February). For today's tastes the bird, particularly when from the marshes, can often have an unpleasantly fishy flavour – reflecting its eating habits. Apicius had an admirable way of dealing with this by parboiling the birds in salt water, flavoured with dill. As with so many ancient ideas, this is still the best method.

SERVES 4
2 wild ducks, hung for 10–14
*   days, then drawn and*
*   dressed*
6 sprigs fresh dill or 2
*   teaspoons dried dill*
75 g/3 oz unsalted butter
2 small onions, peeled but left
*   whole*
1 lemon, cut in half
1 orange, cut in half
2 × 5 cm/2 in cinnamon sticks
Maldon salt
freshly ground black pepper
2 large onions, finely sliced
2 sprigs fresh fennel or 2 dried
*   fennel sticks*
2 sprigs thyme
2 sprigs fresh savory or 1
*   teaspoon dried savory*
1 tablespoon white mustard
*   seed*

*1 tablespoon coriander seeds,
    lightly crushed
1 tablespoon flour
2 tablespoons Dijon mustard
4 tablespoons brandy
4 tablespoons orange juice
400 ml/14 fl oz game or good
    beef stock*

Bring a large saucepan of salted water to the boil, then throw in the dill. Turn the heat low so the water barely simmers, then add the ducks. Leave for 5 minutes, remove, drain and dry thoroughly inside and out.

Melt the butter, when bubbling add the ducks and sear all over. Remove from the pan and stuff them each with 1 onion, half a lemon, half an orange and a cinnamon stick. Season with salt and pepper.

Add the sliced onions to the pan and sauté gently for 15 minutes, then add the fennel, thyme, savory, mustard and coriander seeds and cook, stirring until the mustard seeds start to spit. Stir in the flour and continue stirring for 3–4 minutes, then add the mustard, brandy and orange juice. Return the ducks to the pan, pour over the stock and bring quickly to the boil. Lower the heat and simmer very gently for 2–2½ hours, covered. Test for tenderness by pressing a skewer into the breast – it should slide in easily.

Remove the birds from the pan, carve to give each person half the breast and a leg (keep the carcass for stock) and keep warm. Reduce the sauce slightly, then glaze each portion with a tablespoon, serving the remainder separately.

Mustarded Roast Quail

Quails have been highly regarded for a very long time. They are mentioned in the Bible, when they appeared literally out of the sky and saved the fleeing Israelites along with the manna provided by the Lord. The sudden appearance of the quails is not so fanciful as it might seem for they fly until quite fatigued, often letting the wind carry them along, until they drop exhausted to the ground in flocks. The Romans condemned the birds as food as they are partial to eating hemlock and other poisonous seeds, though strangely this does not seem to affect the eater of the quail. But by medieval times they were highly popular and widely sold in the City of London. Today, they are a protected species, and our supplies are all farm-reared: less gamey than the wild creatures but still an exquisite delicacy.

SERVES 4–6
12 quails
6 teaspoons Five-herb
  mustard (p.59)
125 g/4 oz unsalted butter
Maldon salt
freshly ground black pepper
6 rashers streaky bacon,
  beaten very thin
125 ml/4 fl oz port

Quails used to be cooked undrawn in the manner of snipe and woodcock. Today, however, they are always sold drawn, and they are never hung. Spread each bird lightly with mustard and put in a roasting tin. Melt the butter and pour over the quails, season, then cover with the bacon. Cook in the oven at 200°C/400°F/Gas Mark 6 for 7–10 minutes, basting once or twice. Remove from the oven, turn the heat to 150°C/300°F/Gas Mark 2 and pour off the cooking juices into a small pan. Return the birds to the oven for 2–3 minutes, meanwhile adding the port to the butter in the pan and bubbling hard. Serve the quails surrounded by triangles of fried bread, with the sauce poured over the birds.

Pigeons in Vermouth, Saffron and Mustard

Pigeons provided our ancestors with a great deal of their game; medieval manor houses had their dovecots and by Tudor times many a cottage had a small wooden pigeon house tucked on to the ends of the gables. In 1520 they cost one penny each; now they are nearer a pound. Which is amazing since most farmers are as keen as their medieval forebears to be rid of them: pigeons are not fussy as to how they fatten themselves, so long as it is on the best corn . . .

SERVES 4
4 pigeons
2 tablespoons olive oil
2 red onions, finely chopped

300 ml/½ pint double cream
2 bay leaves
4–5 strands saffron
Maldon salt
freshly ground black pepper
4 tablespoons vermouth
300 ml/½ pint red wine
1 tablespoon Matthew's
    mustard (p.68)

Wash the pigeons inside and out. Reserve the livers if present, cutting out any yellowish bits to avoid bitterness. Heat the olive oil and sauté the onions for 15 minutes; meanwhile, very gently heat the cream in another pan with the bay leaves and saffron. Stir after 2–3 minutes to start the colour of the saffron running.

Push the onions to the side of the pan, raise the heat and lightly colour the pigeons all over, season with salt and pepper, then add the vermouth and bubble hard for 1 minute. Pour in the red wine and stew gently for 20–40 minutes, turning the birds occasionally, until they are tender. (Squabs – pigeons a month old – will need the shorter time, older birds the longer.) Remove the pigeons from the pan and carve off the breasts. Keep the carcasses for soup. Reduce the wine by boiling hard for 2–3 minutes, then strain in the cream. Return the breasts to the pan with the chopped livers and simmer gently for a further 5–10 minutes until the sauce thickens. Stir in the mustard and serve immediately with little croûtons and piles of fresh watercress.

Pheasant with Cremona Mustard

In 1932, there appeared in Italy a rather odd cookbook – *La Cucina Futurista*, written by the famous Futurist poet (and friend of Mussolini), F. Marinetti. Obsessed with the Fascist principles of purity, virility and nationalism, the poet had earlier launched an attack on pasta – a food for the slow and docile, anti-virile and made with expensive foreign flour. There was uproar. Marinetti, undaunted, proceeded to invent the most extraordinary combinations: small blood sausages and pieces of chocolate 'swimming' in a custard sauce; fish with pineapple and bananas; roast beef surrounded by halva; fruit tart on a thin layer of chocolate, covered with tomato and spinach sauces. Some dishes, however, display historical knowledge – lamb served with stuffed dates (familiar to the Arabs) and this pheasant recipe: 'Roast a carefully cleaned pheasant, bathe it for an hour in Moscato di Siracusa [a sweet, heavy Sicilian wine] in a *bain-marie*, and for another hour in milk. To finish, stuff it with Mostarda di Cremona and candied fruit.' Overdoing it certainly, but medieval game birds had often been stuffed with grapes, pears, quinces and nuts, accompanied by a mustard and sugar sauce. And, as Elizabeth David points out, 'pheasant is very often dry, so the baths in sweet wine and milk are not such foolish ideas'.

SERVES 6–8
*1 brace of pheasant, giblets
    reserved*
*125 g/4 oz unsalted butter,
    plus a little extra, softened*
*5 tablespoons Mostarda di
    Cremona (p.68) plus 1
    tablespoon extra of the
    syrup*
Maldon salt
freshly ground black pepper
*4 rashers back bacon,
    flattened thin*
*150 ml/¼ pint Muscat de
    Frontignan (or any good,
    sweetish white wine)*
1 tablespoon flour
2 shallots, finely chopped
2–3 strips lemon peel
1 sprig lemon thyme
lemon juice

Pheasants are usually hung for 5–14 days so talk to your butcher when ordering them. If you buy from a supermarket, there is no choice but they are usually fairly mild. Discard any yellowish pieces from the livers, then chop them and add to the Mostarda, its fruits also chopped quite small. Mix thoroughly into the butter, pat into a sausage shape and chill until firm. Smear some plain butter underneath the skins of the pheasant breasts, then paint with a spoonful of the mustard syrup. When the stuffing mixture is quite firm, cut it in two and put one piece inside each pheasant. Season lightly with salt and pepper, then lard with the bacon.

Place the pheasants in a roasting tin, and pour over the wine. Cook in the oven at 220°C/425°F/Gas Mark 7 for 45–60 minutes – this will depend on the weight of the birds. The usual time allowed is 20 minutes to the pound plus 10 minutes extra. Baste every 10 minutes or so, then 10 minutes before the end, remove the bacon (crumble and reserve it), froth the birds with flour and return to brown the breasts.

While the pheasants are cooking, make a stock with the giblets, shallots, lemon peel and thyme. Cover with cold water, bring to the boil then simmer gently. Strain and keep aside.

Once the birds are cooked, transfer them to a serving platter, carve and keep warm in the oven, covered with foil. Pour the cooking juices into the strained giblet stock and bring to the boil, add the crumbled bacon, season to taste and squeeze in a little lemon juice to offset the sweetness. Serve in a very hot sauceboat.

Salmis of Partridge with Orange Mustard Sauce

A ginger sauce was often recommended for partridge by the medieval cook – a good idea, as its flavour can be bland compared to other game birds. It shares their tendency to dryness though, so this popular Victorian method of cooking game is ideal. The birds are part-roasted, then stewed in a highly flavoured sauce.

SERVES 4
2 brace of partridge
50 g/2 oz unsalted butter
4 rashers bacon, flattened thin
2 shallots, very finely chopped
2 teaspoons white wine
   vinegar
25 mm/1 inch piece fresh root
   ginger, peeled and grated
juice of 1 Seville orange
150 ml/¼ pint port wine
1 teaspoon strong Dijon
   mustard
Maldon salt
freshly ground black pepper
1 teaspoon arrowroot

Smear the partridges liberally with butter, wrap in bacon and roast in the oven at 200°F/400°F/Gas Mark 6 for 20 minutes. Take out of the oven, remove the bacon and cut off the breasts and legs, taking off the skin. Pour the cooking juices into a small pan. Put the skin and carcasses into a pan, just cover with cold water and bring to the boil, then simmer fairly vigorously for 30 minutes, or until reduced to a good 300 ml/½ pint. Strain and reserve.

Melt the butter you poured off the roasting pan, add the shallots and stew gently for 5 minutes. If you have more than about 2 tablespoons butter, pour off the excess then deglaze the pan with the vinegar. Add the ginger, orange juice, port wine and reserved carcass stock and simmer for 10 minutes. Arrange the partridge meat in a shallow flameproof dish. Stir the mustard into the sauce, season lightly with salt and pepper, then mix the arrowroot with a little cold water and stir into the sauce, boiling for a minute to thicken. (This is not the traditional method but it gives a beautifully clear glaze.) Pour the sauce over the meat, then stew gently for a further 10 minutes or so to finish cooking the partridge. Serve from the cooking dish.

Roast Haunch of Venison with Vinegar and Mustard

Venison was the prerogative of the land-owning classes, though even they were restricted by an Act of 1671 which forbade the killing of deer by all except 'qualified persons'. Despite the harsh penalties for poaching, ways were found and venison often appeared on the menus of London coffee houses and City inns. Today we are luckier. Venison is widely farmed and though much goes to the Continent, it is increasingly available from butchers and even supermarkets. It is a lean, rich, sweet meat, ideally suited to the piquant sauces of ancient times. In the Tyrol they still finish venison with a sauce of soured cream and powdered mustard.

SERVES 6–8
1.6–2 kg/3½–4½ lb haunch
of venison
125–175 g/4–6 oz butter
2 tablespoons rowanberry or
redcurrant jelly
1 tablespoon cider vinegar

2–3 teaspoons Dijon mustard
2–3 pinches ground cinnamon
1 tablespoon beurre manié
For the marinade
600 ml/1 pint red wine
2 tablespoons olive oil
2 tablespoons Spicy Italian
    vinegar (p.75)
2 shallots, finely sliced
2 bay leaves
1 cinnamon stick
3 sprigs thyme
Maldon salt
freshly ground black pepper

In a large dish combine the marinade ingredients, using a pinch of salt and a generous amount of black pepper. Immerse the venison, turn it several times, then leave for 1–2 days, turning regularly. Remove the meat and pat well dry. Strain and reserve the marinade.

Melt 125 g/4 oz of the butter in a roasting tin, add the venison and baste well. Cook in the oven at 180°C/350°F/Gas Mark 4 for 1–1½ hours, basting every 10 minutes. Use the extra butter if necessary – it may seem a lot but venison is a dry meat and it will absorb quite a bit. The timing depends on the size of the haunch and how pink you like the meat – test with a pointed knife gently inserted into the thickest part. The colour of the juices will indicate the doneness.

When it is cooked, transfer to a warm serving dish, cover lightly with foil and keep warm. Pour the cooking juices from the roasting tin, scraping up any sediment, into a pan. Add the strained marinade and the fruit jelly. Boil hard to reduce and melt the jelly. Add the vinegar, mustard and cinnamon and bubble for 1–2 minutes, then stir in the *beurre manié* (a mixture of equal volumes of butter and flour), whisking constantly until the sauce thickens. Serve the gravy very hot with the joint, carved thick or thin as you wish.

Roast Goose with Garlic and Mustard Sauce

Goose is such an extravagance nowadays that to do anything be-yond roasting it seems wanton. The French however still follow the medieval habit of buying their geese whole and using the neck, stuffed, to make a 'pudding'. This is delicious, and does prolong the delights of a bird which sadly does not stretch very far: a 4–4.5 kg/9–10 lb goose will really only feed six people. Keep the fat – it is delicious for frying potatoes.

SERVES 6

1 goose, about 4.5 kg/10 lb
  dressed weight, with giblets
  if possible
Maldon salt
freshly ground black pepper
175 g/6 oz prunes, soaked in
  cold water overnight
3 heads of garlic, cloves peeled
  but left whole
150 ml/¼ pint red wine
1–2 teaspoons soft brown
  sugar
1 tablespoon Spicy Italian
  vinegar (p.75)
1–2 teaspoons coarse-grained
  mustard
stuffing of your choice (see
  below)

Remove any pin feathers from the goose, singe the wing tips, and cut away any fat near the vent. Wash inside and out, dry thoroughly then season well with salt and pepper. Lay the goose on a rack in a large roasting tin, prick the fatty bits with a fork then prick the breast skin lightly – try not to pierce the flesh. Put in the oven at 200°C/400°F/Gas Mark 6 and cook for 15 minutes, then carefully drain off any fat in the pan. Repeat this process 2–3 times to remove the excess fat which would make the prunes and garlic (to be put in later) unbearably greasy.

While this preliminary cooking is taking place, make a stock from the giblets if you have them, reserving the liver to add to your stuffing. This can be whatever you like; traditionalists go for sage and onion or you can adapt the earlier stuffings of mixed fruits, or gooseberries. Chestnuts, too, are good with goose while many like to add sausage-meat, enabling the goose to go further. Whichever you choose, make it at this point, place in a shallow buttered tin and bake for the last 45 minutes of cooking time.

After the third draining of fat, mix the drained prunes (keep the soaking water) with the garlic and stuff inside the goose. Lower the oven to 170°C/325°F/Gas Mark 3 and cook for a further 2–2½ hours, draining off the fat from the tin if it seems to be getting dangerously full. Prick the skin occasionally and turn the bird on to its breast half-way through, turning it on its back again for the last 10 minutes of cooking. The thigh joints should wiggle easily when the bird is done.

Transfer to a warmed platter, scrape out the prunes and garlic, put in a blender, and return the goose to the turned-off oven to keep warm. Add 300 ml/½ pint of giblet stock or prune soaking water to the blender and purée the mixture. Pour into a pan, add the red wine, sugar, vinegar and 1 teaspoon mustard. Bring to the boil, then simmer gently for 5 minutes – add a little more stock or prune water if the sauce is too stiff, but it should be fairly thick. Add extra mustard if you wish and adjust the seasoning, then pile into a bowl and serve very hot, with the goose, your stuffing and roast potatoes.

Duck Breasts with Roman Mustard

Many of Apicius's sauces for game sound an incredible hotch-potch – 'mix pepper, lovage, onion, origany, nuts, figdates, honey, broth, mustard, vinegar, oil' – until one realizes that this is basically a vinaigrette. We omitted the dates and the broth, toasted some pine nuts and made a delicious sauce to pour over grilled duck breasts.

SERVES 6
3 large French duck breasts
50 g/2 oz pine nuts
For the sauce
handful lovage leaves,
*   chopped very finely*
1 small red onion, grated
freshly ground black pepper
Maldon salt
½ teaspoon finely chopped
*   fresh marjoram*
1–2 tablespoons Roman
*   mustard (p.65)*
1–2 tablespoons runny honey
50 ml/2 fl oz Spicy Italian
*   vinegar (p.75)*
300 ml/½ pint olive oil

Prick the duck breasts all over with a fork and put under the grill, skin side up. Cook for 7–8 minutes on a high heat then turn over and cook for a further 1–2 minutes: this will give nicely pink breasts. Well done meat will need another 3 minutes at the first grilling.

Sprinkle the pine nuts in a shallow metal dish and grill for 45 seconds–1 minute until nicely pink. Keep aside.

For the sauce, mix together the chopped lovage, grated onion, a good grinding of black pepper, a pinch of salt, the marjoram, the mustard and honey. Stir in the vinegar to make a thick paste, then gradually add the oil little by little, whisking all the time to produce a thick sauce. Taste and add more mustard, oil or vinegar as needed.

Now you need to work quickly, to keep the meat hot. Cut the breasts in half lengthways, then slice across thickly, slightly on the diagonal. Arrange on hot plates, pour over the sauce and scatter with the nuts. Serve immediately: it is very good with a warm potato salad.

7

BEEF

GRUMIO: What say you to a piece of beef and mustard?
KATE: A dish that I do love to feed upon.

The Taming of the Shrew, William Shakespeare

Although we found manufacturers strangely reticent on exact sales figures, we have established that some thirteen and a half million housewives (out of a population of nineteen and half million) bought mustard in 1985. There must be a great many homes with a pot of mustard in the store-cupboard, and we'll warrant that in most of them it only appears on the table with beef. Yet this British marriage of beef to mustard is relatively recent. Though Tudor writings often mention beef and mustard, they still continued the medieval practice of serving mustard also with brawn, salt mutton, game and fish. So why do we single out beef?

Since neolithic times it appears to have been our favourite meat. Cattle bones found in early settlements far outweigh those from any other creature and we were already exporting the beasts to the Continent before Caesar arrived. His soldiers too preferred beef, their garrisons yielding vast quantities of bones.

For much of the year that beef was not eaten fresh. The difficulties and expense of keeping livestock through the winter meant that most was killed in the autumn and salted for preservation during the ensuing months. Salt beef was always served with mustard. Its value as an accompaniment was rated so highly that in the thirteenth-century Welsh manuscript, *Meddygon Myddvai*, a whole paragraph is accorded to the 'Virtues of Mustard'. It was only in the 1600s that the feeding of root crops (particularly turnips) to animals became widespread. This coincided with the introduction from Holland of vetches (clover, lucerne grass) which produced stronger and fleshier cattle,

Colman's *John Bull* advertisement, *c.* 1900

thus enabling the stock to be kept alive for fresh meat all year round. This, combined with the abolition of fast days (by Cromwell), no doubt accounts for the dramatic rise in meat consumption that then took place.

It may also explain why mustard began to be popular with beef other than in its salted state. Certainly Robert May, the great Restoration cook who published his magnificent (and, in many ways, very modern) *The Accomplisht Cook* in 1660, was recommending the combination, particularly deliciously in 'Ribs of beef with garlick, mustard, pepper, verjuice, and ginger'. No longer was mustard merely needed to disguise the rancid flavours of rotten meat; it could be appreciated as a spice in its own right. Over the next century it was more and more served with fresh meat, reaching a peak in the eighteenth century – the heyday of London's steak and chop houses.

Undoubtedly, the mustard served in Samuel Johnson's favourite eating houses would have been English, either Tewkesbury – with its fiery flavouring of horseradish – or possibly the new Durham mustard powder being hawked around by Mrs Clements. And herein is the seed of a long-running battle between the French and the English. For Dijon also reached its heyday in the eighteenth century and no Frenchman would ever consider anything other than Dijon mustard with his steak. The clean pungent taste of English mustard perhaps complements beef better than most meats, and the sharpness of Tewkesbury mustard is very good indeed with steak. What are most emphatically not good are those jars of mustard – sadly English in origin – masquerading as 'French' mustard. They have far too murky a flavour to enhance beef, or anything else for that matter.

Mustard Coated Roast Beef

'A tale without love is like beef without mustard – insipid.' So said Anatole France. And on the beef front, we absolutely agree since first using this glaze for roast beef. However succulent the joint, it is a little disappointing now without its crispy mustard coating. Good with all cuts, though large joints will need double the quantity.

SERVES 6
1.4 kg/3 lb joint of beef, well larded
Maldon salt
freshly ground black pepper
1 tablespoon mustard powder
1 tablespoon beef dripping, lard or oil
2 tablespoons Dijon mustard
1 tablespoon Worcestershire sauce
1 tablespoon red wine vinegar
½ tablespoon soft brown sugar
1 tablespoon olive oil
150 ml/¼ pint red wine
1 tablespoon brandy
1 tablespoon redcurrant jelly

Mix a good pinch of salt with a generous grinding of black pepper and the mustard powder and rub well into the beef. Heat the dripping, then sear the beef on all sides over a high heat.

Transfer the meat on to a rack over a roasting pan. Mix together the Dijon mustard, Worcestershire sauce, vinegar, sugar and olive oil, then paint all over the beef. Cook in the oven at 230°C/450°F/Gas Mark 8 for 15 minutes, then turn down to 180°C/350°F/Gas Mark 4 and roast for a further 45 minutes for very rare, 55 minutes for nicely pink, or 1¼ hours for well-done meat. Put the joint on a warmed platter and let it rest in the turned-off oven while finishing the gravy. At this stage, let us listen to the wise words of M. Boulestin: 'Do not spoil the special taste of the gravy obtained in the roasting of beef . . . by adding to it the classical stock which gives to all meats the same deplorable taste of soup. It is obvious that you cannot out of a joint get the sauceboat full which usually appears on the table.' Put the roasting tin over a medium heat, add the wine and brandy, scraping up all the sediment, then stir in the redcurrant jelly. Let the gravy bubble, constantly stirring until the jelly has melted. Tip into this any juices from the joint platter, then pour into a *hot* gravy boat. It may not be full, but the taste will be superb. Serve with tall puffs of Yorkshire pudding and that other traditional Yorkshire accompaniment, seen too little nowadays, of finely chopped onions which have been strewn with sugar and left to stand for 1 hour. Mustard on the table, of course.

Robert May's Rib of Beef

Robert May's suggestion of 'garlick, mustard, pepper, verjuice and ginger' for ribs of beef was a dish begging to be eaten. The problem in a small household is how to justify the ribs of beef – for the joint to be successful as a roast you need at least two ribs, preferably three. The answer came with Pierre Troisgros – one of the famous French restaurateur brothers. For the 'king' of Beaune has a favourite dish – one rib of beef, freshly cut off the joint (by himself, naturally) pan-fried and served with a Bordelaise sauce. Here was Robert May's chance – and we took it. A memorable dish.

SERVES 2–3
*1 rib of beef, nicely marbled,
    on the bone*
*5 cm/2 inch piece fresh ginger,
    peeled and cut into very fine
    slivers*
*2 fat garlic cloves, very finely
    chopped*
*freshly ground black pepper,
    ground as coarse as possible*

1 tablespoon Dijon mustard
1 tablespoon olive oil
Maldon salt
25 g/1 oz unsalted butter, plus
    a little extra
1 tablespoon red wine vinegar
125 ml/4 fl oz good red wine

Trim any excess fat off the rib – you only want a very thin layer. Mix together the ginger, garlic, a generous grinding of black pepper, the mustard and olive oil, then smear on both sides of the beef. Leave for at least 1 hour, preferably 2–3.

Melt the butter in a large frying pan, sprinkle one side of the rib with a little salt and when the butter is bubbling add the beef. Cook over a moderate heat for 2–5 minutes, depending on how rare you like beef. Turn over, sprinkle on a little salt, add some extra butter to the pan if necessary and cook for a further 2–5 minutes. Remove the rib to a warmed serving platter and rest in a very low oven while finishing the sauce.

Pour the vinegar into the pan, scraping up all the sediment, and bubble for a minute to deglaze. Pour in the red wine and cook fiercely for 2 minutes, stirring constantly. Whisk in a tiny knob of butter if you wish to lightly glaze the sauce.

Cut the beef into slices on the diagonal, pour over the sauce and serve at once.

Medallions of Fillet with Dijon Brandy Sauce

The most prized part of the fillet – the 'eye' – is supremely tender, cutting like butter. It is also extremely expensive, so always buy it from a reputable butcher who will cut the pieces for you – at least 3–4 cm/1¼–1½ inches thick. Such good meat requires the simplest of cooking: this is Maille's suggested recipe.

SERVES 4
4 medallions of fillet steak
    (sometimes called filets
    mignons)
Maldon salt
freshly ground black pepper
1½ tablespoons unsalted butter

3 tablespoons brandy
1 small shallot, very finely
    chopped
225 ml/8 fl oz double cream
3 tablespoons Maille Dijon
    mustard

Donald McGill postcard, 1918

Season the fillets lightly with salt and pepper. Melt the butter in a large frying pan; when bubbling add the fillets. Cook for 2–4 minutes on each side depending on the rarity wanted then pour in the brandy. Ignite and shake the pan until the flames have died down. Transfer the steaks to a hot serving platter. Stir the onion into the pan and sauté for 1 minute, then add the cream and cook over a high heat until it thickens. Stir in the mustard, bubble for another 10 seconds, then pour over the steaks and serve immediately.

Grillade des Mariniers

Do not be fooled by the title – this is no grill but a gloriously rich stew, the meat butter-soft, the sauce thick with a heady concentration of flavours. It is a heritage from the rivermen of the Rhône – each barge would have its own version bubbling away in the galley as the great boats wound their way down to Marseilles, formerly drawn by a team of giant horses, latterly – and much less romantically – chugging away under petrol power. Do they make it still? Or have convenience foods – as in so many other areas of France – won the day?

SERVES 4–6
900 g/2 lb lean rump or
*   topside, cut into 6–8 slices*
3 large red onions, finely sliced
4 tablespoons olive oil
Maldon salt
freshly ground black pepper
1 sprig fresh thyme, leaves
*   stripped off the stalk*
25 g/1 oz unsalted butter
1½ teaspoons flour
2 fat garlic cloves
3 anchovy fillets
1 tablespoon Dijon mustard
1 tablespoon red wine vinegar
4 tablespoons finely chopped
*   parsley*

An earthenware casserole is best for this. Brush 1 tablespoon of oil on the bottom, then make a layer of onions. Top with two slices of beef, then another layer of onions, meat, onions, so on: sprinkle each layer with a little salt and pepper, a few leaves of thyme, as you fill the pot. Mash together the flour and butter, cut into little pieces and strew over the top layer (which should be onions), tucking a couple of pieces down the side of the pot too. Cover with a butter paper, then a tight-fitting lid and cook in the oven at 140°C/275°F/Gas Mark 1 for about 2 hours.

Crush the garlic with the anchovy fillets, then mix in the mustard and vinegar. Lastly whisk in the remaining olive oil and the parsley. Stir into the pot, cover again with the butter paper and lid and cook for another 45 minutes–1 hour. The meat should be so tender you can cut it with a spoon – the aroma so tantalizing, you have to eat *now*.

Carbonnade de Boeuf Flamande

Traditionally the dark Bordeaux mustard is the mustard for this dish. Mild, sweet and dark from the husks that are left in, it has a subtle spiciness. It is not the muddy concoction that passes in England for French mustard. The name of Louit on the pot denotes authenticity, but this is hard to come by. If necessary use a good German sweet mustard.

SERVES 4–6
3 tablespoons beef dripping or
   lard
3 large red onions, finely sliced
4 fat garlic cloves, finely sliced
900 g/2 lb stewing beef,
   trimmed of all gristle and
   fat, cut into 15 mm/½ in
   cubes
1 tablespoon soft brown sugar
1 tablespoon red wine vinegar
1½ tablespoons flour
Maldon salt
freshly ground black pepper
freshly grated nutmeg
1 sprig fresh thyme
3 sprigs fresh parsley
1 sprig fresh marjoram
300 ml/½ pint brown ale

*150 ml/¼ pint good beef
   stock, or water
8–10 slices French bread
1–2 tablespoons Bordeaux
   mustard*

Melt half the dripping in a wide, shallow casserole (essential or the bread won't fit in one layer), add the onions and sauté for 15 minutes or until nicely browned and softened, adding the garlic for the last 5 minutes. Remove the onions and keep aside. Add the rest of the dripping to the pan, put in half the meat and brown over a high heat. Remove, add the remaining meat, sear that and remove.

Sprinkle in the sugar and stir until lightly caramelized, then deglaze with the vinegar. Return the meat and onions to the pan, sprinkle over the flour and stir until all the fat is absorbed. Season – be generous with the pepper and nutmeg, light with salt, then add the herbs (use 1 teaspoon dried mixed herbs if fresh are unavailable) and pour in the ale slowly, stirring all the time. Add the stock and just enough water to cover the meat. Cover and cook in the oven at 150°C/300°F/Gas Mark 2 for about 2½–3 hours, until the meat is really tender and the sauce thickened. Smear the bread with mustard and arrange the slices over the top of the meat, mustard side down, tops just sticking out, and cook uncovered for a further 15–20 minutes until the bread is golden and crisp.

Boeuf en Daube Dijonnaise

A *daube* is traditionally associated with beef, although it can encompass any large piece of meat, either left whole or chopped small, sometimes marinated, then gently braised in a stock (often wine-based) with herbs and seasonings. Ancient pots, or *daubières*, were of earthenware, stoneware, cast iron or tinned copper, usually wider than they were deep and often with a concave lid, for filling with hot embers. Although it is very much a country dish, taking its name from a word which implied a crude execution (hence our word 'daub'), and although the seasonings, herbs and stock vary from region to region, from season to season, it is certainly not slapdash. Richard Olney sums it up perfectly: '. . . the soul of a *daube* resides in pervasive unity – the transformation of individual qualities into a single character.'

SERVES 4–6

*900 g/2 lb piece of rump or
    topside*
*75 g/3 oz fresh pork back fat,
    cut into small narrow strips*
Maldon salt
freshly ground black pepper
½ teaspoon dried mixed herbs
2 tablespoons olive oil
*175 g/6 oz unsmoked streaky
    bacon, in one piece then cut
    into small cubes*
*125 g/4 oz fresh pork rinds, as
    unfatty as possible, cut into
    small pieces*
2 onions, finely chopped
2 carrots, sliced lengthways
1 celery heart, finely chopped
For the marinade
*200 ml/7 fl oz dry white
    Burgundy*
*2 tablespoons white wine
    vinegar*
4 tablespoons brandy
2 cloves garlic, finely chopped
1 bay leaf
1 sprig fresh thyme
3 sprigs fresh parsley
To finish the sauce
*2 tablespoons green
    peppercorns, rinsed of their
    brine and lightly crushed*
1 tablespoon Dijon mustard
1 tablespoon unsalted butter

If you have a larding needle, lard the beef with the pieces of pork fat, then roll the joint in salt, pepper and the dried herbs. Otherwise, make small incisions all over the meat, roll the pork fat in the seasonings and press into the cuts in the joint. Put the meat in a deep bowl, add the marinade ingredients and leave for 3–6 hours, turning occasionally.

Drain and pat dry the meat. Pour the oil into your pot, then make a thin layer with half the bacon cubes and pieces of pork rind. Put in the meat, pack the chopped vegetables around it with a few on top then cover with the remaining bacon and pork rinds. Pour over the marinade and add just enough water barely to cover the meat. Cover with a tightly fitting lid and bring slowly to boiling point – this will take about 45–55 minutes, then transfer to the oven, at 150°C/300°F/ Gas Mark 2, and cook for a further 1½–2 hours until the meat is exceedingly tender. Transfer the meat to a warmed platter, surround with the bacon and rind pieces and keep warm. Skim the excess fat off the sauce and pour into a pan. Add the peppercorns and mustard and bring to a hard boil. Turn to a simmer then whisk in the butter to lightly glaze. Pour over the meat and serve immediately.

Tewkesbury Mustard Casserole

Recipes for casseroles abound – some distinctly better than others. Two requisites are paramount: a long, very gentle cooking and good seasonings. Perhaps not quite such a plethora as Hannah Glasse sometimes recommends – besides several spices, herbs and lemon peel, she has oysters, anchovy, ox palates, gherkins and mushroom powder. Eliza Acton again sums it up with beautiful simplicity in her conclusion to the recipe 'To Stew A Rump Beef': 'Grated horse-radish, mixed with some well-thickened brown gravy, a teaspoonful of mustard, and a little lemon-juice or vinegar, is a good sauce for stewed beef.' It could almost be Tewkesbury mustard casserole.

SERVES 5–6
900 g/2 lb stewing steak,
    trimmed of fat and gristle,
    cubed in 15 mm/½ in pieces
5 tablespoons olive oil
4 large onions, finely sliced
6 fat garlic cloves, crushed
4 teaspoons flour
4 teaspoons mustard powder
freshly ground white pepper
4 tablespoons whisky
400 ml/14 fl oz red wine or
    good beef stock
4 sprigs fresh thyme
2 teaspoons fresh marjoram
3 bay leaves

12 *whole allspice berries,*
  pounded
4 *cloves*
2 *tablespoons soft brown*
  sugar
Maldon salt
freshly ground black pepper
1–2 *tablespoons Tewkesbury*
  mustard (p.67)
lemon juice

Heat the oil in a large, flameproof casserole until just beginning to smoke. Add the beef and sear for 2–3 minutes. Remove the meat, add the onions and garlic to the pan, stirring to coat with the oil. Cover and sweat for 10 minutes.

Sift the flour and mustard powder together, then sprinkle over the onions and stir until all the oil is absorbed. Sprinkle with freshly ground white pepper, then add the whisky and bubble for 2 minutes.

Pour in the wine, stirring all the time, then add the herbs, spices, brown sugar and stir again to mix well. Return the beef to the pan, pushing it down gently to nestle in the sauce, then cover with a tight-fitting lid and cook on the lowest possible heat for 3½–4 hours. The heat must be very gentle so use an asbestos mat if needed and check the liquid level from time to time, topping up with a little water if absolutely necessary.

Test that the meat is tender by pressing in a fork – it should go in like butter. If not, give it another 15–20 minutes, again adding a little more liquid if the sauce is too thick. Transfer the meat to a warmed dish and keep warm. Stir the Tewkesbury mustard and a squeeze of lemon into the sauce, and bubble hard for 1 minute or so until rich, concentrated and not too liquid. Season with salt and pepper then pour over the beef. Serve with mashed potatoes into which a chopped, raw onion has been stirred, and stewed mushrooms.

Glazed Salt Beef with Mustard Sauce

For the Tudors salt beef was still a highly regarded dish on the well-dressed table, but today it is not highly esteemed. Have we been so indoctrinated by the tales of Hanged Beef, 'it may fill the belly and cause a man to drink, but it is evil for the stone, evil of digestion,' that we are still harbouring a deep-held prejudice? The time has come for a revival of this very ancient English dish. So, find a good butcher who brines his own beef – and enjoy this.

SERVES 6–8
1.6–1.8 kg/3 ½–4 lb salted
  silverside or brisket of beef,
  boned and rolled
1 large onion, chopped
1 leek, cut in half lengthways
1 large carrot, chopped
1 celery stick
6 white peppercorns, lightly
  crushed
1 bay leaf
1 parsley sprig
For the glaze
16 cloves
75 g/3 oz soft dark brown
  sugar
1 teaspoon powdered mustard
freshly ground allspice
1 teaspoon ground cinnamon
2 tablespoons honey
1 tablespoon orange juice
For the sauce
300 ml/½ pint medium dry
  cider
1 teaspoon Dijon or
  Tewkesbury mustard
1–2 tablespoons beurre manié
  (equal volumes of flour and
  butter worked to a paste)
freshly ground black pepper
good posy fresh parsley, very
  finely chopped

Immerse the beef in cold water and soak overnight. Drain and rinse very thoroughly, then place the meat in a large pan. Strew on the vegetables, peppercorns and herbs, adding cold water to cover.

Bring slowly to boiling point, skim off any scum and taste the cooking liquid. If it is very salt, pour half away and refill – this will depend on the brine your butcher uses, but most today are fairly light. You do want the stock for the sauce though, so if at all in doubt replenish with some fresh water and bring again to the boil.

Reduce the heat to the lowest possible, cover the pan and simmer very gently until quite tender – about 3½–4 hours. Leave the meat in the liquid to cool.

Drain the meat thoroughly, patting dry the fat, then stick in the cloves all over. Put in a roasting pan. Mix together the glaze ingredients – warm the honey slightly if it is thick until easily pourable – and smear over the beef. Roast in the oven at 180°C/350°F/Gas Mark 4 for 40–50 minutes until deeply glazed. Give it the occasional baste during cooking.

About 10 minutes before serving, measure out 300 ml/½ pint of the stock (keep the rest for soup), skim off any fat and pour into a pan with the cider. Bring quickly to the boil, taste and add a little water if it is too salty, then stir in the mustard. Have the sauce at a gentle simmer and whisk in the *beurre manié*, little by little, until thickened to your liking. Add pepper and finely chopped parsley, then pour into a very hot sauceboat and serve with the salt beef cut into thin slices. Also excellent cold, with Devil Chantilly (p.103).

8

LAMB AND MUTTON

Mustard and mutton, the sign of a glutton,
Mustard and beef, the sign of a thief.

Anon

Almost everybody we asked found this ditty familiar, yet nobody knew its origins. They sound suspiciously Victorian for, apart from the rather sanctimonious air, it seems to have been then that the partnership between mustard and mutton became frowned upon. That it was not the norm is made clear in a little book, written for Keen's in 1892 to celebrate their 150th anniversary: 'It [mustard] is, in fact, the natural piquant accompaniment to roast pork . . . and made dishes, to poultry and to some kinds of fish, and among gourmets, to *mutton*. Let the depreciator of cold mutton try a slice or two with the piquant addition of some fine mustard deftly commingled with a dash of walnut or mushroom catsup, and he will no longer despise the cold roast shoulder or the succulent boiled neck, eaten with a discreetly chosen salad.'

The interesting point is the combination of mustard and walnut catsup. It appears a century earlier in a recipe of Thomas Jefferson's for Cold Stew'd Beef and some thirty years later in the Mustard Club booklet, as a 'reader's' suggestion for Devilled Beef which states also that it is particularly good for cold mutton. Hannah Glasse mentions walnut pickle with mutton, in a hash of cold mutton and in the endpiece to a recipe, 'To Fry a Loin of Lamb': 'You do mutton the same way and add 2 spoonfuls of walnutt pickle.' Now walnuts and mutton are a particularly Arab combination, and the Romans would have known the dish. By medieval times – and right through to the Elizabethan period – mustard was the classic accompaniment to salt mutton. Some 150 years later, the nuts and the condiment were forming a *ménage à trois* with the fresh meat. Who made the link, and when? History gives us clues but not the complete answer.

Curiously, one of the very few references to mustard in the Middle Eastern kitchen combines it with lamb. The ninth-century poem by Ishaq ibn Ibrahim, quoted at the magnificent banquet given by the Caliph of Baghdad in the tenth century, has the lines: 'Last, ladle out into a thin tureen Where appetizing mustard smeared hath been, And eat with pleasure, mustarded about, This tastiest food for hurried diner-out.' A wonderfully evocative description of *sambusaks*, the glorious Arab stuffed pastries, which are still made today almost exactly as described in the poem. And, though the word used in the poem is 'meat', traditionally lamb is that meat. Mustard has disappeared from the modern recipe, nuts have made an entrance. One of the answers given to our oft-asked questions on the Arab indifference to mustard was that perhaps it was due to the area's preponderance of lamb dishes – lamb and mustard not being 'natural partners'. Yet in India there is a huge repertoire of lamb and mustard dishes: lamb baked whole, gently braised, spiced kebabs, meatballs . . .

Mustard, of course, must originally have been used to 'hot' dishes up, but many of the recipes are mild and of direct Moghul descent. And the Arab and Moghul kitchens had extremely close links. Perhaps that most influential of Arab physicians, Galen, did not appreciate mustard's virtues – though it had long been recognized as a benign influence on heavy meats.

With the second highest fat content of our animal foods (28 per cent – even with all visible fat trimmed off, the muscle itself still contains fat), lamb is indeed a heavy meat. The medievals realized that, hence their constant partnership of mustard and salt mutton. Somebody, somewhere (maybe with a knowledge of the Indian kitchen?) introduced it to the fresh meat. Glutton he may have been. But we should thank him.

Baked Lamb Cutlets

Lamb cutlets provide a fertile ground for experiments with mustard. If you know your cutlets come from really young, fresh lamb, simply spread them on each side with a smidgeon of mustard and olive oil, sprinkle with salt and pepper and grill – briefly. They should be pink, tender and juicy. They will not taste too much of mustard – but they will taste of lamb. For frozen cutlets, or meat of a dubious age, a slow baking will give better results.

SERVES 4–6
12 lamb cutlets, trimmed of
   most of their fat
3 tablespoons olive oil
1 bunch fresh mint
300 ml/½ pint red wine
2 tablespoons Five-herb
   mustard (p.59)
lemon juice
Maldon salt
freshly ground black pepper

Sprinkle the cutlets with a little salt and black pepper. Heat the oil, add the meat and sear quickly on both sides. Make a bed of the mint in a roasting tin, place the cutlets on top – in one layer – and pour over the wine mixed with the mustard. Bake in the oven at 170°C/325°F/Gas Mark 3 for 25 minutes, then turn, baste – the liquid will have considerably reduced – and bake for another 15 minutes, by which time the juices should have almost all been absorbed. Transfer to a serving platter, squeeze over the merest hint of lemon juice and serve.

Devilled Lamb Cutlets

Devilling was at its most favoured during Victorian and Edwardian times, with a legion of variations and spice combinations – all subtly different. What they had in common was a reminder of the Raj kitchen and the glories of the British Empire. Note also, the walnut ketchup.

SERVES 4–6
12 lamb cutlets, if possible the
   very thin ones sold as
   'breakfast cutlets'
2 tablespoons mustard
   powder
2 tablespoons walnut ketchup
Maldon salt
freshly ground black pepper
50 g/2 oz unsalted butter
3 small shallots, very finely
   chopped

1 tablespoon soft dark brown
  sugar
150 ml/¼ pint red wine
  vinegar
1 tablespoon Worcestershire
  sauce
few drops Tabasco sauce
2 tablespoons mint jelly
cayenne pepper

Mix the mustard powder with 2 tablespoons cold water and the walnut ketchup to a smooth thin paste. Smear lightly on both sides of the cutlets and leave for 1 hour. Sprinkle lightly with salt and black pepper. Melt 1 tablespoon butter in a small pan, add the shallots and cook for 5 minutes. Sprinkle in the sugar and stir for 2–3 minutes until lightly caramelized, then pour in the vinegar, constantly stirring. Add the Worcester sauce, Tabasco and mint jelly and gently, gently bubble until thick and syrupy.

Meanwhile, melt the remaining butter in a large frying pan (or roasting tin). Add the cutlets and cook: 2 minutes each side is fine for thin cutlets, 3–4 minutes for thicker ones. Transfer to a warmed serving dish, pour the cooking sediments into the 'sauce' pan, stir well and pour over the meat. There will not be much sauce – but it will be very concentrated in flavour. Sprinkle with a *little* cayenne and serve at once.

Mutton Carbonadoes

Especially popular as grilled steaks in Elizabethan times were pieces of mutton fillet: 'Cut a leg of mutton in thin fillets and to make it tender: chop it on both the sides with the back of the knife so that they be not chopped through. Then salt them well and lay them, on a gridiron and broil them till they be enough, and with vinegar and minced onions serve them forth.' A little mustard completes the sauce. 'Gigot' chops have been used here (cut from across the leg of the lamb) but mutton would be equally good.

SERVES 4
4 gigot lamb chops
2 tablespoons olive oil

Maldon salt
freshly ground black pepper
2 large sweet onions, very
finely chopped
150 ml/¼ pint cider vinegar
1 teaspoon sugar
150 ml/¼ pint medium dry
white wine
freshly ground nutmeg
1–2 teaspoons Dijon mustard

Flatten the chops lightly using a large-bladed knife, working around the bone. Brush with oil on both sides. Put the onions into a pan, deep rather than wide, add the vinegar and the sugar then simmer gently, covered, for 10 minutes. Stir, then pour in the wine and cook, covered, for a further 15 minutes until very soft. Season with plenty of nutmeg, then add the mustard (1 teaspoon) and simmer, uncovered, while cooking the chops.

Grill the chops under a medium heat for 10–15 minutes, turning once, depending upon how pink you like your lamb. Season lightly with salt and pepper then give them a further minute on each side under a high heat to brown. The onion sauce should by this time have absorbed almost all the liquid – if not, bubble hard for 1–2 minutes until it has reduced. Check the mustard, adding a little extra if necessary. It shouldn't be overpowering, but the taste should be there. Spread a little 'sauce' over each chop and serve at once.

Grilled Shoulder of Lamb

Not such an illogical idea as it might at first seem. We barbecue lamb quite happily, yet the number of people who exclaim 'Grilled roast lamb . . .' The words are almost instinctive – you have a shoulder of lamb, you have a roast lamb! Yet lamb grilled is very good, and it doesn't take long. It is not a meal for fussy eaters of thin, neat slices of meat: carve it in chunks and let the meat fall off the bone.

SERVES 5–6
1 shoulder of lamb, about 1.6
kg/3½ lb weight

*2 tablespoons finely chopped
mixed fresh herbs, or 1
tablespoon dried mixed
herbs if absolutely necessary
1 teaspoon mustard powder
4 tablespoons olive oil
1 tablespoon Dijon mustard
150 ml/¼ pint dry white wine
Maldon salt
freshly ground black pepper*

Slash the meat right through to the bone, on both sides, making the gashes about 5 cm/2 inches apart. Mix the herbs with the mustard powder and rub all over the joint, pushing well into the cuts. Mix the oil, mustard and wine, pour over the joint and leave for 12–24 hours.

Drain the meat, reserving the marinade. Grill under a moderate heat (on a rack) for 5 minutes. Turn over, cook for 5 minutes then turn again. Sprinkle with a little salt and pepper, cook for a further 5 minutes then turn and repeat with the other side. Continue cooking for 20–25 minutes, turning every 5 minutes and basting with a little marinade until the outside is marvellously charred. Transfer to a hot dish, scrape up the juices from the grill pan and smear over the lamb. Eat.

Baked Lamb Shoulder

It is strange how we get locked into culinary prejudices. Mint sauce with lamb is anathema to the Frenchman. His penchant for garlic causes English noses to wrinkle. Yet both are not merely good in taste but also have a chemical purpose. How many people though think of tomatoes and lamb as a particular partnership? The French have the edge on us: most of their *daubes* and casseroles for lamb are moistened not with stock but tomatoes. With sound reason – the acidity cuts through the fat in the meat (that, too, is why rosemary is traditionally associated with lamb – its essence performs the same function) and the sweetness adds a roundness of flavour. Mustard intensifies the taste of both the lamb and the tomatoes.

SERVES 4–6
*900 g/2 lb lean lamb, cubed
3 tablespoons olive oil*

2 large sweet onions, chopped
  but not too finely
3 garlic cloves, cut in half
1 sprig thyme, leaves stripped
  from the stalk
3 sprigs fresh marjoram, finely
  chopped
2 sprigs fresh savory, finely
  chopped, or 1 teaspoon
  dried savory
400 g/14 fl oz canned plum
  tomatoes
Maldon salt
freshly ground black pepper
1 tablespoon Dijon mustard
150 g/5 oz Cheddar cheese,
  grated
cayenne pepper

Heat the oil, add the onions and garlic and sweat for 10 minutes. Remove from the pan. Add the lamb, lightly and quickly browning it all over. Put the onions at the bottom of an ovenproof dish, and cover with the meat. Mix the herbs together and sprinkle over. Drain the tomatoes – keeping the juice – and chop the flesh. Spread over the meat. Mix the tomato juice with salt and black pepper, then stir in the mustard. Pour over the casserole then cover with grated cheese and a light scattering of cayenne. Cook in the oven at 180°C/350°F/Gas Mark 4 for about 1¼ hours until the cheese is bubbling and golden. Serve very hot, with crusty bread to mop up the juices, and a good green salad.

Saddle of Lamb in Mustard and Port

Traditionally, saddle of mutton was one of the great English dishes. And from medieval to Georgian times it had a traditional stuffing – oysters. It is interesting how the idea of fish and meat was quite clearly defined: anchovies with beef, oysters with mutton, crab with lamb – each type of fish cleverly complementing its meaty partner, and not intruding with any taste of fish at all. Anchovies add piquancy and oysters a sweetness, while the crab seems to take on a delicate nuttiness. Since fresh oysters today are a wild extravagance, for this recipe use either frozen shucked oysters (beginning to be available in Britain, widely so in America) or – for a different but equally good flavour – smoked oysters. Since saddle of mutton is almost as extravagant as oysters – and considerably harder to find – we have used a small saddle of lamb. If you have a reliable source of real mutton, treasure it, and double the quantities of the stuffing. You will of course also feed more people, say 10–12. Either way, ask the butcher to bone (but not roll or tie) the saddle for you, keeping the bones and trimmings.

SERVES 8

1 small saddle of lamb, about
1.6 kg/3 lb boned weight,
bones and trimmings
reserved
2 sprigs lemon thyme
2 garlic cloves, whole but
peeled
Maldon salt
freshly ground black pepper
2 tablespoons Dijon mustard
5 tablespoons port
2 tablespoons redcurrant
jelly
For the stuffing
25 g/1 oz unsalted butter
1 large onion, finely chopped
225 g/8 oz shucked frozen
oysters, defrosted, or 125
g/4 oz can smoked oysters,
drained, plus 125 g/4 oz
white crabmeat
1 bunch watercress, finely
chopped
juice of 1 lemon
freshly grated allspice
For the stock
1 small onion stuck with 6
cloves
1 cinnamon stick
1 celery stick

fresh parsley
1 bay leaf
fresh chervil
small piece lemon zest
2 tablespoons white wine
  vinegar
½ teaspoon sugar

First, make a light stock with the reserved bones and trimmings, the stock ingredients and 1 litre/1¾ pints cold water. Bring slowly to the boil, skim off any scum then simmer gently for about 1 hour, half-covered. Simmer, uncovered, for a further 15–20 minutes until reduced to 450 ml/¾ pint. Strain, cool, skim off the fat and reserve.

To make the stuffing, melt the butter, add the onions and stew gently for 20 minutes until softened but not coloured. Remove from the heat, stir in the oysters, or smoked oysters and crabmeat, then add the watercress, lemon juice and allspice. Season well and mix thoroughly.

Place the lamb, skin side down, on a flat surface and open it out. Lay one thyme sprig and one garlic clove on each side of the saddle, then spread the stuffing evenly down both sides. Carefully turn in the outer flaps of meat, then roll together and tie securely. Place the joint, skin side up, on a roasting rack and season with salt and pepper.

Mix together the mustard and port. Gently heat the redcurrant jelly until melted – add a tablespoon of water to the pan to prevent burning. Stir into the mustard and port then smear the lamb with the paste. Cook in the oven at 200°C/400°F/Gas Mark 6 for about 1½ hours for pink lamb (25 minutes per lb) to just over 2 hours (35 minutes per lb) for well-done meat. Baste every 30 minutes.

Remove the joint to a warmed platter, scrape up the sediments in the roasting tin, pour off any excess fat then add the stock and boil furiously for 3–4 minutes to reduce slightly and heighten the flavours. Pour into a warmed sauceboat and serve with the lamb cut into thick slices.

Lamb Rissoles with Mustard Wine Sauce

One of the favourite methods of cooking lamb in the Middle East is to mince it very finely, then highly spice it, before grilling or pan-frying. Add a French sauce, and you have an excellent dish.

SERVES 6

*900 g/2 lb lean lamb, finely
    minced*
1 large onion, grated
Maldon salt
freshly ground white pepper
3 tablespoons olive oil
*1 tablespoon brown mustard
    seed*
*1 tablespoon cumin, lightly
    crushed*
*1 teaspoon powdered
    cinnamon*
*4 tablespoons finely chopped
    parsley*
2 fat garlic cloves, crushed
For the sauce
25 g/1 oz butter
1 shallot, finely chopped
175 ml/6 fl oz red wine
2 teaspoons Dijon mustard
2 tablespoons crème fraîche

Put the lamb into a food processor, with the onion and a generous seasoning of salt and pepper. Heat 1 tablespoon oil, add the mustard seeds, cover the pan and cook until they start to pop – about 1 minute. Drain and add the seeds to the processor together with the cumin, cinnamon, parsley and garlic cloves. Blend until paste-like. If you don't have a processor, just mix together *very thoroughly* in a large bowl, really pounding the meat until quite smooth. With wetted hands, form into small balls. Heat the remaining oil in the wiped-out frying pan and add the meatballs – give yourself plenty of room to turn them over, so do the cooking in two batches if need be. Cook for about 6–7 minutes, turning fairly constantly until crispy and browned on the outside, still soft within. Keep warm.

Wipe out the pan with kitchen paper, add the butter and sizzle lightly. Add the shallot and sauté for 3–4 minutes, gently, then pour in the wine. Bubble hard for 2 minutes to reduce, then stir in the mustard and *crème fraîche* and cook for a further minute. Pour over the meatballs and serve immediately.

Steamed Marinated Mutton

Steamed mutton is a Moroccan favourite – there, very simply served with salt and cumin seeds sprinkled on top. But the meat is so tender it can be pulled apart in the fingers, and it is a good method for cooking English mutton, which is often of indifferent age: not mature enough to have the richness of true mutton (three to four years old) but old enough to have lost that first flush of youthful tenderness. Soy sauce, incidentally, is no newcomer to the English kitchen – it came with the first East India Company traders in the early eighteenth century.

SERVES 4–6
900 g/2 lb lean lamb, cubed
2 garlic cloves, finely chopped
5 cm/2 in piece fresh root
   ginger, peeled and grated
½ teaspoon ground cinnamon
1 teaspoon black peppercorns,
   crushed
2 tablespoons Matthew's
   mustard (p.68)
3 tablespoons soy sauce
150 ml/¼ pint medium dry
   white wine
1 tablespoon syrup from
   Mostarda di Venezia
   (p.71)
3–4 pieces of quince from
   Mostarda di Venezia, finely
   chopped
lemon juice
fresh mint sprigs, very finely
   chopped

Put the lamb in the bottom of a fairly wide, heatproof dish. Mix together all the ingredients except the quinces, lemon juice and mint, then pour all over the lamb. Cover the dish with greaseproof paper, tied round the top tightly, then with foil or a towel, also tied (much as one does a Christmas pudding). Put into a large pan and carefully pour in boiling water, to come two-thirds of the way up the dish. Have the water hinting at a simmer, cover the pan and cook, very gently, for about 2 hours, topping up with more boiling water as necessary.

Mix the chopped quinces with a little lemon juice to taste, then stir in the chopped mint. (Quinces with lamb was a well-known medieval partnership – again from the Arabs. Today, only the Persians – with their huge quince orchards – follow the ancient tradition, although Morocco still favours many fruit and meat stews.) Put the dip in a small bowl.

Carefully lift out the mutton dish from the pan, dry the bottom, remove the foil and paper and serve while the aroma is still drifting out of the bowl. Accompany with the quince dip.

Lamb 'Oven' Curry

The Oxfam shop one day revealed a little treasure: a small, tatty leatherbound book, marked very firmly in red ink on the inside cover 'Property of the Colonel's Wife – PLEASE do not move, June 6th 1862.' There is no name, no mention of a place, except for one month spent visiting 'The Colonel's Aunt' in Simla. What *is* meticulously recorded though are trips to the market, what she saw, what she bought, what she paid for it and how it was cooked.

This recipe was particularly intriguing as she has noted 'especially good to be cooked in England'. Why? Because it's cooked in the oven, unlike most of her other curries? Or perhaps she has adapted it – there is no Indian title here, as with most of the other dishes. Either way, it is especially good; and it is pleasing to think the treasured book has not met such an ignominious end after all.

SERVES 6
*1.1 kg/2½ lb boned leg of
  lamb (about 1.8 kg/4 lb
  unboned weight)*
*5 cm/2 inch piece fresh root
  ginger, peeled and coarsely
  chopped*
*1–2 green chillies, seeded and
  chopped*
1–2 garlic cloves, peeled
Maldon salt
juice of 2 lemons
50 ml/2 fl oz mustard oil
*2 bay leaves, dried and
  crumbled*

1 large onion, finely sliced
1 tablespoon mustard powder

Cut the lamb into 25 mm/1 inch cubes, trimming off any fat or gristle. In a coffee grinder, blend the ginger, chilli and garlic with a pinch of salt (this stops the chilli juices from becoming bitter). Stir the paste into half the lemon juice, and 1 tablespoon mustard oil. Pour over the lamb and leave for 2–3 hours.

Heat the remaining oil in a roasting pan, add the onions and sweat gently for 10 minutes, turning occasionally. Sprinkle over the crumbled bay leaves. Place the meat in an even layer on top of the onions, pour over the marinade and cook in the oven at 180°C/350°F/Gas Mark 4 for 45 minutes. Mix the mustard powder with 3 tablespoons cold water (there is a note in the original beside this ingredient, which is actually listed as '2 tablespoon mustard seed powdered *very* fine (if no cook-boy available, use COLMAN's M.P.)'). Stir the mustard paste into the remaining lemon juice and sprinkle all over the lamb – do not turn the lamb though. Cook for a further 30 minutes then serve with a pile of pilau rice. The meat is succulently tender, the juices delicately spicy.

9

PORK

It is the one [animal] whose empire is the most universal, and whose qualities are the least in dispute. Without it, there would be no bacon, and consequently no cookery; without it, no ham, no sausage, no *andouille*, no black pudding and therefore no *charcutiers* . . . Everything about the pig is good, what culpable lapse of memory can have transformed its name into a vulgar insult?

Grimod de la Reynière

The pig has always been the poor man's favourite meat, and it is easy to understand why. Not a drop – literally – is wasted. For the medieval peasant the great autumn slaughter was a time of high festivity and activity: the making of blood puddings, salting of sides, curing of hams, flaying of fat for lard were all part of the winter preparations. Not least was the making of Thomas Tusser's Christmas 'souse': the hind joints, ears, snout, cheeks, trotters and, sometimes, tail were all pickled in a strong brine, often laced with ale or wine. For many a family, the pig, however preserved, was going to be their only meat for the next few months. Fortunately, it pickles and salts particularly well. Rich in fat, and succulent, it requires less salt than beef or mutton, so providing a tenderer joint. Its very richness, of course, needed offsetting, and so the range of sharp, spicy sauces – and mustard – became its natural accompaniment.

Apicius gives a mustard sauce for roast pork, and several for boiled boar. Cooked sides of pork are also pickled by him in 'mustard, vinegar, salt and honey, covering meat entirely. And when ready to use you'll be surprised.' Some 2000 years later, the unknown author of *The Indian Cookery Book by a Thirty-Five Years' Resident* – quoted by Elizabeth David in her *Spices, Salt and Aromatics in the English*

Kitchen – was also using mustard as a preservative for cooked pork. Having ascertained that 'The best vindaloo is that prepared with mustard oil', he or she goes on to say that a vindaloo cooked from fat pork will keep long enough 'to be sent Home round the Cape' if stored in stone jars 'well covered with mustard oil'.

Back in medieval England, their hams and sausages saw them through the winter, and mustard had its place. With sausages so much so, according to Dumas's colourful account, that Edward III burning his way through France gave no quarter to those pleading for an end to the fiery destruction: '"Bah!" said the ferocious Plantagenet, "War without burning is sausage without mustard!"'

Ham is a natural for mustard and sugar glazes, and even with no mustard in the glaze, it is the automatic accompaniment to the meat. In the 1840s, when the first ham-sandwich sellers appeared on London streets, two of the requisites for setting up in the business were: '2d for mustard-pot and spoon' and '4d for mustard'. Colman's Mustard Club cleverly exploited the tradition with their gimmick of advertising in the provincial papers that their 'mystery man' would be 'in town' on a certain day, eating ham sandwiches. Any waiter who passed him the mustard would be given £1.

The partnership was not new, of course. Giles Rose, in the enchantingly titled *A Perfect School of Instruction for the Officers of the Mouth* (1682), finishes his recipe For A Gammon of Bacon, 'and when it is boiled raise the skin and stick it with Bays and Rosemary . . . then serve it with mustard.' Apart from the Bays and Rosemary – how much nicer than the ubiquitous cloves – the recipe is most modern. And it was not just gammon that called for mustard. The Frenchman F. Misson, describing the cookshops all over London at that time, writes: 'Generally, four Spits, one over another, carry round each five or six Pieces of Butcher's Meat, Beef, Mutton, Veal, Pork and Lamb; you have what Quantity you please cut off . . . with this, a little Salt and Mustard upon the Side of a Plate, a Bottle of Beer and a Roll; and there is your whole Feast.' Hannah Wolley, in *The Accomplisht Lady's Delight*, a few years earlier, had recommended a sauce 'with butter, vinegar, mustard and sugar' to accompany Broyl'd Leg of Pork while in the Burgundian kitchen whole legs of pork were marinated in wine for a day, smeared with mustard and then roasted – a dish still popular today.

Italy varies her mustard accompaniment. With *zampone* (a stuffed pig's trotter), one is offered delicious fruit pickle, Mostarda di Frutta.

Since the early days when salt pork and mustard sauce opened the feasts, mustard and pork have travelled together. Without micro-

Novelty mustard containers that converted into money boxes after use

scopes, without knowledge of the structure of meat, man's instinct has led the pig to mustard. And wisely so. For the mustard quickens the breakdown of the fatty cells, exposing a greater area of the meat fibres to the gastric juices and thereby encouraging easier and more complete assimilation.

Mustard Seed Sausages

Thousands of tons of sausages are sold each year. Sadly, most of these are far from pleasant, yet to make one's own is not difficult. After all, if the medieval peasant, with no food processor, could do it, so can we. Skins, obtainable from any good butcher who makes his own sausages, keep well in salt, chilled, merely needing a good soaking before use. And if you haven't a sausage-filling attachment, or an obliging butcher, then you can make pretty lacy packages like the French *crépinette*, by wrapping small rounds of the mixture in softened caul fat.

SERVES 4–6
*700 g/ 1½ lb belly of pork,
    derinded and coarsely
    chopped*
*700 g/ 1½ lb lean pork, hand
    and spring ideally, coarsely
    chopped*
225 g/ 8 oz pork back fat
*2 tablespoons brown mustard
    seed, soaked for 24 hours*
2 tablespoons Maldon salt
*freshly ground white and
    black peppers*
1½ tablespoons castor sugar
¼ teaspoon saltpetre
*2 tablespoons crushed
    coriander seeds*
*2 tablespoons finely chopped
    fresh parsley*
*1 tablespoon finely chopped
    fresh thyme, or tarragon, or
    young sage leaves*

For the cooking
3 tablespoons olive oil
2 large onions, finely sliced
4–6 garlic cloves, sliced
   lengthways
150 ml/¼ pint fruity white
   wine
1 tablespoon Dijon mustard

Mince the pork and fat finely or whizz in a food processor. Grind the soaked mustard seed in a spice grinder – it won't pulverize completely, but sufficiently for the purpose. Add to the food processor together with the remaining ingredients and whizz again. If mixing by hand, make sure to distribute the spices evenly. Be generous with the peppers.

Fill the casings, twisting every six inches or so (a refinement only started in the early seventeenth century) and hang for 1–2 days in a dry airy place. This is not vital but greatly improves the flavour which can otherwise be a trifle bland. Half the amount will be adequate for 4–6 people, so freeze the remainder.

To cook the remainder, heat the oil in a large frying or roasting pan, add the onion and garlic and sauté gently for 10–15 minutes until soft and lightly golden. Bring some salted water to the boil, dip in the sausages for 1 minute. Drain and pat dry, then add to the onions. Brown lightly, then add the wine – mixed with the mustard – and bubble hard for 30–40 seconds. Season, lightly, reduce the heat and cook for 30–40 minutes turning the sausages frequently, until they are crisp and cooked through. Particularly good served with new potatoes, dressed while still warm in a *light* mustard vinaigrette. Green salad, of course.

Pork Balls with Mustard-Soy Dip

A constant feature of the medieval kitchen is the dish Pommes d'Or – Golden Apples. Little balls of minced, highly spiced pork were dipped into a batter and fried until golden. Often part of the batter was mixed with a mass of finely chopped parsley, to give little green 'apples' too. With this dip, Japanese in origin, the batter is superfluous but a rolling in finely chopped parsley before frying is still a good idea.

SERVES 4–6
350 g/12 oz lean pork
1 tablespoon mustard oil
1½ teaspoons brown mustard
    seed
freshly grated nutmeg
½ teaspoon ground caraway
5 cm/2 inch piece fresh root
    ginger, peeled and grated
1 small onion, grated
Maldon salt
freshly ground white and
    black peppers
2 teaspoons finely chopped
    fresh marjoram
3 tablespoons fresh parsley
1 teaspoon castor sugar
1 large egg, beaten
50 g/2 oz butter
For the sauce
2 teaspoons mustard powder
4 tablespoons light soy sauce
    (available at Chinese
    supermarkets)

Either put the pork through a mincer two or three times, or chop coarsely, then mince in a food processor.

Heat the oil in a small frying pan, add the mustard seeds, cover and fry until popping. Drain and add to the pork, together with the remaining ingredients, except the butter. Blend until thoroughly mixed and quite pasty.

With wetted hands, take a walnut-sized piece of the mixture and roll into a small ball. Test fry in a little butter until golden and crispy. Taste for seasoning, adjusting if necessary, then form the rest of the mixture into little balls. Melt the butter in a large pan, when bubbling add the meatballs and fry – in batches if necessary – until golden and cooked through. Keep warm while cooking the remainder.

Mix the mustard with 2 tablespoons cold water, then whisk in the soy sauce – adding a little more water if the sauce is too strong. Serve the pork balls with the sauce in tiny individual bowls, for people to dip into.

Fillet of Pork Seville with Mustard

Although the early crusaders must have eaten sweet oranges on their travels in the Middle East, the first oranges to arrive in England were the bitter Spanish type, in the late thirteenth century. They soon found their way into the cooking pot, usually with sugar to provide those ever-present bitter-sweet sauces. The Elizabethans particularly used them with fish and chicken, but their sharp flavour also provides a good counterfoil to pork.

SERVES 4–5
550 g/1¼ lb pork tenderloin,
    cut into ½ inch thick slices
Maldon salt
freshly ground black pepper
50–75 g/2–3 oz butter
juice of 2 small Seville oranges
1–2 teaspoons castor sugar
125 ml/4 fl oz chicken stock
½ teaspoon ground caraway
1 egg yolk
6 tablespoons double cream
2 teaspoons Dijon mustard

Season the meat lightly with a little salt and black pepper. Melt the butter in a large frying pan, or two, add the pork slices and sauté for 2 minutes or so until firm and opaque.

Add the orange juice, sugar, stock and caraway, then simmer for 5–6 minutes turning the meat once. Test for doneness, giving it 1–2 minutes more if necessary. Whisk the egg yolk with the cream and mustard. Remove the meat to a warm serving dish, lower the heat and beat in the cream mixture. Heat through gently, stirring all the while until the sauce slightly thickens. Do not boil or it will curdle. Pour the sauce over, or around, as you prefer, the meat and serve.

Pork Fillets with Mustard Seeds and Lovage

Sage, which we regard as the particular herb for pork, only came into the greatest favour during the seventeenth century, although it is still the traditional flavouring for Cumberland pork sausages. Lovage, with its slight pepperiness and hint of celery, is another apt partner: the leaves for fresh cuts, the seeds good in sausages.

SERVES 4
550 g/1¼ lb pork tenderloin
  cut into 5 cm/2 inch
  medallions
50 g/2 oz butter
1 tablespoon white mustard
  seed
10 lovage leaves, finely
  chopped
1 tablespoon granular
  mustard
3 tablespoons medium dry
  white wine
Maldon salt
freshly ground black pepper

Put the slices of pork in one layer between two sheets of greaseproof paper and flatten lightly with a meat bat. Melt half the butter, add 3–4 slices of pork so they fit neatly in one layer. Sauté for 2–3 minutes on each side until opaque and cooked right through. Remove from the pan, keep warm and cook the rest.

Add the remaining butter to the pan, and when just melted, add the mustard seeds and cook for 2 minutes until beginning to splutter. Add the lovage and cook, stirring constantly until soft and dark green.

Stir in the mustard, then pour over the wine. Raise the heat and bubble for 2 minutes, then season with a little salt and pepper. Pour over the pork fillets and serve immediately. Whatever the vegetables, keep the flavours very simple: this is a subtle and delicate dish.

Gammon with Sherry Mustard Sauce

Ham-curing methods have varied little over 2000 years. Anne Wilson, in *Food and Drink in Britain*, describes how in Italy, *c.* 150 BC, 'hams had to be covered with salt and steeped in their own brine for 17 days, dried in a draught for 2, rubbed over with oil and vinegar, and then smoked for a further 2 days . . . Barring the oil and vinegar dressing', little has changed.

Today, in some areas the tradition of home-cured ham still persists. If you can get one of these, so much the better. If not, you could try curing a ham yourself: for the best recipes and meticulous detail – most important in home curing – turn to Jane Grigson's *Charcuterie and French Pork Cookery*. Otherwise, buy a good lean gammon joint – smoked or not as you prefer. Incidentally, Maldon salt, a staple as you will have noticed, gives excellent results if home-curing hams. Hannah Glasse on the subject: 'Yorkshire is famous for Hams; and the Reason is this: Their Salt is much finer than ours in London, it is a large clear Salt, and gives the Meat a fine Flavour. I used to have it in Essex from Malding, and that Salt will make any Ham as fine as you can desire; it is by much the best Salt for salting Meat.'

SERVES 8–10

1.8 kg/4 lb gammon joint, soaked overnight (even unsmoked joints benefit from a soaking; the salting process inevitably hardens the meat a little and soaking restores the succulence)
1.7 litres/3 pints bouillon (pp.226–7)
300 ml/½ pint amontillado sherry, plus extra if necessary
1 tablespoon light soy sauce
2 tablespoons soft dark brown sugar
freshly ground allspice
freshly ground black pepper
2 tablespoons Dijon mustard
1 tablespoon flour
1 tablespoon unsalted butter

Bring the ham to the boil in a large pan of cold water, simmer for 10 minutes then discard the water. Cover with the bouillon and bring to a good but gentle simmer. Cook for 1 hour 40 minutes – allowing 20 minutes per pound plus an extra 20.

Remove the joint from the pan and skin, then place in an ovenproof dish into which it fits snugly. Cover with the sherry and 150 ml/¼ pint of the cooking liquor. Cook in the oven at 180°C/350°F/Gas Mark 4 for 50–60 minutes, until the meat is quite tender when pierced with a fork.

Transfer the meat to a roasting tin, mix the soy sauce, sugar, allspice, pepper and mustard with 2–3 tablespoons of the sherry liquor, and smear over the ham. Raise the oven to 220°C/425°F/Gas Mark 7 and return the meat for 10–15 minutes until the glaze is melted and golden. Be careful that it doesn't burn.

Meanwhile, taste the braising liquid, adjust the seasoning if necessary, adding a little more sherry, soy, or some of the initial cooking juices if it seems too strong. (Keep the remaining stock for soup.) Stir in a touch of Dijon mustard if wished – but this sauce should be subtle – then bring to the boil, lower the heat and whisk in the flour and butter, previously mixed to a smooth paste. Beat until lightly thickened, then pour into a hot sauceboat. Serve with the ham cut into thick or thin slices as you prefer.

Roman Mustard Pork Chops in Red Wine

The Romans enjoyed their pigs in many guises: Virgil wrote about them, Roman soldiers took them on their marches – fresh food after the battle – and languishing banqueters had their appetites stimulated between courses by performing pigs (the Etruscans apparently trained them to march to music). Nero and his Senators preferred simply to eat the creature, pork far outstripping mutton as the favoured meat, especially salted pork, eaten with cabbage. The ancient Roman mustard, flavoured with almonds and pine kernels, goes particularly well with the fresh meat.

SERVES 6
6 spare rib pork chops
Maldon salt
freshly ground white pepper
3 garlic cloves, finely sliced
   lengthways
15 g/½ oz flaked almonds
2 rosemary sprigs
2 tablespoons Roman mustard
   (p.65)
350 ml/12 fl oz red wine
2 tablespoons olive oil
25 g/1 oz pine kernels

Rub the chops all over with a little salt and black pepper, then make 4–5 slits on both sides of each chop and slide in a sliver of garlic and almond flake. Arrange on a roasting pan on top of the rosemary sprigs. Mix the mustard and wine with 1½ tablespoons of the oil and pour over.

Cook, covered, in the oven at 180°C/350°F/Gas Mark 4 for 1 hour, turning the chops once. Then uncover and cook for a further 20–30 minutes, basting every 10 minutes.

Heat the remaining oil, and sauté the pine kernels for 45 seconds until they turn pink. Scatter over the chops and serve with mashed potatoes.

Mustard Pork in Milk

This Italian method of cooking pork is unusual but excellent. Traditionally the rolled loin is used but the recipe is obligingly adaptable: loin chops, spare rib chops and belly rashers can all be substituted, the last in particular making for a very rich sauce as the melting fat combines with the milk.

SERVES 6
6 spare rib chops
Maldon salt
freshly ground black pepper
2 tablespoons Dijon mustard
3 tablespoons olive oil
2 large onions, finely sliced
2 garlic cloves, crushed
2 thyme sprigs
1 tablespoon fresh coriander
  seeds, lightly crushed
1 tablespoon brown mustard
  seeds
about 600 ml/1 pint milk
350 g/12 oz fresh young broad
  beans (or frozen, if
  necessary)
finely chopped fresh parsley

Rub a little salt and pepper over each side of the chops, then smear both sides with mustard. Heat the oil in a large heavy-based pan (vital if the dish is not to burn), add the onions and cook for 10–15 minutes, covered, until nicely softened. Stir in the garlic, add the thyme sprigs and arrange the chops on top. Sprinkle over the seeds, a little extra salt and a good grinding of black pepper. Add the milk and bring to the boil, gently, then cover and cook, at the slowest possible simmer, for about 1 hour. Do not disturb the contents of the pan, but check after about 50 minutes that the liquid is not evaporating too quickly.

Blanch the broad beans in salted water for 2–3 minutes if young and fresh, 5–7 if frozen, then drain and add to the pan. When you lift off the lid, the milk will have formed a golden translucent veil. Stir into the meat, adding a little extra milk if need be – you don't want too much liquid but there must be enough to prevent sticking, all too easy at this stage. Cook, very gently, again covered, for a further 8–10 minutes. Sprinkle with lots of finely chopped parsley and serve.

Crispy Roast Pork Belly with Sesame Mustard

At St Faith's Fair, held annually in Norwich, the tradition was to serve crackly roast pork – with pots of mustard. The purveyors of the mustard were not always over-generous and supplies ran out very quickly. In Norfolk, if you have a near-empty mustard-pot, they still call it 'St Fay's Fair Mustard'. Well-crackled pork is not just an English tradition – the Chinese love it, especially pork belly. One word of warning: we have found gas and electric ovens very variable in their production of crackling. While this dish has never failed in a gas oven, it has proved less reliable in an electric one. If the worst comes to the worst, cut off the crackling 5 minutes before serving and crisp it under the grill. Chop it into small pieces and strew them over the pork, and disaster will be averted.

SERVES 4–6
12 slices thick end pork belly,
  ½ inch thick
12 tablespoons Sesame
  mustard (p.64)
4–5 tablespoons peanut oil
1 teaspoon sesame oil
Maldon salt

freshly ground black pepper
12 cloves
700 g/1½ lb spinach, washed,
*   thoroughly drained and*
*   finely shredded*
4 tablespoons toasted sesame
*   seeds*

Heat the oven to 200°C/400°F/Gas Mark 5 (the difference in oven temperatures is deliberate). Mix the mustard with 1½ tablespoons of the peanut oil, season lightly, then spread both sides of each pork slice with the mixture. Sprinkle over the sesame oil. Stick a clove into each slice.

Place the pork, skin upwards, in a roasting pan – put crumpled foil on either side if necessary to keep the meat upright.

Sprinkle over 12 tablespoons boiling water, then put into the oven for 40 minutes – do not baste. Turn the oven down to 140°C/275°F/Gas Mark 1, and leave for a further 15–20 minutes.

Meanwhile, heat half the remaining oil in a large pan, or wok, over a medium heat, add half the spinach and stir-fry for 5 minutes. Transfer to a warmed serving plate, then repeat with the rest of the spinach. Stir constantly while cooking. Add to the serving dish, and sprinkle with the toasted sesame seeds. Check the pork crackling, crisping under the grill if need be, then arrange the pork on top of the spinach. Sprinkle with a little extra black pepper and serve.

10

OFFAL AND VEAL

Good husbands and huswife now chiefly be glad,
Things handsome to have as they ought to be had,
Good bread and good drinke, a good fier in the hall,
Brawne, pudding, and souse, and good mustards withal . . .

Thomas Tusser, 1557

So the poet farmer from East Anglia set the Christmas scene. It is interesting that, from very early times, offal dishes were considered great delicacies. Although originally brawn could mean any cold meat, it normally indicated leg of wild boar. By the thirteenth century, it was being made from the animal's forequarters, though all the carcass could be used except the head. This, more often than not, was boned, stuffed and highly decorated to provide the centrepiece of the main course. Brawn usually followed at the end of the banquet, either highly spiced and peppered, or sliced in sweet sauces of wine and honey, or almonds and sugar. Within the next 100 years, however, it was to gain a different companion, and move its place in the feast.

In 1387, the Bishop of Durham gave a magnificent banquet at his London palace for Richard II and the Duke of Lancaster. Among the hundreds of dishes to emerge from the ecclesiastical kitchens was a newcomer – 'Brawne with Mustard'. Sixteen years later, the dish appeared again, in the second remove, at the celebratory marriage feast of Henry IV and Joan of Navarre and by the middle of the century the combination was firmly established. 'Set forth mustard and brawne,' said Russell in his *Boke of Nurture* in 1460, advice faithfully followed by George Nevill, Archbishop of York at his grand enthronement banquet in 1467. More significantly, the brawn appeared as an appetizer – 'First brawn and mustard out of course, served with malmsey', its place still sufficiently unusual to cause comment. From thereon it tended always to be the opening dish, and mustard its traditional accompaniment.

By Tudor times brawn had come to be particularly associated with the Christmas table, although still occupying a high place of honour at banquets. By now it was being made from the domesticated pig as its wild cousin was extinct. The art of brawn-making started to decline in the eighteenth century, although it still appeared at Christmas, together with hogs puddings – black and white puddings or gallotines. These had been popular since Roman times, when they were served (according to Apicius) with mustard, although the recipe had been simplified over the centuries.

What had – indeed has – not changed during all those years was the traditional accompaniment: mustard. In fact, in all the ancient manuscripts, mustard was the constant companion to almost every offal dish, a point repeatedly made by Samuel Pepys. Many a dinner is described in his diary, and not only is his enjoyment obvious, so, too, is the necessity for mustard. 24 October 1662 saw him having 'a dish of tripes of my own directing covered with mustard, as I have heretofore seen them done at my Lord Crewe's'. The next day he 'Dined at home with my wife upon a good dish of neats' feet and mustard, of which I made a good meal.'

The lack of mustard in the house on 23 April 1663 had unfortunate consequences: 'At cards till late, and being at supper, my boy being sent for some mustard to a neat's tongue, the rogue stayed half an hour in the streets, it seems at a Bonfire, at which I was very angry and resolve to beat him tomorrow.' The morrow dawned, Pepys was 'up betimes, and with my salt Eele went down in the parler and there got my boy and did beat him till I was fain to take breath two or three times.'

One hundred years later, mustard was still making frequent – although less colourful – appearances in Hannah Glasse. Her recipes for Ragouts of Hogs Feet and Ears, To Fry Tripe, To Stew Tripe all have mustard, either in the cooking or as a sauce, 'Butter and Mustard in a Cup'. The association continued through to the next century although by this time much offal was considered 'lowly' food. The presence of mustard was logical: offal is often not only rich but at the same time rather bland. Some piquancy is needed to balance these qualities, as indeed it is to spice the rather delicate taste of veal. For that too, in the past, was given a sharp sauce, often of mustard.

Veal and the British have an ambivalent relationship. The Romans were partial to the meat and undoubtedly introduced it to England. Apicius has several veal recipes, including a fricassée which calls for

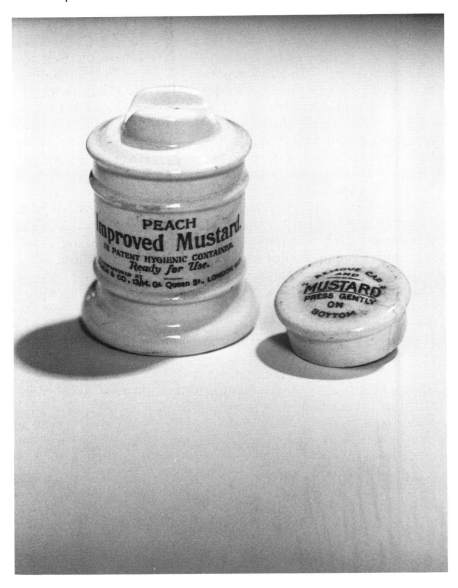

Peach's mustard dispenser filled with cartridges
of mustard from below. The scoop is to fit a knife.
c. 1860s

mustard. But with the break-up of the Roman Empire, and the rise of the Anglo Saxons – who measured their wealth in cattle – veal disappeared from the menu until the Normans arrived. Probably the earliest recipe we have is in *The Forme of Curye*. Richard II must have been fond of veal for this is a simple, but delicious, dish using the leftovers in Veal Fritters. The meat appeared in many other guises, particularly on 'skuets' (small skewers) and as an Easter highlight. Along with the side of bacon (and, for the rich, milk-fed lamb) was veal pie, made from the minced meat, dried fruits, spices, wine and eggs. For the Tudors, big was beautiful, and whole legs, roasted, were the festive norm.

By the seventeenth century, the new influx of French-trained cooks were both harking back to and moving away from the medieval influences. Elegant and highly popular was the veal olive: a thin slice of meat, rolled round a spicy forcemeat, then roasted. Mustard was particularly recommended with certain veal dishes, typically breast of veal, especially when 'collared' (boned, stuffed, rolled, then roasted) or 'soused' in a strong pickling brine and boiled. An early eighteenth-century manuscript, discovered by Beverly Nichols in the 1930s, is quite explicit in its directions for this dish: 'you may make sauce w[ith] butter Vinegar & mustard it w[ill] eat very well Cold.' Similar sauces appear repeatedly through the century while the repertoire of dishes is considerably widened, often to include one, or more, offals.

Veal was potted with tongue and called 'Marbled Veal', mixed with pork to make sausages (still so in Germany today, particularly *brat-wurst* which is usually eaten with a coarse-grained mild mustard), or ragouted with 'a dozen veal kidneys and 2 sweetbreads' – all to be served with mustard. By this time, meat was generally of a fine quality, a fact much appreciated by the food cognoscenti, such as Samuel Johnson. Many were the gossipy suppers he enjoyed at the Mitre in Fleet Street, where he tucked into veal pies – and mustard. By now, the pies often contained the veal kidneys and sweetbreads as well as chopped meat. The association of veal with offal continued well into Victoria's reign, but with the Edwardians offal came into its own. Sweetbreads, liver and kidneys were especially favoured.

Today, the price of these delicacies is positively regal when calf is their origin, perhaps reflecting a certain snobbishness. Or perhaps it was always so: a calf's head was the vital factor in 'mock' turtle soup, a dish that graced many a grand eighteenth-century dinner table. And veal tripe in Italy is considered far superior, with a price to match, to that of the older ox.

What is sad is the turnabout in fortune of those dishes once considered fit to put before a king: the Shield of Brawne, the Hot Puddings, the Soused Collars. Dishes, which, though cheap of ingredient, reflected the care, ingenuity and skill of the cook if the right balance of texture and taste was to be achieved. Dishes which have been mustard's main companions for a very long time.

Brawn with Lombard Mustard

If the thought of making brawn is daunting – let it not be. On the medieval principle of using anything *but* the head, it is indeed a simple dish. Brining is not essential but does add vastly to the flavour: if you don't have an obliging butcher to salt the meat for you, it *is* worth the little extra trouble.

SERVES 8_10
900 g/2 lb hand and spring of
  pork, or a blade piece, on
  the bone
2 pig's trotters
Maldon salt
freshly ground white pepper
freshly ground allspice
lemon juice
For the brine
350 g/12 oz rock or sea salt
175 g/6 oz brown sugar
25 g/1 oz saltpetre
3 litres/5 pints of water
For the bouillon
1 large onion, coarsely
  chopped, some skin
  reserved
1 thyme sprig
3–4 parsley sprigs
1 mace blade
2 cloves
4 juniper berries, lightly
  crushed
nutmeg (end pieces, too small
  for grating, are ideal)

6 black peppercorns, lightly
  crushed
2 garlic cloves, peeled but left
  whole
1 celery stick
For the mustard sauce
2 tablespoons coarse-ground
  mustard powder
1 1/2 tablespoons cider vinegar
2 teaspoons honey
2 tablespoons sweet, fortified
  wine – sherry, Marsala,
  Madeira (ginger wine is also
  good) – plus extra

Hand and spring joints are often pre-cut and quite large, so if you don't have a butcher who will cut it to size for you, buy a blade. To make the brine, bring all the ingredients to the boil and simmer – quite hard – for about 20 minutes, skimming off the scum occasionally. Strain and leave to cool then pour into a large earthenware crock or bowl. Add the pork joint and the trotters, making sure all are completely covered by brine, then weight them down – an old round bread board is ideal for this (it must of course be scrupulously clean) with a non-porous rock or stone on top, or else a heavy china bowl. Leave for 24 hours (longer if more convenient, but the meat may then need soaking before cooking to rid it of excessive salt).

Drain the meat, then place in a large pan, add the bouillon ingredients and plenty of cold water to cover. Bring to the boil, cover, and simmer at the gentlest of heats for 2–2 1/2 hours. Remove the meat from the pan and cool. Strain the stock and taste. If it is quite salty, simply season – fairly highly – with freshly ground white pepper and allspice, then stir in the lemon juice – 1 whole small lemon should do. If the stock is not too salt, then reduce by hard boiling, tasting every 5 minutes, to about 600 ml/1 pint, before seasoning.

Pick out all the meat from the trotters, discarding the skin and gristle. Take the meat off the main joint and chop finely. Do not be tempted to mince or chop it in a food processor – you will have a nasty mush on your hands. Taste the meat for salt, no extra should be needed, unless it was not brined. Place in a large bowl, round cake tin or loaf tin, then pour over enough seasoned stock to cover well, mixing thoroughly. Leave to cool, then cover with greaseproof paper and weight it with a plate (or another loaf tin) which will fit just inside your bowl or tin. Chill for 12–24 hours (it can be left for 2–3 days).

About one hour before serving, make the sauce (of medieval origin, taken from *The Forme of Curye*). Heat the honey, gently, with the vinegar and sweet wine. Plunge the bottom of the pan in cold water to cool quickly, then stir the mixture into the mustard powder. Leave for 30 minutes, by which time the mustard will have thickened considerably. You can either serve it as it is, or thin it down with a little extra wine as you please. Richard II's cook made 'it thynne with wyne' – we prefer it thicker, but this does depend on the powder's absorbing capacity, the time it has been left and your taste.

Black Pudding and Apple Fritters with Mustard and Apple Juice Sauce

In nearly all the medieval illuminated manuscripts which depict the great slaughter, there appears in the background a group of people making black puddings. These had to be made swiftly after the kill since fresh blood was of the essence – a point still agreed upon by the black-pudding makers of today.

For the best of these we have – once again – to turn to the North, to the old market towns of Bury, in Lancashire, and Barnsley, in Yorkshire, with their 'black pudding' stalls: Chadwicks, established in Bury in 1865, and Albert Hirst, their Barnsley rival – one of the few Englishmen to excel at the black pudding contests held in Mortagne-au-Perch where black puddings are serious business. Wiltshire, long famous for its pigs, has black puddings too – slender and elegant, like the puddings of the Shires rather than the fat and round shapes preferred in the North. Ireland has her own version, drisheen, similar to the French *boudin*. Unlike the French, no one on this side of the Channel marries apples to these blood sausages – despite our predilection for apple sauce and pork. Yet it is a natural partnership, the cleanness of the apple cutting through the richness of the pudding. Apple pancakes are good, so, too, simply sautéd slices of apple, but best of all are these apple fritters much loved by the medievals.

SERVES 4
about 350 g/12 oz black
pudding, sliced
lemon juice

For the sauce
*100 ml/3½ fl oz mild chicken
   stock*
*100 ml/3½ fl oz apple juice,
   unsweetened*
2–3 teaspoons Dijon mustard
¼ teaspoon arrowroot
For the fritters
3 small Cox's apples
1 large egg
275 g/10 oz flour
pinch of salt
oil for frying

Squeeze a little lemon juice over the black puddings and leave aside. Heat the chicken stock and apple juice gently. Mix 2 teaspoons mustard with a little warm stock to a thin paste, then stir into the pan. Mix the arrowroot with a little cold water and reserve.

Make the batter by beating the egg with 225 ml/8 fl oz cold water until frothy, then fold in the flour whisking thoroughly until lump-free and smooth. Or simply combine the whole lot in a food processor. Core and peel the apples then slice. Pour about half the batter into a shallow dish, add the apples and turn them over several times to coat thoroughly, adding a little more batter if necessary. (Make pancakes with the leftover batter – easier than measuring half an egg!)

Pour a good inch of oil into a wide pan and heat gently until just beginning to smoke. Put the black pudding under a medium grill. When the oil is hot, add a few slices of apple – don't overcrowd the pan or they'll stick together. Cook for 2–3 minutes each side until golden and puffy. Drain on to absorbent paper and cook the rest, meanwhile turning the black pudding. Turn the heat up under the sauce, when just simmering whisk in the arrowroot to thicken *very* slightly (this is a thin dipping sauce). Pour into small bowls. Drain the remaining apple fritters and serve at once with the hot black pudding.

Calves' Liver
with Lime Juice, Pine Kernels and Mustard

Calves' liver today vies with, and sometimes beats, steak in price. However it is one of the finest offals and deserves luxurious treatment.

And if the price is too daunting, you can use lamb's liver (pig is a little strong in flavour for this dish) *provided* it is cut finely – almost onion-skin thin – and soaked in milk for about half an hour before cooking. Without a very obliging butcher, the best thing to do is buy the liver in a piece (about 450 g/1 lb for 4), lightly freeze, then cut it yourself.

SERVES 4
450–550 g/1–1¼ lb calves'
liver, cut very thinly
a few strips of lime zest, pith
removed
juice of 2 fresh limes
1–2 teaspoons mild Dijon
mustard
Maldon salt
freshly ground black pepper
50 g/2 oz unsalted butter
50 g/2 oz pine nuts
1 tablespoon sweet sherry
a little finely chopped parsley

Lightly wash the liver in cold water just to remove any blood. Shred the lime zest, blanch in boiling water for 3–4 minutes, drain and reserve. Mix together the lime juice and mustard and dip the liver slices into the juice before lightly seasoning with salt and pepper.

Melt the butter in a large heavy frying pan. When it is bubbling add the pine nuts and cook for a minute, tossing until pink. Remove with a slotted spoon and reserve.

Add the liver to the pan and cook quickly on both sides – 30–45 seconds per side will be enough if it has been finely cut. It should be just lightly pink on the inside and golden without. Put on a serving plate, add the lime juice mixture and sherry to the pan, bubble for another minute then pour over the liver. Scatter on the nuts, the lime zest and the parsley and serve immediately. This is not a dish to be kept waiting.

Veal Kidneys Sautéed with Juniper Berries, Sage, White Wine and Mustard

Devilled kidneys, or steak and kidney pie, tend to be our answers to kidneys. Nothing wrong in that: they are perfectly good dishes, particularly for pig's kidneys which are stronger in flavour and better suited to such rumbustious treatment. But veal kidneys possess a certain delicacy, requiring greater subtlety.

SERVES 4
4 small or 2 large veal kidneys
25 g/1 oz unsalted butter
1 tablespoon olive oil
Maldon salt
freshly ground black pepper
8 juniper berries, lightly
   crushed
3 small fresh sage leaves, finely
   chopped and lightly crushed
150 ml/¼ pint fruity white
   wine
½ teaspoon mild Dijon
   mustard

Remove the fat from around the kidneys (keep it and render for future occasions) then slip off the thin outer membrane. Cut in half through the middle and snip out the fat from the 'heart'. Cut, slightly on the diagonal, into thin slices. Melt the butter with the oil in a large frying pan, *lightly* season the kidneys with salt and pepper then add to the pan and cook, flipping over the slices for about 45 seconds – they should be opaque in colour with tiny droplets of blood on the surface. Remove to a serving dish. Add the juniper berries and sage leaves, then pour in the wine. Raise the heat and bubble fiercely for 30 seconds, then whisk in the mustard. Do not be tempted to add more – it should hardly taste. Pour over the meat and serve at once. Croûtons are the classic garnish, particularly nice if dipped into finely chopped parsley when just out of the frying pan. And, in an ideal world, Gewürztraminer would be the wine used. Drink the rest of the bottle with the kidneys.

Braised Lamb Tongues

Neat's tongue (ox tongue) was a highly popular dish and tongue was also used as an ingredient in the original, and complex, mince pies. François Misson wrote about 'Christmas Pye . . . being eaten everywhere . . . it is a most learned Mixture of Neats-tongues, Chicken,

Eggs, Sugar, Raisins, Lemon and Orange, various Kinds of Spicery . . .'
Not quite our taste today and, with ox tongue the price it is, rather an
extravagance. Lambs' tongues, however, are economical and we can
take a tip from the flavourings in that pie, for orange and lemon juices
add a nice touch of sweet sharpness to the sauce.

SERVES 4
700 g/1½ lb lambs' tongues,
   root end trimmed
Maldon salt
2 tablespoons olive oil
25 g/1 oz unsalted butter
6 leeks, cut in half lengthways
6 large carrots, quartered
   lengthways
24 small button onions, peeled
   but left whole
6 inner celery stalks
50 g/2 oz streaky bacon,
   derinded and cut across into
   thin strips
3–4 garlic cloves, peeled but
   left whole
juice of 1 large sweet orange
   or, even better, 2 blood
   oranges
juice of 1 small lemon
1 bay leaf
1 thyme sprig
small posy of parsley, stalks
   cut off and tied in a bundle,
   curly tops finely chopped
   and reserved
freshly ground black pepper
freshly ground allspice
1 tablespoon Moutarde Soyer
   (p.62)
½ teaspoon tomato purée
2 tablespoons beurre manié
   (equal volumes of flour and
   butter mashed together to a
   paste)

Put the tongues in a large bowl and cover with cold water, mixing in 1 tablespoon of salt to every litre/1¾ pints water. Leave overnight. This mild brining vastly improves the flavour. Drain the meat and place in a pan covered with fresh cold water. Slowly bring to the boil, skim off any scum, then cover and simmer on the lowest possible heat for about 1½ hours. Remove the meat and leave until cool enough to handle, reserving the stock.

Trim the bones and any gristle from the root end of the tongues then peel by slitting down the middle with a sharp pointed knife. The skin should then easily peel away. Either cut the tongues in half through the middle or into thickish diagonal slices.

Heat the oil and butter in a large flameproof casserole, add the onions and sweat for 5 minutes, then add the leeks, carrots, celery stalks, garlic and bacon. Glaze the vegetables then make into a flat bed for the meat.

Taste the reserved stock: if it seems salty, bearing in mind that the final sauce will be reduced by a good third, measure out 300 ml/½ pint and make up to a generous 450 ml/¾ pint with water. If it is not too salt, then simply measure out the full amount. Pour over the vegetables, add the orange and lemon juices and the herbs, including the parsley stalks but not the curly tops. Bring the liquid to boiling point, lower the heat and lay the tongues on their bed. Season with black pepper and a little allspice, lay a buttered greaseproof paper over the tongues, then cover the pan and cook very gently for a good hour, until the meat is quite tender.

Remove the tongues from the pan, then the vegetables, arranging them on a large serving dish and placing the meat on top. Cover with foil and keep warm in a low oven.

Bring the juices in the pan to a rapid boil and reduce by about a third. Mix the mustard with the tomato purée and whisk into the sauce, then add the *beurre manié*, little by little and constantly whisking until the sauce is thickened. You may not need all the *beurre manié* – this depends both on your reduction and preference as to thickness. Pour over the tongues and scatter with the chopped parsley. Season again with a little more black pepper and freshly ground allspice.

Noisettes of Veal with Mostarda di Venezia

One of the problems in buying veal is that different countries joint the animal in different ways. Properly, the noisettes, or medallions, are taken from the 'silverside' – a lengthwise-cut, small joint from the back of the leg above the knuckle. It looks very similar to the fillet in shape and size, although close comparison will reveal that the medallions have a more pronounced grain. To add to the confusion, it is often called the fillet which truly comes from the inside of the loin (like beef), although technically any boneless cut can be called a fillet. Even more confusingly, the *noix de veau* is a larger joint, also cut lengthwise, but higher up from the chump end of the loin (similar to topside of beef). This will not do for your noisettes although, if your butcher follows the traditional English cuts for veal, you are not likely to encounter that problem for the leg is usually cut *crosswise* into roasting joints. The obvious solution is to know your butcher and which method of butchering he practises, and make sure he tells you whether the medallions are from the leg or the true fillet. The latter is fine of course, but will probably be more expensive and will not need quite so long a cooking time.

SERVES 6
6 noisettes of veal, about 2
    cm/3/4 inch thick
Maldon salt
freshly ground black pepper
40 g/1 1/2 oz unsalted butter
200 ml/7 fl oz white wine
50 g/2 oz Parma ham, cut into
    fine dice
4 tablespoons Mostarda di
    Venezia (p.71)
lemon juice
Dijon mustard (optional)

Lightly flatten the noisettes, season with a little salt and black pepper and leave aside. Melt the butter gently, and when sizzling add the veal. Cook for 1 minute each side then pour in the wine. Bubble for a minute or two, then sprinkle in the diced ham. Turn the heat low and simmer, covered, very gently for 20–25 minutes until the meat is very tender when pierced with a skewer. Meanwhile, mix the Mostarda di Venezia with a tablespoon or so of lemon juice to lightly sharpen.

Transfer the noisettes to a warmed dish, add the Mostarda to the pan and stir over a high heat until bubbling and very hot. Taste and add a touch more lemon if necessary and a spot of Dijon mustard if you wish. Serve at once.

Fricassée of Veal with Fennel and Mustard Seed

Fricassées entered our kitchens in the late sixteenth century, quite a few years before the *daube*. Since we now tend to lump the two together with ragouts and casseroles to denote any kind of stew, its earlier appearance has no apparent significance until we remember that the fork at this time was a rare, and treasured, implement of the very rich – mainly used to eat pears and ginger in syrup. And *fricasser*, from the early French, originally meant to mince, later to chop very small, thus rendering meat suitable as 'spoon' fare. Early gravies were thin, often simply highly spiced wine, reminiscent of medieval potages – though without the mustard that Apicius recommends for fricassée. By the late seventeenth century (when forks were more familiar) the meat was still chopped, though not so small, and the gravy had become a thicker sauce with more subtle flavourings.

SERVES 4–6
*900 g/2 lb pie veal, trimmed of
    any fat and gristle*
2 tablespoons flour
*1 tablespoon black pepper,
    freshly ground*
1 tablespoon oregano
Maldon salt
3 tablespoons olive oil
1 tablespoon unsalted butter
3 tablespoons pine nuts
*1 tablespoon white mustard
    seed*
1 large onion, finely chopped
*75 ml/3 fl oz Cinzano or dry
    white wine*
*600 ml/1 pint veal or chicken
    stock*
*3 fresh fennel stalks, feathery
    sprigs removed and*

reserved, or 2 dried fennel
stalks and 5−6 sprigs fresh
fennel
150 ml/¼ pint double cream
lemon juice
2−3 tablespoons Dijon
mustard

Mix the flour with the pepper, oregano and a good seasoning of salt, then sprinkle all over the veal. Heat the oil, add the pine nuts and cook for a minute until pink, then remove. Add the mustard seeds to the pan and cook, covered, until they start to spit. Drain them and reserve with the pine nuts, return the oil to the pan, add the butter and, when melted, the veal. Sear lightly. Remove the meat, add the onions and sweat, gently, for 10 minutes.

Return the meat to the pan, pour in the Cinzano and bubble hard for 1 minute, then pour over the stock. Bury the fennel stalks in the meat, cover the pan and cook, the merest hint of a simmer, for 2 hours until the meat is meltingly tender. Remove the fennel stalks. Beat the cream with a squeeze of lemon juice and the mustard and stir into the pan. Cook over a highish heat for a couple of minutes until the sauce thickens slightly then pile into a tureen. Sprinkle with the reserved pine nuts and mustard seed. Chop the fennel sprigs very finely and strew on top. Serve at once.

Cold Loin of Veal with Sour Mustard Sauce

Loin of veal has always been considered one of the great or 'gross' meats: usually roasted, to be served, said Master Chiquart, with 'the proper sauce'. Often this was a Camelyne sauce – sweet, spicy and sharp, with raisins, currants, ginger, cloves and vinegar. Italy uses veal perhaps most deliciously in the glorious Vitello Tonnato – cold veal with a tunny sauce. We've adapted that principle, poaching rather than roasting the veal to ensure maximum tenderness and succulence, adding a sour cream mustard sauce, spiced with the medieval flavourings.

SERVES 4−6
900 g/2 lb loin of veal, boned
  weight
50 g/2 oz unsalted butter

2 *tablespoons olive oil*
300 ml/¹/₂ pint dry white wine
1 bay leaf
1 sage sprig
2 parsley sprigs
freshly ground black pepper
Maldon salt
finely chopped chervil
For the sauce
175 ml/6 fl oz soured cream
1–2 tablespoons lemon juice
1¹/₂ teaspoons icing sugar
1 slightly heaped tablespoon
  Dijon mustard
¹/₄ teaspoon four-spice
  mixture (p.63)
25 mm/1 in piece fresh root
  ginger, peeled and grated

Roll and tie the veal into a neat sausage shape, then season lightly with salt and black pepper. Melt the butter with the oil in a pan into which the meat will fit snugly. Add the veal and brown on all sides, lower the heat, add the herbs and pour in the wine. Bring to a simmer, then cook, covered, *most* gently, for 1¹/₂–2 hours until the meat is very tender. If necessary, use a heat-diffusing mat, checking the pan occasionally and adding a little water (or stock ideally) to prevent the pan from becoming dry. You don't want too much juice at the finish of cooking, but you do want 4–5 tablespoons nicely concentrated liquor.

Remove the meat from the pan and cool. Add 2–3 tablespoons water to the juices in the pan and deglaze over a high heat. Cool slightly. Mix together all the sauce ingredients, then whisk in the cooking liquor. Slice the veal thickly, arrange on a platter and pour over the sauce. Leave for at least 2 hours before serving, liberally sprinkled with finely chopped chervil.

VEGETABLES AND PICKLES

'Very true,' said the Duchess: 'flamingoes and mustard both bite. And the moral of that is – "Birds of a feather flock together."'

'Only mustard isn't a bird,' Alice remarked.

'Right, as usual,' said the Duchess: 'what a clear way you have of putting things!'

'It's a mineral, I *think*,' said Alice.

'Of course it is,' said the Duchess, who seemed ready to agree to everything that Alice said: 'there's a large mustard-mine near here. And the moral of that is – "The more there is of mine, the less there is of yours."'

'Oh, I know!' exclaimed Alice, who had not attended to this last remark, 'it's a vegetable. It doesn't look like one, but it is.'

Alice's Adventures in Wonderland, Lewis Carroll

Throughout history, mustard is mentioned as being grown for its leaves, and it still is in China, India, parts of Europe, Africa and the south-eastern states of America, where considerable quantities are produced. No one knows when exactly the plant started to be cultivated for its greenery, although it was first introduced as such into Louisiana by the French. The Negro slaves soon took it into their kitchen – the peppery taste perhaps reminding them of home. It quickly became a staple and made an early – and lasting – marriage with salt pork and bacon, still a classic dish of the Black South. Nutritionally, however, it has occasionally caused problems in poor, inland communities. For mustard greens contain minute traces of 'goitrogens', which, in people on an iodine-deficient diet eating vast quantities of the leaf, can affect the thyroid's ability to use iodine, thus causing the gland to swell. The problem is rare and, for most, mustard greens are highly beneficial providing a good source of calcium, Vitamins A and C, iron and potassium. The flavour, raw, is pungently biting and a few young leaves mixed with other salad greens add a nice pep. Cooked, the flavour is less pronounced – a mildly peppery spinach would be an apt description. The Chinese – who frequently use mustard greens as a vegetable – also have a spinach salad which is dressed with mustard, sesame oil and vinegar which is remarkably similar in taste to a cooked mustard leaf salad.

The French seem first to have appreciated the mustard plant only for its vegetable qualities: Charlemagne (*c.* AD 800) merely states of mustard that it is a plant whose leaves can be eaten raw or cooked. There is not a mention anywhere of its use as a spicing ingredient. Centuries later, the leaf was still important in its own right. Thomas Jefferson appreciated it highly and grew it in his garden.

The precedents were ancient. Aesculapius wrote of the 'green plant' that it was a 'wholesome and agreeable herb', while Apicius has a 'dish of field vegetables' – a purée thickened with beaten eggs – which, according to some translations, contains 'green mustard' though other sources state that should read 'green peppers'. We do know, however, that the Romans pickled mustard leaves in vinegar and in AD 300 Diocletian noted that his subjects in the East ate mustard as a condiment *and* a vegetable. Far away, in China, the ancients were also pickling mustard greens. They still do, and their famous 'snow pickle' is a classic winter dish.

It is as a component in pickling, rather than as a pickle itself, that mustard has had one of its oldest and most consistent roles. The white seed in particular has highly preservative qualities, and is one of the prime ingredients in pickling spice mixes. Menandiers, around 300 BC, was pickling turnips in vinegar with mustard seed, a relish the Romans enjoyed as an appetizer: as a pickle they added mustard seed to beetroots.

Pride of place for pickles and chutneys though must go to India. The use of the seed in their pickles – hot, mild or sweet – is legion, although on fast days in certain regions only pickles without mustard seed are permitted. So, too, with the *tarkas* – a mixture of seeds fried in hot oil, often with chilli and/or garlic. Mustard seed is a prime component of these, except on a fast day, when cumin is substituted.

However, for normal pickling purposes, mustard is vital. Perhaps not in such quantities as those proposed in a charming little pamphlet probably from the twenties: 'Receipts for Cooking the Most Favourite Dishes in general use In India, Also for Preparing Chatney and India Pickle by Hadjee Allee Native of Calcutta'. Three-quarters of a pound of mustard (seed and paste) in addition to four ounces of cayenne and eleven ounces of other spices, to a mere six pints of vinegar is a trifle alarming. However, modern recipes from Bengal for vegetables with mustard are enticing. Interestingly, the combination of ground mustard and sugar – so beloved of medieval Europe – also appears here: especially in dishes of mixed vegetables, cooked in a little oil, the mustard and sugar then stirred in at the finish.

For vegetable curries, mustard oil is considered the best cooking medium, and the seeds are also used to spice many individual vegetable dishes. Moving northward, one finds the leaf – 'mustard spinach' – prominent on the table, most notably in the famous Punjabi dish, Sarson ka Saag (p.241).

If you mention mustard greens to the British, most will think of mustard and cress. Yet the greenery here is actually the cress, mustard supplying its seed. But one can also sow the seed (white) on damp absorbent paper and within a couple of days harvest a little forest of sprouts. Delicious for scattering like parsley, and perfect for delicate sandwiches.

Mustard Greens in Coconut Milk

China, as well as the American South, combines mustard greens with salt pork in a delicious soup. And many of the Caribbean islands have a traditional soup/stew with salt pork, crab and coconut milk combined with another green leaf often called callaloo (actually from the taro plant). Crab contains iodine – the ideal nutritional partner for mustard greens – and coconut milk sweetens their peppery flavour.

SERVES 4–6
450 g/1 lb mustard greens,
    washed and shredded finely
1.5 litres/2½ pints chicken
    stock
3 onions, finely chopped
3 garlic cloves, crushed
1 thyme sprig, leaves stripped
    off the stalk
125 g/4 oz salt belly of pork,
    finely diced
175 g/6 oz white crabmeat

50 g/2 oz creamed coconut
freshly ground white pepper
Maldon salt (if necessary)

Pack the greens into a large saucepan, pour over the chicken stock, then add the onions, garlic, thyme and pork belly. Bring to the boil, then simmer gently for 30 minutes until the meat and greens are tender (mustard greens will never go completely limp like chard or spinach but they shouldn't be tough and chewy).

Add the crab and the creamed coconut, raise the heat slightly and stir for a few minutes to start melting the coconut. Simmer for a further 20 minutes, stirring occasionally and checking that the coconut has completely dissolved.

Season generously with pepper, add salt if necessary – this will depend on how salt the pork was – then pour into a large tureen.

Mustard Spinach – Sarson Ka Saag

When India was partitioned in 1947, the displaced refugees were often given a bag of mustard seed – as a 'start in life'. Quickly and easily, the leaves provided a nutritious food, the seeds an income and next year's harvest – their oil could even be used as fuel. This dish, using the greens, is one of the Punjab's most famous though is rarely met with in the West.

SERVES 4
900 g/2 lb mustard greens
2 turnips, finely chopped
2 celery stalks, finely chopped
3 tablespoons vegetable oil
2 large onions, finely chopped
25 mm/1 inch piece fresh root
  ginger, grated
¼ teaspoon chilli powder (or
  less)
Maldon salt

Wash the greens and shred finely, then shake off excess water. Pack into a large saucepan then sprinkle over the turnip and celery. Cook very gently, until softened – the greens should produce enough liquid for the cooking but check after 10 minutes and add a little water if necessary. 30–40 minutes stewing should be enough. Purée in a blender then return to the pan. Heat the oil until nearly smoking, add the onions and ginger and cook until golden. Stir in the chilli powder, then pour the mixture over the spinach purée. Season with a little salt, stir lightly and serve immediately.

Green Beans with Mustard

A curious similarity is displayed in two recipes for green beans with mustard from two kitchens many thousands of miles apart. Eastern India has a traditional dish of beans mixed with a mustard seed, garlic and green chilli paste, the whole garnished with a *tarka* of fried mustard seed and chilli powder. Apicius cooked his beans in broth, then added a paste of mustard seed, nuts, rue, honey and cumin. His garnish was a light sprinkling of vinegar. We have married the two recipes, using Roman mustard to provide the nutty element and adding cumin to the *tarka* to give an oriental flavour.

SERVES 4
450 g/1 lb green beans, topped
and tailed, then sliced
diagonally into 25 mm/1
inch pieces
Maldon salt
1/2–1 small green chilli, seeded
and finely chopped
1 fat garlic clove, crushed
1 teaspoon Roman mustard
(p.65)
2 tablespoons mustard oil
1/2 teaspoon brown mustard
seed
1/2 teaspoon cumin seeds

Cook the beans in salted boiling water for 5–8 minutes, depending on their age. They should be tender but with a slight bite still. Drain them and return the empty pan to the heat with 1 tablespoon of oil.

Blend the chilli, garlic and mustard together with a pinch of salt, add to the pan and stir-fry for 30 seconds. Add the beans and stir thoroughly, over a very low heat. In another small pan, heat the remaining oil, add the mustard seed and cumin, cover, and cook until they start to splutter. Pour over the beans and serve immediately.

Braised Leeks with Mustard

Leeks, onions and garlic all display a great affinity with mustard, the spice greatly enhancing the sweetness of the Allium family. Perhaps it is not so surprising: the leaves of many of the Cruciferae contain oil of garlic, and the Alliums have certain chemical substances also found in mustard seed.

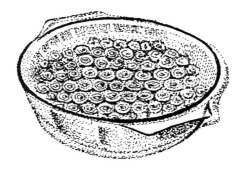

Braised leeks with mustard

SERVES 4
900 g/2 lbs medium leeks,
    washed and trimmed
300 ml/½ pint medium dry
    white wine, dry cider or
    chicken stock
2 teaspoons Dijon mustard
40 g/1½ oz unsalted butter
freshly ground black pepper
Maldon salt

Cut the leeks into 4 cm/1½ inch lengths. Arrange them, standing upright, in a large, fairly shallow and preferably circular dish, packing them tightly together (see illustration above). Mix the cooking liquid of your choice with the mustard and pour over, then dot with flakes of butter. Season, generously with black pepper, very lightly with salt.

Cook in the oven at 180°C/350°F/Gas Mark 4 for 30–40 minutes until the leeks are very tender and about two-thirds of the liquid is absorbed. Should there be any leftovers, they make a heavenly soup.

Stewed Red Cabbage with Mustard Cream

Despite other nations' views on British vegetable cooking, we have an extraordinarily rich heritage of delicious and seemingly, nowadays, unusual vegetable recipes. Pickled red cabbage seems to be the staple today: braised with apples, sugar and vinegar the vegetable is acknowledged as a good 'foreign' accompaniment to pork or goose. Yet it was a commonplace eighteenth- and nineteenth-century dish, simply stewed in butter with peppers – black and cayenne – with either gravy or a dash of vinegar added at the finish. Eliza Acton adds cream to Savoy cabbage; we have moved the idea to red cabbage, adding juniper berries and mustard.

SERVES 4–6
*1 small red cabbage, core
    removed*
125 g/4 oz unsalted butter
8 juniper berries
Maldon salt
freshly ground black pepper
150 ml/1/4 pint double cream
1 1/2 teaspoons Dijon mustard

Shred the cabbage very finely, wash under cold water, then shake lightly. As Maria Rundell charmingly puts it in *Domestic Cookery* (1806), the cabbage needs no water 'but what hangs about it'.

Melt the butter in a large heavy-bottomed pan (essential, to prevent burning), and crush the juniper berries. When the butter begins to bubble, add the berries to the pan, then tip in the cabbage and stir thoroughly. Cover with a very well-fitting lid and cook over the lowest possible heat for 3–4 hours until the cabbage is meltingly tender. Check frequently, stirring to prevent sticking, and only add water (or a little stock) if absolutely vital. Season with salt and a good helping of freshly ground black pepper, then mix the mustard with the cream and pour into the pan.

Raise the heat and cook, stirring, until the cream is bubbling and has thoroughly coated the cabbage.

Stewed Cucumbers in Mustard Cream

Cucumbers appeared in many guises in the eighteenth century: pickled, preserved, or in salads as today. They were also cooked – an idea we seem to have lost, but a good one, especially for those who are prone to indigestion after eating the vegetable raw. It is an excellent method for dealing with older cucumbers. Traditionally they were cooked in butter, or veal gravy, with sliced onions. Hannah Glasse added mustard – we've cut down on the butter, but added a touch of cream.

SERVES 6
3 medium-sized cucumbers,
    peeled, seeded and cut into
    5 cm/2 inch strips
3 small onions, finely sliced
50 g/2 oz unsalted butter
3 tablespoons chicken or veal
    stock
1 mace blade
Maldon salt
freshly ground white pepper
100 ml/3 1/2 fl oz double cream
lemon juice
1 teaspoon Dijon mustard
handful of finely chopped
    fresh chervil, parsley, fennel
    or tarragon

Melt the butter in a large pan, add the onions and sweat gently for 10 minutes. Add the cucumbers and sauté for 2 minutes, then stir in the stock, together with the mace blade, salt and a good grinding of white pepper. Cover the pan and stew gently for 6–10 minutes until the cucumber is soft but not mushy. Pour in the cream, add a squeezing of lemon juice, then stir in the mustard. Bubble for 1–2 minutes until the sauce is lightly thickened. Strew liberally with the herb of your choice and serve.

Potatoes with Mustard Seeds

Today there is a revival of interest in the potato: growers list varieties by the hundred, and it is once again, in many supermarkets and kitchens, being accorded the respect it received when Sir Francis Drake first brought it to England. We owe the partnership of mustard seed and potatoes to Western India, where garlic, cumin, turmeric, tomatoes and chilli are also added to give a spicy bed for eggs. Here, in a much simplified recipe, they make a delicious course by themselves.

SERVES 4–5
450 g/1 lb large new potatoes,
  scrubbed but not peeled
Maldon salt
1½ tablespoons peanut oil
1 small garlic clove
1 medium onion, very finely
  chopped
¼ teaspoon Dijon mustard
1 teaspoon brown mustard
  seed
finely chopped parsley or fresh
  coriander leaves

Boil the potatoes in salted water, drain and slice thickly. (If you must peel them, do so at this stage.)

Heat the oil in a large pan, add the onion and fry briskly until softened and golden. Crush the garlic with a pinch of salt and mix in the mustard. Add to the pan and cook for another 2 minutes to crisp the onions slightly and release the aroma of the garlic. Push to the sides of the pan. Add the mustard seeds, cover and cook until they start to spit. Add the potatoes, mixing gently so as not to break them up, then cook for a further 2 minutes until lightly browned. Pile on to a serving dish, scatter liberally with chopped parsley or coriander and serve.

Mustard-stuffed Lotus Root

The lotus flower – so beloved of romantic writers and, floating on the lakes of Kashmir, of tourists – is more prosaically enjoyed by the orientals for its culinary qualities. The roots are used by both Indian and Chinese cooks, the latter also cooking the seeds and employing the leaves as a flavour-imparting wrapper for steamed foods. The roots are long, thin and, when cut across, reveal an intricate network of holes – ideal for stuffing as in this recipe from Elizabeth Lambert Ortiz' *Japanese Cookery*.

SERVES 4

*1 medium-sized lotus root,
    about 18 cm/7 inches in
    length (available canned
    from Chinese and Japanese
    food stores)*
2 teaspoons rice vinegar
375 ml/13 fl oz light stock
¼ teaspoon soy sauce
¼ teaspoon salt
*2 teaspoons mirin (Japanese
    rice wine)*
*3 tablespoons dry Japanese or
    English mustard*
*3 tablespoons white bean
    paste*
1 teaspoon sugar
1 large egg yolk
1 small egg
50 g/2 oz flour
vegetable oil for frying

Peel the lotus root and drop into a pan of briskly boiling water and the vinegar. Simmer for 5 minutes, then drain. Return the pan to the heat, add the stock, soy sauce, salt and mirin together with the lotus root. Simmer for 5 minutes until the root is tender – there should be enough liquid to keep it covered. Remove the lotus root from the pan and cool.

Mix the mustard to a thick paste with 2–3 tablespoons hot water. Add the bean paste, sugar and egg yolk and mix until smooth. Using chopsticks and fingers, stuff the mixture into the holes running along the length of the root.

Break the egg into another bowl and whisk. Stir in 1 tablespoon of cold water, then add the flour mixing lightly with chopsticks to a batter. Coat the root with the batter.

In a heavy frying pan, heat enough oil to cover the root until bubbles form on chopsticks when they are stirred in the oil (180°C/350°F on a fat thermometer). Put the batter-coated lotus root into the pan and fry for 5 minutes, turning 2–3 times until lightly coloured. Lift out, drain on paper towels then cut into 15 mm/½ inch slices. Arrange on small plates.

'Cucumbers Pickled Like Mangoes'

Pickled mangoes reached Britain in the latter part of the seventeenth century and quickly attained great popularity. Since the fresh fruit was unobtainable, imitations soon appeared using cucumbers, marrows or melons as the base ingredient. The cucumber itself, although familiar to the Romans and possibly grown in English gardens during their occupation, had virtually disappeared until the fifteenth century when it was still considered a rarity. Although more widely cultivated over the next 200 years, it was still small and almost round (similar to a variety grown in Iran today) and therefore a more logical substitute than one might, at first, imagine. Oddly, when cucumbers were pickled as a preserve for the winter, there were no mustard seeds in the recipe. Only when they began to be pickled 'like mangoes' does the seed appear.

> *1 kg/2¼ lb small cucumbers,*
> *   ideally pickling ones*
> *2 teaspoons white mustard*
> *   seed*
> *4 large garlic cloves, very*
> *   finely chopped*
> *1 tablespoon freshly ground*
> *   allspice*
> For the spiced vinegar
> *1.7 litres/3 pints white wine*
> *   vinegar*
> *2 teaspoons black*
> *   peppercorns*
> *2 tablespoons Maldon or rock*
> *   salt*
> *1 tablespoon allspice berries*
> *5 cm/2 inch piece fresh ginger,*
> *   peeled and finely sliced*
> *2 teaspoons white mustard*
> *   seed*

Bring the vinegar to the boil with the pickling spices, remove from the heat and leave for 2–3 hours.

If you can get pickling cucumbers they merely need to be sliced lengthways and the seeds scooped out with an apple corer. Ordinary salad cucumbers will need to be cut into smaller lengths (to fit into the preserving jars) before deseeding. Mix together the mustard seed, garlic and freshly ground allspice, then pack into the spaces left by the seeds. Reassemble the cucumber pieces by tying two halves together with fine string and pack into sterilized jars.

Strain the vinegar, bring it again to the boil, then pour over the cucumbers. Cover the jars and leave for 24 hours. Drain off the vinegar, strain it (returning any floating spices to the jars) and heat to boiling point. Pour over the cucumbers, seal and again leave for a day. Repeat this procedure for 9 days by which time the cucumber should be 'of a good green'. You may need to add a little extra vinegar towards the end of the week. Keep for at least 3 weeks before use. Yield: about 1 kg/2¼ lb.

Mango Pickle

The pickled mangoes so popular with our ancestors cannot have been very hot, to judge by the cucumber/marrow recipes that abounded in imitation. Yet the traditional mango pickle of the Gujerati and Maharashtran kitchens in Western India is hot indeed – even this 'mild' version is not unpiquant, but the original recipe has 125 g/4 oz red chillies.

> 900 g/2 lb green mangoes
> 2–4 red chillies (to taste),
>   seeded and finely chopped
> 2 teaspoons fenugreek seed
> 50 g/2 oz Maldon salt
> 3 tablespoons brown mustard
>   seed
> ½ teaspoon ground asafoetida
>   (available from Indian
>   grocers)
> 1 tablespoon turmeric
> 450 ml/¾ pint vegetable oil

Cut the mangoes into quarters, slicing them away from the stone. It is almost impossible to do this job tidily, so do the best you can and place a bowl underneath to catch the juices. Chop the quarters coarsely, then scrape the remaining flesh off the stone and add to the bowl.

Blend the chillies with the fenugreek, salt and mustard seed – the mustard won't pulverize, but no matter – then mix into the asafoetida and turmeric. Bring the oil almost to boiling point and pour over the spice mixture. Stir into the mangoes, mixing quite thoroughly. Spoon the pickle into sterilized jars, making sure each has a good covering of oil. Cover and seal, then store in a cool place, shaking the jars well every day for a week. Yield: approximately 700 g/1 ½ lb.

Banana, Apple and Mustard Chutney

Intrigued by an Uncooked Apple and Banana Chutney in *The Apple Book* by Jane Simpson and Gill MacLennan, we added mustard and ground ginger. Very fruity, slightly piquant – extremely good.

> *3 medium-sized bananas,*
> * peeled and mashed*
> *450 g/1 lb onions, peeled and*
> * chopped*
> *450 g/1 lb cooking apples*
> *450 g/1 lb sultanas*
> *225 g/8 oz currants*
> *450 g/1 lb brown sugar*
> *300 ml/½ pint red wine*
> * vinegar*
> *1 teaspoon Maldon salt*
> *½ teaspoon cayenne pepper*
> *1 teaspoon freshly grated*
> * dried ginger root*
> *250 g/9 oz Dijon mustard*

Put the bananas and onions into a large bowl. Peel, core and chop the apples – add to the bowl. Then stir in all the remaining ingredients. Mix very thoroughly, then pot in sterilized jars. Keep for at least 2 weeks before using. The authors of the original recipe state that it will keep for up to a year. With the added mustard the preserving powers should be even greater though we found that, once opened, a jar rarely lasted very long. Yield: about 2.5 kg/5 ½ lb.

Piccalilli

Piccalilli is probably the most famous pickle of all – and certainly the best known mustard pickle, although it is actually turmeric which gives it that bright yellow colour. The recipe, and the name, have changed little through the years. *The Receipt Book* by A. Blencowe (1694) gives the delightful title 'To Pickle Lila – an Indian Pickle'.

> 900 g/2 lb cauliflower florets –
>   about 1.4 kg/3 lb
>   unprepared cauliflower
> 450 g/1 lb pickling onions,
>   peeled and quartered
> 450 g/1 lb carrots, cut into fine
>   matchsticks
> 450 g/1 lb white cabbage,
>   shredded
> 1 large cucumber, cut into
>   chunks
> 400 g/14 oz coarse rock or sea
>   salt
> 1.2 litres/2 pints cider vinegar
> 2 tablespoons mustard
>   powder
> 3 tablespoons white mustard
>   seed
> 4 tablespoons brown mustard
>   seed
> 3 mace blades
> 6 cloves
> 1 tablespoon turmeric
> 10 cm/4 inch piece fresh root
>   ginger, peeled and grated
> 1 teaspoon freshly ground
>   allspice
> 4 fat garlic cloves, cut into fine
>   slivers
> 175 g/6 oz castor sugar
> 2 tablespoons cornflour

Place the vegetables in a very large bowl (or 2), sprinkle with the salt and leave for 24 hours. Drain off the brine, rinse the vegetables in cold water. Put the vinegar, with the remaining ingredients except the cornflour, into a preserving pan (*not* aluminium) and bring to the boil. Turn the heat low, add all the vegetables and simmer gently for about 15–20 minutes until they are cooked but still have a 'crunch'. Mix the cornflour to a paste with 2 tablespoons cold water, stir into the pan and boil for a couple of minutes, stirring, to lightly thicken the juices. Ladle into sterilized jars and keep for at least 1 month before using. Yield: about 2.7 kg/6 lb.

PUDDINGS ET AL

I'm mad about mustard – even on custard! – Ogden Nash

Although it was a special 'mystery' pudding that started this mustard quest, we did wonder in the beginning how mustard would fare at the meal's end. Savouries, obviously, are no stranger to the condiment, particularly those of a cheesy nature. Welsh Rabbit is famous, the Scottish, English and Buck versions perhaps less so today. Devilled dishes of sardines, herring roes, crab, kidneys or lobsters all knew mustard and were popular dinner finales in the 1930s.

Mustard is no newcomer either to baking: cheese scones and straws spring immediately to mind. Mustard bread is perhaps less obvious, but the partnership is old. Medieval and Victorian peasant alike enjoyed bread and dripping but, with no dripping to hand, the rough dark brown bread would often be enlivened with a dip into the mustard pot. In certain parts of the North of England, a pinch of mustard was – indeed still is – mixed with the dripping before it went on to the bread. And Drover's Bread (a kind of northern Cornish pastry) was made with a mustard-spiced dough, stuffed with mustard-seasoned steak. Whether Northerners would knowingly countenance mustard in their gingerbread, or parkin, is a moot point. But undoubtedly at some stage they would have consumed it, since ginger was often adulterated with mustard to ease its exorbitant price. And a conscious addition of mustard makes for a deliciously spicy gingerbread (p.258). The French equivalent, *pain d'épices*, though usually translated as gingerbread, should perhaps be rendered literally – spiced bread – since it rarely seems to contain ginger. Dijon is the centre today for most of France's *pain d'épices*, and not surprisingly mustard is often one of the spices.

Tea time can see mustard with other partners. Chocolate's flavour is considerably strengthened and coffee, too, is given a boost. Frederick

Said Brother Bill to Simple Sue,
"Let's tuck into this custard."

But when they dipped their peckers in
They found the stuff was MUSTARD!

Postcard, *c.* 1900

the Great, an inordinate coffee drinker by all accounts, always added a pinch of mustard to his brew to bring out the flavour. It is curious, this chemical reaction that mustard has with certain flavourings and spices. Those with a bite – ginger, pepper, cayenne – are themselves heightened but also allow mustard's nip to come through. Where sweetness is of the essence – chocolate, nutmeg, cinnamon, allspice – mustard melds into the background leaving merely the full glory of the spice concerned.

The tang of the seed in Mostarda di Venezia or Cremona is of course quite noticeable, though for those in ignorance of mustard's presence, the flavour is not definable. This led us to experiment with other fruits. Chestnuts, curiously, became quite chocolatey; mango, rhubarb and plums were intense in their fruitiness whilst pears added to a mustard blancmange (p.256) proved Ogden Nash oddly correct. But the flavour of the mustard was greatly softened, absorbed to a good degree by the bland sweetness of the fruit leaving the custard with a definite – though again indefinable – piquancy. Bananas are another fruit made intense by mustard, which is useful for making banana bread with less than very black bananas. We found a strange recommendation, made by a Mustard Club member, of mustard with Christmas pudding. Yet strangely, a little dab of mustard spread on hot Christmas puddings does bring out the full richness of the fruits.

There is a huge field here open to exploration: chocolate and rhubarb mousses – add mustard to the melting chocolate before mixing with puréed rhubarb and whipped cream; iced mousses of *mascarpone* and Mostarda di Venezia; perhaps some Mostarda di Cremona mixed into a fresh fruit salad. Most simply, one could combine the sweet and the savoury with a beautifully mature farm-house Cheddar, a pot of Matthew's mustard (p.68) and some perfectly ripe fresh fruit. With a glass of fine port, or a lightly chilled, slightly fruity, Francken wine – what better way to end this pursuit of mustard?

Mostarda di Venezia and mascarpone served with La Colomba in Venice

La Colomba's 'Mystery Special'

La Colomba in Venice, home of the pud that started it all, is enchantingly decorated with paintings of doves – all originals from great artists including Braque and de Chirico. The special dessert echoes the theme, and is served in the form of two doves: pastry beaks and wings cleverly transform the spoonfuls of soft cheese and quince purée into tiny little birds.

Mascarpone – the soft creamy cheese so often used in Italy for sweet dishes – is simplicity itself to make but a thermometer *is* essential. Over- or under-heating will spell disaster.

SERVES 6
450 g/1 lb Mostarda di
  Venezia (p.71)
For the mascarpone
1.7 litres/3 pints double cream
scant ½ teaspoon tartaric acid

To make the *mascarpone*, start the day before. Pour the cream into the top half of a double boiler or into a bowl placed over a pan of simmering water. On a medium heat, bring the cream to a temperature of 80°C/180°F. Remove the pan from the heat and add the tartaric acid (a vegetable acid commonly used in baking powders and fizzy drinks, available from chemists). Stir for 30 seconds, then take the top part of the double boiler, or bowl, off the hot water. Stir for another 2 minutes, then pour the cream into a cheesecloth-lined large bowl. Leave in a cool place, or the lowest shelf of the refrigerator, for 12 hours before using.

To assemble the pudding, simply put 2–3 tablespoons each of the Mostarda and the *mascarpone* on to individual serving dishes and chill lightly. Decorate if you wish with tiny shortcrust pastry beaks and wings to make little doves.

Mustard and Pear Ring

We found the opening quote and illustration almost simultaneously. We wondered about mustard and custard, and then came upon an American recipe for a savoury blancmange to be served with a sweet fruit pickle. The combination did not quite work – but add pears and you have a deliciously piquant pudding.

SERVES 4–6
4 eggs, beaten
225 ml/8 fl oz cold water
125 ml/4 fl oz cider vinegar
200 g/7 oz sugar
1 sachet powdered gelatine
1–1½ tablespoons mustard
  powder
½ teaspoon turmeric
¼ teaspoon salt
3 ripe pears
225 ml/8 fl oz double cream,
  plus extra to serve
  (optional)
lemon juice
borage flowers

Combine the eggs, water, vinegar, sugar, mustard, turmeric and salt in a double boiler (or place in a bowl over a pan of simmering water).

Whisk constantly until the sugar is melted and everything amalgamated and slightly thickening. Sprinkle the gelatine over 2 tablespoons cold water in a small bowl, then place the bowl over another pan of simmering water and dissolve. Whisk into the custard, then leave to cool and slightly set.

Peel, core and finely chop or roughly mash one of the pears and stir into the custard. Whisk the cream until soft peaks form, and fold in. Pour into a ring mould and chill until set.

Just before serving, peel the remaining pears, slice finely and sprinkle with a little lemon juice. With a sharp pointed knife, run round the edges of the custard, dip the bottom of the ring in very hot water, put a plate over the mould, then turn over quickly – the ring should plop out neatly. Pile the sliced pears in the middle, scatter over the borage flowers and serve with extra cream – chilled – if wished.

Spiced Chestnut Cream

Strangely, mustard seems to make chestnuts taste of chocolate, rather than heightening their natural earthiness. Cacao intensifies this of course, but the effect is similar whatever the liqueur.

SERVES 4–6
225 g/8 oz unsweetened
    chestnut purée
125 g/4 oz unsalted butter
125 g/4 oz sugar
2 teaspoons cacao
1 tablespoon mustard powder
150 ml/¼ pint double cream,
    whipped
175 g/6 fl oz double or single
    cream, chilled, to serve

Heat the purée with the butter and sugar, stirring constantly until melted. Add the cacao and mustard powder and cook for a further 2 minutes. Remove the pan from the heat and leave to cool for 30 minutes.

Whisk in the whipped cream very thoroughly, then spoon into small bowls – old-fashioned custard glasses are nice – and chill overnight. Serve with chilled cream handed round separately.

Mango and Dill Mustard Iced Fool

Lovely as a starter with a mass of very finely chopped fresh dill – and refreshing as a dessert too, with caraway seeds or eau-de-Cologne mint to garnish.

SERVES 6
3 large or 6 medium-sized
    mangoes
3 tablespoons icing sugar
4 tablespoons natural yoghurt
3/4 teaspoon Dill mustard
    (p.60)
eau-de-Cologne mint or
    caraway seeds, to garnish

Peel the mangoes, then slice into a food processor or blender. Add the icing sugar and purée. Blend in the yoghurt and mustard then pour into six 125 ml/4 oz dariole moulds. Freeze overnight. Unmould about 5 minutes before serving and sprinkle with caraway seeds or finely chopped mint.

Spiced Gingerbread

Gingerbread has been a favourite for centuries: the medievals coloured it red with sandalwood, the Tudors black with ground liquorice. By Charles II's time, treacle was appearing on the scene and the ginger-bread reputedly enjoyed by him was dark and rich with candied orange and lemon peel, spicy with ground coriander and ginger. We have kept the coriander, and added fresh ginger and mustard to make a lovely sweet-spicy bread with a bite.

50 g/2 oz butter
50 g/2 oz soft dark brown
    sugar
125 ml/4 fl oz treacle
2 tablespoons soured cream
1 large egg, beaten
125 g/4 oz flour
1/4 teaspoon bicarbonate of
    soda

1 tablespoon coriander seeds,
    well crushed
1 tablespoon mustard powder
1 tablespoon ground ginger
40 mm/1 1/2 inch piece fresh
    root ginger, peeled and
    grated
1/4 teaspoon ground cinnamon

Heat the butter, sugar and treacle (to measure out the last, lightly oil a measuring jug and spoon – the treacle will then pour off easily), stirring until melted and well mixed together. Cool a little, then beat in the soured cream and egg, whisking very briskly. Stir in the sifted flour, bicarbonate of soda, coriander, mustard and ground ginger, then add the grated fresh ginger and cinnamon. Beat hard for 4–5 minutes, then pour into a greased 600 ml/1 pint loaf tin, or shallow ring or heart-shaped mould. Bake in the oven at 170°C/325°F/Gas Mark 3 for 35–40 minutes until it springs back when gently pressed with a finger. Cool then unmould. The bread can be iced if wished – a lemon and cinnamon glacé icing is good – but it is also excellent alone. Makes 8 slices.

Mustard Seed and Allspice Biscuits

Nutty from fried mustard seeds, sweet with allspice – the only disadvantage of these biscuits is that one never seems to make enough.

225 g/8 oz butter
175 g/6 oz sugar
6 tablespoons strong coffee
2 teaspoons mustard powder
few drops pure vanilla extract
275 g/10 oz self-raising flour
2 tablespoons brown mustard
    seed
1/2 tablespoon peanut oil
freshly ground allspice

Blend the first five ingredients in a food processor, or beat well together in a large bowl. Add the sifted flour and blend well in. Fry the mustard seeds in the oil in a covered pan until they start to spit. Drain.

Break off walnut-sized knobs of dough and roll between wetted palms, then flatten and place on greased baking sheets.

Scatter some mustard seeds over each biscuit, then sprinkle generously with freshly ground allspice. Bake in the oven at 180°C/350°F/Gas Mark 4 for 15–20 minutes until lightly golden at the edges. Remove from baking sheet and cool. Makes 40–45 biscuits.

Chocolate Fingers

On our visit to Colman's we were told that mustard greatly intensifies the flavour of chocolate. Indeed it does, particularly when cocoa powder is used for baking.

> 225 g/8 oz *unsalted butter or*
> *soft margarine*
> 225 g/8 oz *vanilla sugar*
> 2 *tablespoons natural yoghurt*
> 2 *tablespoons fresh orange*
> *juice*
> 1 *tablespoon mustard*
> *powder*
> 7 *tablespoons cocoa powder*
> 275 g/10 oz *plain flour*
> 1 *teaspoon baking powder*
> ¼ *teaspoon salt*
> *freshly ground black pepper*

Cream the butter and the sugar, either by hand or in a food processor. If you are using the latter, the remaining ingredients can then all be added at once, otherwise add one by one. Mix until thoroughly blended, then roll the dough into a long sausage shape. Place on a piece of foil or greaseproof paper, then flatten slightly – so that the biscuits will be finger-shaped. Roll and chill for at least 1 hour: although you can bake the biscuits immediately, it is more difficult to slice the dough finely. When it is chilled, very thin slices can easily be shaved off. Place on a greased baking tin, and cook in the oven at 190°C/375°F/Gas Mark 5 for 10 minutes if the slices were ⅛ inch thin, 12–13 minutes if a little thicker. For a slightly spicier biscuit, sprinkle with a little freshly ground black pepper before baking – this may sound odd, but black pepper and chocolate have met before. And it makes a deliciously piquant, very chocolatey biscuit. Any unused dough can be rewrapped and kept in the fridge for up to 2 days. Or freeze it and cut off slices with a freezer knife, giving them an extra minute or so in the cooking. Makes 55–60.

Mustard and Spring Onion Bread

Spicy with spring onions, this bread has a lovely earthy flavour which is brought out by the mustard. It is from Gail and Mick Duff's *Food from the Country*.

SERVES 4–6
1 teaspoon active dried yeast,
*   or 2 teaspoons dried yeast,*
*   or 15 g/½ oz fresh yeast*
1 teaspoon honey
150 ml/¼ pint milk, warmed
225 g/8 oz wholemeal flour
6 spring onions, finely
*   chopped*
3–4 teaspoons coarse-ground
*   mustard powder*
1 teaspoon Maldon salt

If using active dried yeast, mix all the dry ingredients together first, then stir the honey into the milk, pour into the bowl and mix thoroughly to a dough. Dried yeast will need to be scattered over the honey and milk and left to froth for 15 minutes, while fresh should be creamed with the honey and milk *before* being poured over the flour mixture. Turn the dough out on to a floured board and knead well, then return to a lightly oiled bowl, make a cross in the top and cover with a tea towel. Leave to rise for at least 1 hour until doubled in size. Knead again and form into a round, then lightly flatten. Cover with the cloth and prove for 20–30 minutes, then bake in the oven at 200°C/400°F/Gas Mark 6 for 25–30 minutes until golden. Cool on a wire rack.

Roast Cheese

A Georgian supper dish, often served after late card games or when the master of the house returned home late. Since even the most junior in the servants' hall could easily prepare it, there was no danger of upsetting Cook by keeping her up till all hours. It is one of the many variations of the famous Welsh Rabbit which abound in English early cookery.

SERVES 4
1 egg yolk
25 g/1 oz unsalted butter,
    softened
50 g/2 oz fresh white
    breadcrumbs
50 g/2 oz Farmhouse
    Lancashire or Cheshire
    cheese, finely grated
¼ teaspoon mustard powder
¼ teaspoon anchovy paste
Maldon salt
freshly ground white pepper
4 large slices of warm toast,
    cut into fingers

Mix together the egg, butter, breadcrumbs, cheese, mustard and anchovy paste, adding a little salt if using Cheshire but not with Lancashire – *real* Farmhouse Lancashire is deliciously salt on its own. Divide the mixture between four ramekins, cover with foil and bake in the oven at 180°C/350°F/Gas Mark 4 for 5–8 minutes until melted and bubbling. Remove the foil and cook for a further 2–3 minutes until very lightly browned. Serve, sprinkled with freshly ground white pepper, accompanied by toast fingers to dip into the cheese. Good port on the table, of course.

Glamorgan Sausages

Wales has always had fine cheeses, and made innovative use of them. Glamorgan sausages make a delicious supper or breakfast dish and fully warrant George Borrow's description, 'not a whit inferior to those of Epping'. Since the Epping sausage was noted for its meatiness, this was praise indeed.

SERVES 4
150 g/5 oz fresh white
    breadcrumbs

125 g/4 oz Caerphilly cheese,
  grated
5 cm/2 inch piece leek, very
  finely chopped
2 tablespoons finely chopped
  parsley
½ teaspoon thyme leaves,
  stripped from the stalk
1 teaspoon mustard powder
Maldon salt
freshly ground black pepper
1–2 egg yolks
1 egg white
day-old breadcrumbs for
  coating
lard or butter for frying

Mix together the breadcrumbs, cheese, leek, herbs and mustard powder, season with a little salt and lots of black pepper then bind with 1 egg yolk. If the mixture seems a little dry, add the second yolk. Form into small, thin sausages about 5 cm/2 inches long. Lightly beat the egg white, and dip in the sausages, then roll them in the dried breadcrumbs. Fry in lard or butter until golden brown, about 5–6 minutes, turning constantly but gently. Good hot or cold.

Trieste Spread

Tucked away, at the end of a reply to a reader's query in a back issue of *Bon Appétit*, was an intriguing comment on *mascarpone*. It stated that in the Trieste region it is mixed with gorgonzola, leek, caraway, anchovy and mustard to make a spread. Despite intensive research in Italy we found no evidence of this delicacy, however it sounded so interesting and the combination of ingredients so unlikely that we started to make it and eventually produced Trieste Spread. The name has now stuck though later we discovered in George Langs' *The Cuisine of Hungary* (where we should have looked, as Trieste was part of the Austro-Hungarian Empire until 1920) a spread called Lipto using sheep's-milk cheese. The result is delicious. A warning though: the proportions given have been arrived at after much experimenting and it is very important that the exact balance is maintained for each flavour to come out individually. Too much of this, too little of that, and the harmony is lost.

A tango from the 1930s

SERVES 6–8
250 g/10 oz mascarpone,
  (p.255)
50 g/2 oz gorgonzola, roughly
  chopped
50 g/2 oz green end of a leek,
  cut into 6 mm/¹/₄ inch rings

2 anchovy fillets
2 teaspoons Dijon mustard
¼ teaspoon caraway seeds
½ teaspoon Maldon salt
freshly ground black pepper
    (about ¼ teaspoon)
olive oil (optional)

Blend everything, except the leek and olive oil, quickly in a food processor. The consistency should be soft and buttery. If it is too dry or crumbly – and this will depend largely on the ripeness and age of the gorgonzola – add a little olive oil (not more than 2 tablespoons should be needed). Add the leek rings and whizz again for a few seconds. Do not overprocess or the mixture will clot and become grainy. It has always been eaten too quickly for us to test its keeping qualities. Delicious on new potatoes or on steaks (cod as well as fillet), it is best of all served at room temperature with black bread, thin water biscuits and a pile of the season's first walnuts.

SELECT BIBLIOGRAPHY

ACTON, ELIZA, *Modern Cooking for Private Families*, London, 1845

ALEE, HADJEE, *Receipts for Cooking the most Favourite Dishes in General Use in India also for Preparing Chatney and India Pickle*, Calcutta, c.1920

APICIUS, MARCUS GABIUS, *Cooking and Dining in Imperial Rome 80 BC–AD 40*, translated Vehling, Dover, 1936

ARTUSI, PELLEGRINO, *L'Arte di Mangiar Bene*, Florence, 1950

AVADA, FATHER DOMENICO, *Practica de Speciali*, Rome, 1678

AYRTON, ELIZABETH, *The Cookery of England*, London, 1974

Baileys Agricultural Durham, 1810

BEETON, MRS, *Every Day Cookery and Housekeeping Book*, London, 1865

BENNETT, JAMES, *History of Tewkesbury*, London, 1830

BINSTEAD, RAYMOND, *Pickle and Saucemaking*, Food Trade Press, London, 1939

BLATHWAYT, RAYMOND, *As a Grain of Mustard Seed*, Colman's, Norwich, 1923

BLENCOWE, A., *The Receipt Book*, 1694

BLONDEL, MADELEINE, *Catalogue of Moutarde de Dijon Exhibition, 1984 in Dijon*

CAREME, M. A., *L'Art de la Cuisine Française*, London, 1836

CLAIBORNE, CRAIG, *Cooking with Herbs and Spices*, New York, 1970

COGAN, DR THOMAS, *Haven of Health*, 1605

COLMAN'S, *Mustard Users Mustered by Baron de Beef*, c.1930

COLMAN'S, *Mustard Seed Crop Husbandry*, 1982

COLMAN'S, *The Advertising Art of J. J. Colman Ltd. Yellow, White and Blue*, Norwich, 1977

COLMAN'S, *History of the Mustard Pot*, c. 1920

COLUMELLA, *De Re Rustica*, AD 42

COOKE, ALASTAIR, *America*, BBC 1973

CULPEPER, NICHOLAS, *The English Physician or Herball*, London, 1653

CURNOSKY, *Bon Plats, Bon Vins*, 1949

DAVID, ELIZABETH, *Spices, Salt and Aromatics in the English Kitchen*, London, 1970

Declaration of Academy of Dijon, 1853

DECLOQUEMENT, FRANÇOISE, *Moutarde et Moutardiers*, Paris, 1982

DE FONTENELLE, JULIA, *Manuel du Moutardier, Manuels-Roret*, Paris 1827 and 1887

DENCE, *Season to Taste*, Food Trade Press London, 1985

DIGBY, SIR KENELM, *The Closet Opened, 1669*, A. McDonnell, 1910

DIOSCORIDES, *De Materia Medica, c.* AD 100

DUMAS, ALEXANDER, *Dictionary of Cuisine*, Paris, 1973

EVELYN, JOHN, *A Discourse of Sallets*, London, 1699

GERARD, JOHN, *Gerard's Herbal*, 1597

GLASSE, HANNAH, *Art of Cookery Made Plain and Easy*, 1747

'GOODMAN OF PARIS', *Le Menagier de Paris*, Paris, 1390.

GORDON, VICTOR, *The English Cookbook*, London, 1985

GRIEVE, MAUD, *A Modern Herbal*, London, 1931

GRIGSON, JANE, *Charcuterie and French Pork Cookery*, 1967

HAMMER, STEPHEN, *French's Centennial*, New York, 1980

HIPPOCRATES, *Medicorum Graecorum Opus*, translated E. Littre, Paris, 1861

HOLLAND, LADY, *Memoirs of the Rev Sidney Smith*, 1855

IRELAND, ARTHUR, *The Story of the Grain of Mustard Seed*, London, 1914

JOBARD, *Essai sur L'Histoire de la Moutarde de Dijon*, (undated)

KEEN, ROBINSON AND CO., *Gossip About London City 1742 to 1892*, London 1892

KETTNER, AUGUSTE, *Book of the Table*, 1877

KIMBALL, MARIE, *Thomas Jefferson's Cook Book Virginia*, 1976

KITCHENER, WILLIAM, *Apicius Redivivus the Cook's Oracle*, 1817

LANG, GEORGE, *The Cuisine of Hungary*, New York, 1971

LEYEL, MRS, *The Gentle Art of Cookery*, London, 1925

LIVINGSTONE, *The Book of Spices*, New York, 1969

MARINETTI, F., *La Cucina Futurista*, Rome, 1932

MAY, ROBERT, *The Accomplisht Cook*, 1660

MESSEGROVE, *Health Secrets of Plants and Herbs*, London, 1976

MISSON, FRANCOIS, *Memoires et Observations*, 1719

MUFFETT, DR THOMAS, *Health Improvements*, 1655

NEASHAM, *North Country Sketches*, London, 1893

OCKERMAN, J., *Source Book for Food Scientists*, A.V.I., London, 1978

OLNEY, RICHARD, *Simple French Food*, London, 1981

ORTIZ, ELIZABETH LAMBERT, *Japanese Cookery*, London 1986

— *Latin American Cooking*, London, 1969

Stere Hit Well, PEPYSIAN LIBRARY, Magdalene College, Cambridge, No. 1047

POULTNEY, S. V., *Vinegar Products*, London, 1949

REYNIERE, GRIMOD DE LA, *Almanach des Gourmands ou Calendrier Nutritif*, Paris, 1803–1810

ROSE, GILES, *A Perfect School of Instruction for the Officers of the Mouth*, 1682

RUNDELL, MARY, *A New System of Domestic Cookery*, London, 1806

RUSSELL, J., *Boke of Nature*, 1460

SHAW, NANCY, *Food for the Greedy*, 1936

SMITH, MICHAEL, *Fine English Cookery*, London, 1973

SOYER, ALEXIS, *Gastronomic Regenerator*, London, 1846

SPENCER, EDWARD (NATHANIEL GUBBINS), *Cakes and Ale*, London, 1897

TOKLAS, ALICE B., *The Alice B. Toklas Cook Book*, London, 1954

WILSON, C. ANNE, *Food and Drink in Britain*, London, 1973

WOLLEY, HANNAH, *The Queen-Like Closet*, 1670

— *The Accomplisht Lady's Delight*, 6th edition, 1686

YARWOOD, DOREEN, *The British Kitchen*, London, 1981

INDEX